The
Professional
Trainer

SECOND EDITION
REVISED AND EXPANDED

The Professional Trainer

A Comprehensive Guide to
Planning, Delivering, and
Evaluating Training Programs

Robert H. Vaughn

BK

BERRETT-KOEHLER PUBLISHERS, INC.
San Francisco

Berrett-Koehler Publishers, Inc.
235 Montgomery Street, Suite 650
San Francisco, CA 94104-2916
Tel: (415) 288-0260   Fax: (415) 362-2512   www.bkconnection.com

Ordering Information

Quantity sales. Special discounts are available on quantity purchases by corporations, associations, and others. For details, contact the "Special Sales Department" at the Berrett-Koehler address above.

Individual sales. Berrett-Koehler publications are available through most bookstores. They can also be ordered directly from Berrett-Koehler: Tel: (800) 929-2929; Fax: (802) 864-7626; www.bkconnection.com

Orders for college textbook/course adoption use. Please contact Berrett-Koehler: Tel: (800) 929-2929; Fax: (802) 864-7626.

Orders by U.S. trade bookstores and wholesalers. Please contact Publishers Group West, 1700 Fourth Street, Berkeley, CA 94710. Tel: (510) 528-1444; Fax (510) 528-3444.

Production Management: Textbook Writers Associates, Inc.

Berrett-Koehler and the BK logo are registered trademarks of Berrett-Koehler Publishers, Inc.

Printed in the United States of America

Berrett-Koehler books are printed on long-lasting acid-free paper. When it is available, we choose paper that has been manufactured by environmentally responsible processes. These may include using trees grown in sustainable forests, incorporating recycled paper, minimizing chlorine in bleaching, or recycling the energy produced at the paper mill.

Library of Congress Cataloging-in-Publication Data

Vaughn, Robert H., 1946–
    The professional trainer: a comprehensive guide to planning, delivering, and evaluating training programs / by Robert H. Vaughn.—2nd ed., rev. and expanded.
        p. cm.
    Includes bibliographical references and index.
    ISBN-13: 978-1-57675-270-8
    1. Employees—Training of. 2. Employee training personnel. I. Title.

HF5549.5.T7V338 2005
658.3'12404—dc22   2004062776

Second Edition
10 09 08 07 06 05   10 9 8 7 6 5 4 3 2 1

This book is dedicated to:

My colleagues, for their support over the years;

My students, for all they have taught me;

My family, for the richness of purpose they have provided.

Contents

Foreword

I am delighted that Bob Vaughn and his publisher, Berrett-Koehler, have asked me to write a foreword to this book. Delighted because the 13 chapters will guide you through the "soup-to-nuts" steps that professional trainers regard as essential to success.

As Professor Vaughn mentions in his Preface, if you're an experienced trainer in the HRD field, you will probably want to read selectively rather than from cover to cover, picking those chapters that best meet your immediate needs. Of course, as readers go you may be the exception rather than the rule: most of today's trainers are relatively new to the field. (Membership in ASTD changes by about one-third every year.)

Who are these new trainers? Many are experienced employees whose skills and proficiency on the job led a senior manager to invite each of them to become a trainer in order to impart these skills and proficiencies to others.

In many organizations the role of trainer is either a part-time responsibility or a full-time job held for one or two years. These trainers then can move on with their chosen career path. (Incidentally, many of these "pro tem" trainers opt to remain in the HRD field and thus launch a new career path!)

We live in an age of innovation. Some 25% of the jobs that exist today were not known as recently as ten years ago. Recently Bill Gates of Microsoft made this statement: "In three years every product we make will be obsolete. The only question is whether we'll make them obsolete or someone else will."

Change requires training, and the rate of change is accelerating at a breathless pace. Do you remember what a slide rule is? A typewriter? Carbon paper? A clothes line? A coffee percolator? A mimeograph machine? A dot matrix printer? To be sure, the one thing that remains constant is change.

A half century ago the image most people had of corporate training included a classroom with an instructor up front, often "good ole Charlie" who had three years to go before retirement.

Not knowing what to do with him, the company made him a trainer. The seating was arranged auditorium style or around U-shaped tables. This arrangement is still appropriate for courses that have a large audience and relatively stable course content that won't change from month to month (e.g., management development, supervisory skills, time management, writing, interviewing job applicants, etc.)

However, rapid changes in technology mean that yesterday's task-specific courses soon became obsolete in today's workplace. As a result:

- more than 90% of today's job skills are now taught on the job rather than in the classroom;
- the instructor is usually a supervisor or experienced employee trying to do a professional job as trainer;
- the group size is small, given today's demand for "just-in-time" training, with one-on-one training being quite common.

Where do you fit in among these options? Will you be teaching in a classroom or on the job? Does your expertise lie in human resources development or in the workplace skills you'll be imparting to your trainees? Are you more comfortable imparting information to a group or coaching and tutoring individuals?

Whatever the case, you want to do the best job you possibly can. You want to be a professional trainer.

Hence this book. Its chapters are chock full of the how-to-do-it guidelines that will give you the confidence and the competence needed to impart new knowledge, skills, and attitudes to your learners. What's more, the writing is well organized and presented in bite-size, easy-to-digest segments that will make your journey an enjoyable one.

The payoff? You'll become quite effective in shaping the behavior of your trainees in ways that you planned and they implemented. And that's what being a professional trainer is all about!

Scott B. Parry, Ph.D.
Chairman, Training House, Inc.
Member, HRD Hall of Fame

Preface

As the pace of technology and change increases, organizations are required to train employees, clients, or customers increasingly more often, more efficiently, and at less cost. In today's business world, people are the critical difference, and sometimes the only difference, between organizational success and failure. And training is the primary way to develop the people in your organization.

Almost anyone can be called upon to be a trainer. Some people seem to take to this role quickly and easily, but most approach it with uncertainty or even downright panic. Left to their own devices, most folks try to train others in the same way that they were taught. Yet, there are some major differences in teaching a fifth grader how to write a good sentence, a twenty-five year old how to operate a lathe, and a fifty year old how to sell advertising or write a computer program. We've all had good and bad experiences in learning things, so simply doing unto others what was done unto us is a poor model for effective training.

Who should read this book?

The Professional Trainer is written to help anyone who finds him or herself in the role of training in an organization. This group includes people who are full-time technical or soft-skills trainers, but also the many who do training now and then, as a part of their larger jobs:

- Salespersons and technical experts who must help customers or co-workers learn to use a new process or new equipment.
- Supervisors who must orient and train new hires and help to upgrade the skills of their current employees.
- Co-workers who are asked to help other employees learn tasks that they are currently doing.

- Help-desk employees and other customer service people who help customers, clients, or other employees work through problems in a systematic way.

- Medical personnel, such as nurses or occupational therapists, who must help patients learn to deal with illnesses, medications, rehabilitation exercises, and so on.

- Professionals in any field, such as librarians, athletic coaches, and personal trainers, who work with adults as they develop unfamiliar skills or learn new information.

- Police, fire, and other safety personnel, all of whom undergo extensive and continuing training themselves, and who often are required to give training programs for others, ranging from peers to schoolchildren to senior citizens groups.

- And many more.

People who are brand new to the field of training should find it useful to read through the whole process from beginning to end. So much detail is offered, however, that frequent references to the appropriate sections of the book will be needed as a training program is planned and implemented. Others who have done training before may choose to just read the parts of the book that focus on what they need right now. It can be a valuable reference to provide lists of ideas for brainstorming or implementation.

What will you learn from reading this book?

The Professional Trainer will take you step-by-step through the entire process of organizational training. We begin with some big-picture issues, such as how training is different from teaching at a school and how adults learn differently than children do. Next, we cover the extremely important concept of making sure that the training really meets the needs of the employee and the organization. There's no value in training people on things that the organization doesn't require, nor in training them on things that they already know or can do. Once you know what people need to learn, the book will take you through the steps of planning and designing the training, designing measures of the training, choosing the best way to approach it, choosing and designing media and facilities to support it, actually delivering the training, and finding out whether or not it worked.

This book can be used as a text for a train-the-trainer program, but also as a personal handbook for anyone who manages or conducts training. The suggestions should work equally well for large or small organizations, and in for-profit companies as well as government or social agencies. Often, you won't need to develop a training program from start to finish. Perhaps you will be doing just a small part of a lesson or are looking to improve an already existing training program. *The Professional Trainer* can help you with these tasks, too, because the individual chapters largely stand on their own. Maybe you just need ideas on, say, how to get a group more involved in discussion, or ways to encourage trainees to actually take their skills back to the job and use them. This book is an excellent reference to keep on your shelf, to consult when you need a troubleshooting guide.

What's different about this book?

Most books about training focus on a single subject in the process, and many are written with more emphasis on an "academic," rather than practical, approach. *The Professional Trainer* is a basic primer that covers the entire process, yet it still includes plenty of detail to support the novice trainer. Even somewhat experienced trainers will be pleased with a number of useful checklists and different approaches. Each topic covered also has references to other, more detailed sources of information, if the reader wishes to delve more deeply into a topic. Some of the particularly helpful topics include:

- An overview of the field of training, including a list of what trainers actually do, plus some useful websites where you can get further information (Chapter 1).
- A list of ways to help make the learning experience more attractive and effective for adults (Chapter 2).
- A nine-step process for figuring out what skills and knowledge must be included in a training program, and a list of tools to help refine those concepts (Chapter 3).
- A brainstorming checklist to help create an effective proposal for a training program (Chapter 4).
- Techniques for understanding how to structure training objectives in a way that leads to appropriate levels of training to meet organizational needs (Chapter 5).
- Logical pro and con checklists for different types of learning evaluation (Chapter 6) and a variety of different training delivery techniques (Chapter 7).

- Several checklists to help make appropriate business decisions about technology-based training (Chapter 8).

- Specific suggestions for when and how to use a variety of media support techniques (Chapter 9).

- A guide on how to develop practical and useful training plans, including a checklist for on-the-job training plans (Chapter 10).

- Suggestions on a variety of ways to involve individuals and effectively use small groups, as well as many other ideas useful during the delivery stage of training programs (Chapter 11).

- A step-by-step training program-assessment process, which includes a model, to determine whether the training was done efficiently and effectively (Chapter 12).

- A look into the future of training, including what sorts of changes and challenges can be expected for the field (Chapter 13).

- And many more ideas, models, checklists, and references throughout.

This book also includes a few ideas that you won't find in other books on the subject, such as a comparison of the traditional training model of four levels of objectives to the more academic style model of Bloom's Taxonomy. Also unique to this book are the Training Styles Grid, the Cost Model for Technology-based Training, and other features.

What perspective does the author bring to this book?

As someone who has taught train-the-trainer programs for more than two decades, this book reflects my ideals of what it takes to succeed in this interesting career. It has a good breadth of coverage and a reasonable depth of coverage in the various activities that make up the role of an organizational trainer. It's appropriately referenced but not overly academic. It includes factual, procedural, and conceptual information in a form that is accessible and useful on the job.

Writing, editing, and publishing a book such as this one is no small commitment in time for the author and in money and effort for the editor and publisher. I appreciate, especially, the work of my developmental editor Roger Williams, who saw some merit in this approach and has been helpful in a number of ways in bringing this book to life. A number of helpful suggestions came from the four reviewers, and my thanks goes out to them. My colleague Corrie Bergeron was quite helpful in helping me deal with many of the concepts of the technology-based training. I also gratefully acknowledge the support and many useful suggestions of my wife Susan, also a trainer and educator, who brought a technical training viewpoint to this work. The people at Berrett-Koehler have been a delight to work with in making this book a reality. Finally, I acknowledge the many suggestions from over 1,000 former students and trainees who used the first edition of this book and its predecessor forms as they learned about the business of training. All good trainers learn from their students.

Robert H. Vaughn
Mentor, Ohio
May, 2005

1 The Training Field

> *"Corporate America is now built on intellectual capital rather than bricks and mortar—and that's changing everything."*
>
> —*Thomas A. Stewart*

Being a professional implies that an individual is aware of the history, vocabulary, major theories, tools and techniques, publications, organizations, key individuals, current trends, and ethical considerations related to a given field. This book provides the foundation on which the reader can build toward becoming a professional trainer.

■ ■ ■

An organization's success will depend on its ability to compete, often within a global economy. Coping with today's market changes requires organizations to take a variety of actions: They are merging. They are internationalizing. They are downsizing. They are becoming more flexible in a variety of areas, as exemplified by the flexibility in work arrangements, dress codes, and work hours. Organizations are also investing more in training. Human skills are frequently the most important resource an organization has to offer. All other resources are transferable or easily copied by competitors, but the individual is unique, and *training* is the key to making the best use of individual skills.

The role of the organizational trainer is gaining more importance on a daily basis. The chapter-opening quote from Thomas A. Stewart, an author and member of *Fortune* magazine's editorial board, highlights that change. How big is the training business, and how is it likely to change? What do trainers do, and what should they be doing? This chapter will help put the important and growing role of training into perspective and prepare the reader for the remaining chapters.

What, exactly, is training?

Defining some key terms seems an appropriate place to begin. What is training, and how is it different from development or education?

Training is providing information and direction in a planned and structured manner to employees on how to accomplish specific tasks related to organizational needs and objectives. Training should lead to permanent behavioral change and measurable improvement in job performance. *Training may also be provided to customers or clients, but the same principles apply. Therefore, this book will simplify the phrasing by just using the term "employees" throughout to refer to trainees of any category.*

One way of categorizing the content offered by training is to divide it into three sub-categories: factual, procedural, and conceptual content.

Factual content is pure data and information. Examples of factual content are the price of an item sold by the company, the name of the department manager, the location of the fire extinguisher, or the version number of the software used by the accounting department.

Procedural content provides detailed information about how to do things. Examples of procedural content include the steps required to enter and complete a sales transaction, operate the copy machine, approach a customer in the lobby, or set up the CNC machine to produce a component for the valves the company makes.

Conceptual content includes information about the "why" as well as the "how." An example is a training session that explains that cash received at the register should not be put into the drawer until the change is counted out, so no disagreement can arise as to what amount the customer handed to the cashier. Adults learn better and remember facts more easily when they have a context in which to structure that information. Knowing the reason behind laying the cash received on the top of the register will actually help them to learn to do it.

Training in business and other organizations is often sub-categorized into three levels: *orientation, skill training, and development*.

Orientation is training that relates to providing the information (knowledge, but not usually skills) necessary to function within an organizational setting. It is usually done with new hires immediately or shortly after they start working for the organization. Typical orientation content includes the history and structure of the organization and its position in its industry, work rules and procedures, benefits, and other essential information such as the location of the rest rooms and fire extinguishers and the procedure by which the employee gets paid. Orientation in some form must be done by all organizations. Some will delegate it to each supervisor, while others will centralize it, often in the Human Resources department.

Skill training provides information, including both knowledge and skills necessary to perform the work for which the individual was hired. When a skilled worker is hired, this type of training is usually not required, or is required to a lesser degree than with an unskilled new hire. The skilled hire may simply need to learn this organization's way of doing something they have done before. Certain other skill training may also be relevant to all new hires, such as how to use the phone system or fill out administrative forms. This training may be done during the orientation, even though it includes simple cognitive or physical skills.

Development prepares employees for advancement in their jobs, the organization as a whole, or (sometimes) for personal growth. It may include formal within-company training, other experiences such as job rotation, or even tuition rebates for attending relevant external programs. Developmental activity is not generally tied to specific positions in an organization but relates to broader skills and concepts necessary for growth within the organization.

Note that all these categories of training relate to needs of the organization, and not to needs of a broader society. *Education*, unlike training, provides information and guidance in an organized manner about concepts and knowledge, both general and specific, of all kinds. Education includes offerings by public and private schools, as well as by some organizations and corporations. Education is essential to functioning in society as well as in specific organizations, and—in a strict learning sense—will lead to a relatively permanent change in behavior.

Some of the topics covered in this book also apply to education and development, but the main focus is on training. The reader should emerge with a basic but thorough understanding of the process and vocabulary related to training within an organization.

Table 1-1 compares some of the key differences between learning in an academic setting and receiving training in an organization.

Table 1-1   Some Differences between Academic Learning and Organizational Training

FACTOR	ACADEMIC LEARNING	ORGANIZATIONAL TRAINING
Trainer Credentials	Academic—often only academic. Some colleges, especially two-year and teaching schools, also consider work experience and skills in interpersonal communications.	Skill or knowledge in relevant subject regardless of academic achievement; also, skill in interpersonal communications is more critical.
Course Content	Usually broad and theo-retical. Certain fields, such as computer studies, may also have practical element.	Focused and application oriented. Deals mostly with facts and procedures, only rarely with concepts.
Objective Levels	The most common are knowledge-based and occasionally skill-based objectives. Job perfor-mance objectives are usually only peripheral issues.	Although training often includes knowledge and skill-level objectives, job performance is the outcome of most concern.
Time Basis	Usually lock-step and tied to a semester or quarter system.	Typically short-term; more self-paced; new groups start as needed.
Grading System	"A" through "F."	Usually pass-fail; many programs are not graded at all. Some are proficiency-based.
Common Presentation Style	Lecture and other inductive forms, though cases and lab applications are becoming more common.	Often uses participative experiences, even in a classroom form; a hands-on format is most common for on-the-job training.
Reason for Participation	To obtain a degree, certificate, or other credential. Sometimes for self-satisfaction, but probably for career and employment reasons.	Required by employer in order to support the organization's needs. May be a condition of keeping a job or getting a promotion.

Table 1-1   Some Differences between Academic Learning and Organizational Training (*Continued*)

FACTOR	ACADEMIC LEARNING	ORGANIZATIONAL TRAINING
Student Unit	Individual; working together is considered cheating for most types of assignments. "Client" is individual student.	Group learning is much more common. "Client" is the organization in which the trainee works.
Training Materials	Comprehensive textbooks and outside research materials.	Company materials and trainer-designed materials. Only rarely are books used.

What do trainers really do?

The typical training job requires an individual who understands the skills and knowledge being taught and who has effective interpersonal communication skills. Most trainers will also need to understand how to design training, use various kinds of media, and measure the results of training. Some will also be required to determine training needs through job analysis and evaluation of employee skill levels. Obviously, the job of training can include a wide spectrum of basic skills.

According to a recent report by **ASTD** (formerly the American Society for Training and Development), these are the major areas of expertise needed by trainers[1]:

- Career planning and talent management
- Coaching
- Managing organizational knowledge
- Managing the learning function
- Facilitating organizational change
- Measuring and evaluating
- Delivering training
- Improving human performance
- Designing learning

To develop those areas of expertise, the professional trainer needs to build on a foundation of personal, interpersonal, and business and management competencies. Finally, the professional trainer may be called upon to serve the roles of project manager, professional specialist, learning strategist, and business partner. To see the entire model, go to www.mymodel.astd.org, or see *The ASTD 2004 Competency Study: Mapping the Future.*[2]

Does a trainer really have to be able to do all those things? In a small organization with only one or two trainers, they may indeed be responsible for most of those activities. In a large organization, the labor will be divided, and trainers will specialize, each needing only some of the competencies listed above.

What should trainers do?

A better question than what trainers do might be, what *should* trainers do? An ASTD Leadership Conference report[3] stressed that *trainers should spend their time on the activities that create the most value for businesses*. These activities include:

- Linking training to the results that business units are expected to achieve.
- Designing and developing new training programs to address emerging business needs.
- Conducting training programs.
- Selecting and managing training suppliers.
- Handling logistics and administration of training.
- Measuring the effectiveness of training.

A serious misalignment exists between what senior executives say is value added and what Training and Development people do day-to-day. As Table 1-2 illustrates, most executives believe that trainers should work much more on linking business needs to training and measuring the results of training in terms of its effect on the business' bottom line. The table compares the importance that executives assign to various training activities with the time actually spent on those activities. It ranks each item on a scale of zero to four, with four being the most important effort and most common use of time. The discrepancy column shows how far the reality is from the executives' desires.

The implications are clear: trainers spend too much time in the "administrivia" of their jobs, and not enough time working with managers and the larger organization to make sure the training actually provides something of value.

Table 1-2 Executives' versus Trainers' Views on How Trainers' Time Should be Spent

ACTIVITY	SENIOR EXECUTIVES' DESIRED LEVEL OF EFFORT	TRAINING STAFF'S ACTUAL ALLOCATION OF TIME	DISCREPANCY	CONCLUSION ABOUT TIME SPENT BY TRAINERS IN THIS ACTIVITY
Business Linkage	4.0	0.4	-3.6	Way too little time
Training Design	2.6	2.6	0.0	About right
Development Activities	1.0	3.9	2.9	Way too much time
Training Delivery	2.6	3.9	1.3	Too much time
Sourcing (Finding external information and providers)	1.4	1.5	0.1	About right
Registration and Administration	0.4	4.0	3.6	Way too much time
Measurement	4.0	0.5	-3.5	Way too little time

Scale: 0 = least important, should be allotted least time; 4 = most important, should be allotted most time

Source: Basic chart from ASTD, with explanatory column added for this book.[4]

How large is the training industry?

U. S. business and industry surpassed $51 billion in direct-cost spending on formal employee training in 2004.[5] This figure does not include the huge cost of personal or government spending on work-related training or the costs of elementary and secondary schools and college education. Academic learning, of course, often leads young adults to their first employment opportunity, and work-related training can garner older adults substantial job upgrades or career changes. In 2002, companies in the U.S. spent, on average, less than 2% of payroll, or only about $649 per eligible employee. By comparison, China spent 3.2% of payroll, Asia (excluding China) 3.8%, and Europe 2.5%.[6] Other factors, of course, influence these figures, and not all U.S. companies spend equal amounts. For example, in recent years IBM reportedly spent over 5% of payroll on training, Fidelity First and Xerox over 4%, and Federal Express over 3%. Conversely, some companies have no training budget at all.

The question of "How much training is enough?" is difficult to answer and will vary from one industry to the next. The U. S. is well below average among industrialized nations in per capita expenditures on training. Tony Carnevale, an author and former economist for ASTD, says that U.S. training expenditures are weak, both because we do too little of it and because we do it for too few people.[7] In terms of what kinds of training are offered, the 2003 ASTD survey of 276 training "benchmark" organizations[8] reports that the most common topic for training is technical processes and procedures, followed by information technology skills.

Most organizational training still happens on the job and informally. For off-the-job business training, 85% of all companies use traditional classroom-based training "often" or "always," with only 3% reporting "never," based on *Training* magazine's 2004 survey. ***Technology-based training***, however, is the fastest-growing category, with considerable increases in recent years. It now accounts for over 25% of all training done in organizations, and 26% of organizations report having a separate technology-based training budget.[9] Classroom trainers will need presentation and delivery skills, though exactly how they present and deliver will vary from one situation to another. Trainers who are involved with distance learning or technology-based training will need a different set of skills from those who meet in person with the trainees. These topics are covered in much more depth in Chapters 8 and 9.

What are the various organizational options for providing training?

Training serves two broad categories of employees: current employees and new hires. With the newly hired, there may be a basic option of hiring them already trained—thereby requiring only an orientation—or hiring them untrained. For either category of employees who need skill training, several other basic choices are required. The first choice is whether to conduct training on the job or off the job. If the choice is off the job, the options then become to do it inside the company or to arrange for outside training. Figure 1-1 shows the basic tree of choices.

Each of these choices has certain advantages and disadvantages. Hiring someone already trained means that they can start to work immediately after orientation. The organization gets immediate productivity and eliminates training costs. The new hires may also add a fresh perspective on how the organization accomplishes a technical task. On the other hand, trained individuals will be more expensive than untrained ones to hire, and they may bring bad habits or methods that don't fit the organization's needs or culture. Untrained people come with a clean slate and can learn how to do everything through training. Organizations may also get some financial incentives from certain government, union, or industry sources to hire unskilled workers. And, in fact, they may be the only choice in certain industries if no trained people are available, either because the skills needed are new or in very high demand.

Figure 1-1   Basic Training Choices for New Hires

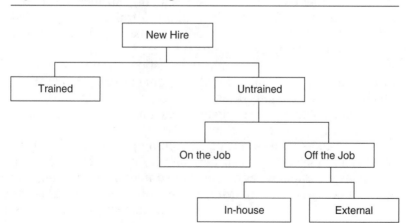

If an untrained person is hired, the organization must choose whether to conduct the training **on the job (OTJ)** or **off** the job. On-the-job training is by far the most common for new hires in business and industry, and it is further discussed in Chapter 7 and others. The company immediately gains at least some productivity from the new hire and minimizes any **transfer of training** problems. Transfer of training problems result when an employee is trained a specific way in a classroom or other training environment, then asked to perform in a real-world environment that does not match the classroom. An example is training workers using Windows XP® in the classroom, then sending them to a job where Windows 98® is still in use.

On the other hand, new employees may be very slow during early on-the-job training and perhaps even pose a hazard to themselves and others. They detract from co-workers' or supervisors' productivity while they are being trained. They may pick up bad habits and may not get to see all parts of the job. The training is not likely to be systematic or effectively evaluated. Off-the-job training, however, requires setting up a separate learning station and using a trainer. Both of these approaches are costly and mean that the worker won't be productive at all during training. Off-the-job training, though, is likely to be much more systematic and focused; thus, it is often more efficient. Many times companies will use a combination of the two techniques in order to gain the benefits of both.

If the decision to train off the job has been made, the question of whether to train inside or outside the organization must be answered next. In-house training offers the major benefit of ensuring the training is relevant to the organization. As mentioned, however, it may be more expensive. The organization must support designing a curriculum, setting up a training facility, and hiring a trainer or borrowing a good worker or supervisor and training him or her to be a trainer. If hiring a company nurse as a new employee, for example, an organization certainly won't opt for this method. External training can come in many forms, all of which share one obvious disadvantage: they're not in-house. The trainer may not know the company, the equipment may not match the company's, the organization has limited control over curriculum, and—in general—transfer of training problems are exacerbated. Conversely, the trainer may be very good and the content very relevant. Much depends on the source of the training and that source's track record with the organization that needs the training. Figure 1-2 shows one manner of modeling these options.

Figure 1-2 Differences among Training Options

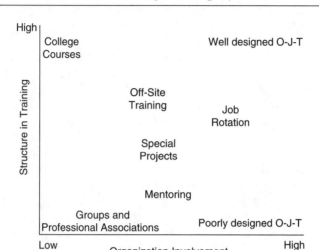

This figure shows a comparison of several training methods as they relate to the control or involvement of the organization in their design and presentation, and the degree to which the training is structured. College courses are typically highly structured, but an outside organization usually has no input at all regarding their content. On-the-job-training can be highly structured (or not, if it's poorly designed), and the organization has a high degree of input to that design—in fact, it controls it completely.

How is training delivered within the organization?

One way of categorizing training delivery within an organization is that it can be delivered in a fragmented, formalized, or focused manner.

The first, *fragmented training delivery*, describes an environment in which no clear link to organizational goals is evident. In this situation, training is often perceived as a luxury or a reward, the emphasis is usually on knowledge-based courses, training is done exclusively by trainers or outside vendors, and the training needs are not assessed. Trainees may sign themselves up or be signed up by their supervisors from a list of available courses being offered.

In *formalized training delivery*, there is an effort to link training to human resource needs. Skill-based courses are emphasized, and pre- and post-course activities are commonly used to facilitate the transfer of learning back to the job. Managers may appraise the training in addition to the trainees.

A *focused training delivery* environment exists in what is called "the learning organization." Training is perceived as necessary for survival. It is linked to organizational strategy and individual goals. The main responsibility for training rests with line management, and accurately measuring the effectiveness of training is important. Pre- and post-course objective tests and other quantitative techniques are used in this environment.

Training can be managed and provided from a variety of different locations in the organizational hierarchy. In a large organization, the training department is often housed as part of the Human Resources operation. In some large companies, though, it is decentralized and apportioned into the various departments that use it. Smaller companies may have no one directly responsible for training. Instead, on-the-job training is left to the supervisors, and any other formal training that must happen is contracted out.

External training may be provided by consultants, colleges, trade schools, correspondence schools, vendors, suppliers, industry associations, and a host of other sources. The problem for the organization becomes one of finding and selecting from among viable options. *Training* magazine's 2004 Industry Report shows that 26% of traditional training programs and 31% of technology-based training are delivered by outside contractors, and even more—35% and 41%, respectively—is *designed* by outside contractors.[10] Historically, training has been seen as a staff responsibility, but the trend is for line managers to be more involved—sometimes even doing the training themselves.

How is training viewed by top management?

The opening quote for this chapter from *Fortune* magazine and other evidence illustrate that training is becoming a more important factor in business today than it has been previously. For example, a two-year measurement of stock performance indices was run in the late 1990s, comparing the stock value of companies heavily involved in training and development to the Standard and Poor's 500 index at large.[11] During this time, the value of the S & P rose 68%, while the value of companies investing heavily in training and development rose 229%. Of course, confounding or external factors (e.g., the performance of the technology industries, which are heavily invested in training) may have skewed these results, but the point remains that organizations that focus on training generally do better than those that don't.

Look for the influence of training to increase substantially in the near future. How much of an increase is difficult to predict, since the nature of training will change both because of the technology used in training and because of the need for technology training within the organization.

How does the organizational environment influence training?

The organizational environment influences training in literally hundreds of ways. It determines how much training is offered, where it is offered, who does it, who gets it, how much support management gives it, and whether the trainees support it.

How much training is offered to employees depends on a number of organizational factors. A company operating in an industry that changes quickly and is heavily invested in high technology probably needs more training than others do. If employee turnover is high, orientation training, at least, will be needed frequently. Whether skills training is needed will depend on hiring practices. Another obvious factor is the organizational budget. If cash supplies are short, training is often one of the first things to go, though this measure may be a false economy. More will be said on that subject later in the book.

Where the training is done can be influenced by management attitudes, the number of trainees at any given time, the organizational resources available to support training, and many other factors. If the company has just one or two people at a time who need training, it may well be done on the job or by sending people to an outside source, such as the manufacturer of the equipment that they need to be trained to use. If many need to be trained, training will more likely be done in-house or by contract.

Who will do the training depends, first of all, on whether people who have the technical skills (and ideally instructional skills as well) are available within the company. If not, training will be done by outsiders. A supervisor or skilled employee, if available, can be chosen to do training, or a professional trainer can be employed. This decision is further influenced by the complexity of the knowledge or skills being taught.

Who gets the training is influenced by such factors as how management feels about training, where problems exist or changes are occurring, how important status levels are in the organization, and so on. This mix of factors is sometimes referred to as part of the organization's *culture*. (See Schein[12] and others on this topic.) Training may be seen as something that everyone needs, or something that is a "perk" (perquisite) reserved for higher-level employees or just certain groups. It may go only to those who ask.

Management support for training is influenced by a myriad of factors, most importantly the budget and whether or not the training department is credible. If top management supports training, or if the experience of people who have been trained is good, probably more training will be done in the organization. Management will also be swayed by their own predilections, other things that are going on that require their attention, and so on.

Finally, *trainee support* has to do with whether the trainees see training as a useful, interesting experience, a total waste of time, or something in between. The attitude people have as they arrive for training is often contagious. Usually if the boss sees it as important, so will the employees, but this perception depends on their own background and experiences. Frankly, most adults find classrooms threatening, and adult learners may require lots of motivation and appropriate conditions for good learning.

How can these influences be controlled?

Most of these influences can't be completely controlled, of course. The most basic ways to deal with the organizational environment are for the trainer to work closely with the organization's management and to do the best possible job in designing and presenting effective training programs. Many of the suggestions throughout this book will help the trainer to design the best possible proposals and do all that can be done to ensure that training is effectively presented and applied in such a manner as to benefit the organization and develop trainees' skills and knowledge.

It also may be useful to enlist the aid of a professional *OD* (organizational development) person or consultant who can help support training or the training department in the areas that are outside the trainers' expertise. In the world of professional management, change is everyone's responsibility, but designing and implementing organizational change is a specialty of the professionals in the organizational development field.[13] OD is concerned with the "big picture" of how organizations operate, including such aspects as their formal structure, culture, communication patterns, and so on. For training to be effective, it must be designed to teach the right people to do the necessary jobs, allowing for the organization's method of operation. This requirement means that a great deal of training must be designed and delivered with a clear understanding of the organization's structure and its visible and invisible (unarticulated) culture.

Factual and procedural training (as opposed to conceptual) can be accomplished without excessive emphasis on organizational culture. Unquestionably, much of training is and should be at the factual and procedural levels. If the conceptual level is ignored completely, however, training will produce employees who know how to handle everything except a new situation. Without conceptual training, employees do not understand the larger context of what they're doing. The result is employees who tend to operate mechanistically. This outcome is not good for any business, and certainly not good for a growing business. It means a more frequent need for retraining, much more supervision required for the employees, and—ultimately—frustrated customers. Yet, the conceptual level is often resisted the most by managers, who may characterize it as giving the employees more than they need to know and keeping them away from productive work.

It is this need to understand how the organization operates that pushes the trainer to be involved in OD-type activities. Such involvement is particularly relevant for the trainer who also designs the training she or he is delivering. The chapters that follow attempt, in general, to deal with all three levels of training: factual, procedural, and conceptual, and to suggest ways in which the trainer can work within the larger organization.

Where can I learn more about the training field?

The premier professional association in the field is **ASTD**, formerly named the American Society for Training and Development. The name changed to simply its initial letters several years ago in recognition of a large and growing percentage of membership outside of the U.S. ASTD is headquartered in the Washington, D.C. area and has over 70,000 members worldwide, many of whom belong to the 140 or so local chapters around the U.S. ASTD welcomes anyone working in positions related to the training field, including vendors, consultants, training managers, media specialists, and trainers in any subject. ASTD provides such member services as the monthly *T+D* magazine (Formerly *Training and Development*), several other quarterly or monthly newsletters and special interest publications, research studies, conferences, a national events presence, a wide variety of training books, and so on.

Another long-time and highly regarded training-related professional association is the **International Society for Performance Improvement**. ISPI members also include persons who are interested in non-training approaches to performance improvement. Like ASTD, ISPI is also headquartered in the Washington area and has numerous local chapters.

Many other professional associations and publications exist, which serve the needs of more narrowly focused trainer groups. Professional organizations with a broad focus, such as the American Management Association, the Society for Human Resource Management, and so on, often have subgroups or special-interest groups of trainers within the larger group.

The primary periodical in the field is *Training* magazine. This magazine is quite readable, widely available, and covers just about all aspects of training. A number of other monthly or quarterly publications come from various professional training associations (Box 1-1), or from other sources such as private or commercial publishers. Certain book publishers also specialize in training-related materials. Box 1-1 provides a list of major training-related resources, including publishers, professional organizations, and websites.

Box 1-1   Selected Professional Resources for the Training Field

---

Note: The field of training is much too large and diverse to give a comprehensive list, so these listings focus on major companies in the business. As most web users know, links from one source will lead you to others, and web searches can be constructed to find specific areas of interest. This information was correct at the time of publication, but is certainly subject to change.

Training-related professional associations:

ASTD (Formerly The American Society for Training and
    Development)
    1640 King Street Box 1443
    Alexandria, VA 22313-2043
    800.628.2783
    www.astd.org

Box 1-1   Selected Professional Resources for the Training Field (*Continued*)

International Society for Performance Improvement
   1400 Spring Street Suite 260
   Silver Spring, MD 20910
   301.587.8570
   www.ispi.org

Society for Human Resource Management
   1800 Duke St.
   Alexandria, VA 22314
   800.283.7476
   www.shrm.org

Society for Industrial and Organizational Psychology
   PO Box 87
   520 Ordway Ave
   Bowling Green, OH 43402-0032
   419.353.0032
   www.siop.org

Selected Training-related publications:

Training magazine
   www.trainingmag.com

T+D magazine (Published monthly by ASTD)
   www.astd.org

Performance Improvement (Journal Published monthly by ISPI)
   www.ispi.org

Learning & Training Innovations magazine (formerly *e-learning*)
deals mainly with e-learning topics
   www.LTImagazine.com

Presentations magazine deals with inductive training techniques
(lecture) and equipment to support them
   www.presentations.com

Chief Learning Officer magazine is targeted to the senior
training persons in an organization
   www.clomedia.com

(*continued*)

Box 1-1   Selected Professional Resources for the Training Field (*Continued*)

Berrett-Koehler Publishers
    Business related books, including many on training
    235 Montgomery, Suite 650
    San Francisco, CA 94104-2916
    800.929.2929
    www.bkconnection.com

Other training related websites:

Tooling University (as discussed in Chapter 8)
    On-line classes in manufacturing technology
    15700 South Waterloo Road
    Cleveland, Ohio 44110
    866.706.8665
    www.toolingu.com

Lakeland Community College
    Regionally accredited Credit and Non-credit
    Train-the-trainer on-line courses
    7700 Clocktower Drive
    Kirtland, OH 44094
    440.525.7100
    www.lakelandcc.edu

The Trainer's Warehouse
    Books, supplies, toys, etc.
    89 Washington Ave.
    Natick, MA 01760
    800.299.3770
    www.trainerswarehouse.com

Information on corporate universities can be found at
    www.corpu.com

Information of web-based training can be found at
    www.webbasedtraining.com

Information on adult learning and cognitive skills can be found at
    www.learnativity.com

Information on one of the several web-based learning platforms
    can be found at www.blackboard.com

One of the largest train-the-trainer companies can be found at
    www.langevin.com

2 Designing Training for Adults

"Actually, learning is only difficult in connection with teaching and studying; otherwise, people seem to learn without much effort."
—Klaus Mellander, The Power of Learning

The professional trainer is very aware that adults learn in many different ways and understands which techniques are appropriate to the trainee. The design of a training program must be based on a well-thought-out process that will minimize later problems and lead to a successful learning experience for all persons concerned.

■ ■ ■

How adults learn is often not explored carefully in books about organizational training. The chapter-opening quote by Klaus Mellander suggests that learning is a natural, lifelong activity, but—in fact little agreement exists on exactly how people learn. This lack of consensus makes it a difficult subject to discuss with trainers, and perhaps this difficulty explains why adult learning is often left to courses in education or psychology, in which the process can be analyzed in more detail. On the other hand, Mellander's quote makes it clear that training, in general, is not done well. In the terminology of the previous chapter, the training of trainers may be too concerned with the factual and procedural aspects of training, when some of the conceptual points about how adults learn would really be useful.

Adult learning

Everyone who's going to train adults should understand something about the process of adult learning. But, as Goldstein puts it, ". . . there's a wide gulf separating learning theories from what's actually needed to improve performance."[1] For most readers, the following pages should provide a good starting point. Those who want more information will find dozens of books listed in the reference section at the end of this text.

How do adults learn?

Because learning is extremely complex and can't actually be observed, researchers must resort to models and theories. A *model* is a simplification of reality, created to help us better understand reality. For example, a model of an airplane might be used in a physics lesson to describe and help a student understand airflow over the wings. Intangible models also exist. The economic concept of supply and demand is one such model. A *theory* is a speculative model of how things work. Theories put together facts that appear to explain a process, situation, or result. Kurt Lewin has said that, "There's nothing so useful as a good theory." W. Edwards Deming adds that, "Experience teaches us nothing without the theory." Theories help us structure, classify, categorize, and sort data until it becomes information.

Some of the established theories about learning in general include Ivan Pavlov's *Classical Conditioning* (you've probably heard of his salivating dog studies), and B. F. Skinner's *Instrumental Conditioning*. Both of these theories are behavioral theories, as are Thorndike's and others. Behavioral theories rely on changes in behavior by the learners as an indication that learning has occurred. This behavioral requirement contrasts with the cognitive learning theories of people such as Piaget, Gagné, Bruner, and others. Cognitive theorists believe that learning need not be tied to behavior. It can be a matter of what a learner knows (cognitively) and how he or she mentally stores and processes information following training.

Perhaps the best way to understand adult learning is to think about your own learning experiences so far. Most people have been taught in a predictable fashion during childhood. The adults (teachers) had the knowledge, and the children (learners) didn't. The authority figure "dispensed" the knowledge. Children learn because they trust the authority figures, who say they need to learn what is being taught, or sometimes even because the children really want to learn it. Children also trust that the teachers know what they are talking about. When you were young and naïve (an "open book"), that learning style was necessary and maybe appropriate. Adults, however, come to a training program under entirely different circumstances.

Adults change in their ability to learn rapidly as they age, but they are almost always capable of learning. As they age, most adults work better using **crystallized intelligence** rather than **fluid intelligence**. The part of intellectual functioning learning theorists assume is the result of knowledge acquisition and experience is called "crystallized" intelligence. It encompasses knowledge such as vocabulary, general information, conceptual knowledge, judgment, and concrete reasoning. Both research and conventional wisdom validate that this type of intelligence is equated with the age of the learner. The word "crystallized" does not, in this case, mean hard and inflexible. Instead, it has to do with structure and orderliness. A crystalline substance is made up of predictable, recurring patterns. Just as a computer stores information in a specific place on its hard drive, then knows where to find it, so too does our mind store acquired information in some way in which it can be retrieved, manipulated, and used to understand new data. "Fluid" (also called *innate*) intelligence has to do with the ability to store specific facts or strings of numbers in short-term memory, to react quickly, to see spatial relations, and to engage in abstract reasoning. Older adults may lag behind their younger counterparts in this type of learning. Thus, adults often need to be able to put new learning into a context or frame of reference based on their existing knowledge.

Another major difference between the way children and adults learn is explained in terms of what each brings to the learning situation. Adults usually bring a better understanding of *why* they need to learn certain skills and facts. They also bring more background experiences than children do, and are more often used to being in charge; they dislike the lack of control they experience in a typical classroom. The trainer who uses the same approach for both adults and children will, for most topics, be missing the needs of one group or the other.

The style of teaching you experienced as a child and, frequently, even as an adult is called **pedagogy**. *Peda* comes from the Greek *pais* which means "child," and *ago* is from the Greek word for "leading." Therefore, pedagogy means *"leading the child."*

The late Malcolm Knowles is an American theorist who popularized a word that better describes the appropriate way of teaching adults: **androgogy**. *Andra* is Greek for man or adult; thus, *"leading the adult."* Table 2-1 compares some of the characteristics of child and adult learners.

Table 2-1   Differences between Child and Adult Learners

	CHILD	ADULT
Method of operating in general	• Dependent and varied, with few common experiences. • Doesn't know own needs and is not asked. • Has trouble relating learning to real world. • Often unable to understand relevance because experience is limited. • Often willing to try and fail.	• Independent, yet with many common experiences. • Capable of self-direction. High need for relevance. Will ask: "What's in it for me?" and expect a good answer. • Seeks out training to cope with life change events. • More accurate; avoids trial and error.
Method of operating during training	• High dependence on trainer. • Child-to-parent relationship. • Trainer develops curriculum. • Learns mostly for future use.	• Can learn from other learners as well as from trainer. • Adult-to-adult relationship. • May help to define own needs. • Learns for immediate needs as well as future use. • May need time to unlearn ideas and challenge current beliefs.

Source: L. Kelly, ed., The ASTD Technical and Skills Training Handbook. New York: McGraw-Hill, Inc. Used by permission.

Table 2-1   Differences between Child and Adult Learners
(*Continued*)

	CHILD	ADULT
Implications for the trainer	• Trainer is the expert—the giver of information. • Needs to provide simple, common illustrations. • Must give frequent examples to learners. • Hard to find common denominators to build on. • "Survey" courses (i.e., a superficial overview of topics) work well.	• Trainer is the catalyst—the arranger of training experiences. Also mediator, facilitator, processor, and occasionally expert. • Can and should draw on learners' prior experience and use their examples to illustrate points. • Instructor can use analogies, similes, etc. • Avoid survey courses; focus on specific problems and issues.

What is the difference between inductive and deductive learning, and when should each be used?

Part, but not all, of the difference in the approach to training between children and adults has to do with whether the trainer uses a style that could be termed **inductive** or **deductive**. With the inductive style, the trainer tells the trainee what needs to be known. A lecture is typical of the inductive style.

The deductive style is also known as the "Socratic method," named after Socrates, the philosopher and teacher who supposedly never told his students anything, but simply asked questions of them. Some also call it the "aha!" style of training, in which the trainer guides the trainee to an understanding by posing situations and asking questions of the trainee. This method leads to the trainees synthesizing previously known facts into higher level knowledge. Case studies are an example of a deductive style. Most training is some combination of both inductive and deductive styles, though not always in the right places or proportions.

Children are frequently taught using the inductive style because of their limited experience with a particular topic as well as with life in general. Adults, on the other hand, will only occasionally need a totally inductive style of training. Adults may need to be trained inductively if the subject matter is: (1) quite new to them, (2) unstructured or illogical, (3) physically dangerous, or in certain other situations, such as those in which damage or loss of productivity could occur. In those situations, even adults should be told facts or procedures, not left to discover them for themselves. Most of the time, however, the deductive approach works better for adults for a variety of reasons, not the least of which is that it *involves* them in the learning. Adults learn best as active learners working on simulations or problems that they perceive to be relevant to the workplace.

Adults need to feel respected, and may see inductive training as being "talked down" to. The deductive approach to training also helps the trainees learn the concepts behind the facts and procedures, instead of just the facts and procedures themselves. This combined approach helps them integrate new information with old, instead of trying to just add on more data. Table 2-2 suggests situations in which each of the two styles is appropriate for adult training.

Table 2-2   Inductive versus Deductive Training for Adults

VARIABLE	USE INDUCTIVE WHEN	USE DEDUCTIVE WHEN
Trainees' entering knowledge	The learner has no (or at least a very limited) relevant background.	The learner knows facts or has experience in related areas.
Nature of subject	Procedure to be learned goes step-by-step; is not intuitive OR when safety or other cost concerns (scrap, etc.) apply.	A variety of means will achieve the desired end; structure is logical and intuitive; **AND** when such things as safety and scrap costs are not an issue.
Trainer's ability	The trainer has a limited grasp of subject or not much experience teaching.	Knows subject and can deal with interactive dynamics.
Time limitations	Lots of material must be covered in a little time; preparation time is limited.	More time is available to train. Adequate preparation is possible.

Do all adults learn in the same way?

The two previous tables highlight many differences between adults and children as learners. But the classifications of "adults" and "children" can be rather broad and subjective. Not all learners are the same. It should be no surprise that humans, irrespective of age, vary from person to person and topic to topic on how they learn best. A number of models exist to describe how individual adults prefer to learn. For the past decade, much of this research has been categorized under the rubric of "learning styles."

Kolb's model of learning styles,[2] for example, uses a test that categorizes learning styles into four general types: the converger, the diverger, the assimilator, and the accommodator. The **converger** learns mainly through abstract conceptualization and active experimentation. This approach means that the person who prefers this learning style can deal with theories, and wants to try things out to prove these theories. The **diverger** pairs concrete experiences with reflective observations. So, this person learns best by doing things, then thinking back over what happened and reflecting on those experiences to develop a fuller understanding. An **assimilator** learns through abstract conceptualization and reflective observations. This type of person doesn't necessarily need to do anything but can cognitively process ideas. Finally, an **accommodator** employs both concrete experience and active experimentation. The accommodator learns to swim best by jumping into the middle of the lake.

Another model of how people learn is offered by R. M. Gagné. He lists eight types of learning, which he calls "varieties of learning (a taxonomy)."[3] They range in increasing complexity from **signal learning** (Pavlovian-type classical response to stimuli) through **problem solving** (recall and integration of multiple previously known data into higher level information). Box 2-1 outlines Gagné's eight types of learning.

Another way of classifying learning styles—according to perceptual categories—is to equate whether learners learn best in visual, auditory, or kinesthetic styles. Visual learners are most comfortable receiving information from sight. Auditory learners take in oral information as a primary means of learning, and kinesthetic learners need to be actively involved in neuromuscular activities to effectively understand skills and concepts. Langevin[4] offers a quick test that categorizes learning preferences under this model. Visual is the most common of these preferences, with kinesthetic a distant second, and auditory third. This perceptual

Box 2-1   Gagné's Eight Learning Styles

Signal learning	Learning a general response to a specific signal.
Stimulus-response	Learning a single response to a stimulus situation.
Shaping	Learning to join together two or more stimulus-response associations.
Verbal association	Learning to associate two or more verbal, specific stimulus-responses.
Multiple discrimination	Learning to make different and appropriate responses to different stimuli.
Concept learning	Learning to generalize and make appropriate responses to stimuli based on classes or character of the stimuli.
Principle learning	Developing a formal logic that relates two or more concepts.
Problem solving	Retrieving and combining two or more previously learned principles into a higher order principle, which is previously unknown to the learner.

model provides a good way to think about designing training, because you can ask yourself what in the lesson is catering to the visual learner, what to the kinesthetic learner, and what to the auditory learner. A pure lecture provides only auditory stimulation. Add a video showing the whole process, or even something as simple as writing the key words on a flip chart, and the visual learner is more engaged. Finally, have the learners manipulate something—practicing a process or even just writing down notes—and the kinesthetic learner gains more.

Many other ways of categorizing learners exist in the adult-learning literature. Regardless of the model employed, probably everyone *can* learn in more than one way. The models only indicate individuals' preferences or most expedient ways of learning.

What can the trainer do with this information? Trainees can be tested to determine their preferred learning styles. If the trainer knows which category an individual trainee matches, she or he may be able to design a more effective or efficient one-on-one training program for that trainee. If there are a number of trainees, it might be possible match them into teams of like-minded peers—all the assimilators in one group, the divergers in another, etc. If several instructors with different training style strengths are available, it may be possible to assign trainees to them, matching the trainees' orientation with the instructors.'

Realistically, in most training situations the trainer won't know the trainees' preferred learning styles. Trainers simply need to be aware that different people learn differently and should try to design the training incorporating a variety of techniques, so that most people are trained in their best learning style at least some of the time. This approach will be explained in greater detail in subsequent chapters.

How can I make the learning experience attractive for adults?

A number of options exist to help make training more palatable for adults. Effective training is, of course, actually a lot more complicated than just following this checklist. Otherwise, there would be no need for the rest of this book. For now, here are some effective ideas for training adults:

Help set positive expectations, so people can relax. Keep training as risk free as possible. Many adults have been negatively conditioned by poor training experiences in the past. Trainees frequently approach a training session with some concerns. Adults don't want to look foolish with their peers, so the trainer should do whatever is reasonable to establish the experience as positive and non-threatening. The trainer creates the environment, but the trainees can help develop and buy into the expectations for the learning experience.

Use appropriate motivations and rewards. Reduce ambivalence to learning. Blanchard and Thacker state that "Most learning isn't something that happens automatically or unconsciously. It's an activity that we decide to do or not do."[5] Given this situation, the trainer needs to clearly spell out the benefits to learning. Motivation can be positive or negative, of course. One can motivate by saying, "Learn to do this and you will enjoy your job more, get a raise, and be able to retire happy and fulfilled." Or, one can motivate by saying, "Learn to do this by next week, or you're fired." Positive motivation is usually preferable, but the negative approach may work (expect consequences, however). Which will work best depends in large part on the individual trainees.

Allow for unlearning time, if necessary. Sometimes the experience that adults bring to the training can be excess baggage instead of useful information. Keep in mind that some people show up with good ideas and experience, others with poor ideas or experience that doesn't match the situation, and still others with no idea or experience at all. If they show up with incorrect ideas or old ways of doing things—e.g., the wrong methods for doing a task—then allow some extra time and clear reasons to *unlearn* before the trainees can tune themselves in to learning the correct method.

Make the training clearly relevant. Adults want specific, practical, and life-like situations that will satisfy their needs and interests. Adults want to see immediate benefits from the material they're learning. Explain why they need to learn what you are teaching. Relevance will be easier to explain if the trainer follows the processes outlined in the next chapter and works with the supervisors of the trainees before, during, and after the training sessions.

Use the concept of "just-in-time" training. Training that can be immediately applied provides additional motivation and a sense of urgency. If possible, schedule technical training just before the skill or knowledge will be used in the workplace, allowing enough time for assimilation and practice, of course.

Sequence the training appropriately. A popular book in the field is titled "Telling Ain't Training."[6] Simply presenting a collection of relevant information to trainees does not qualify as training. The data must be organized in some logical, cohesive fashion, using principles of instructional design. Frequently, ideas are presented starting with the easiest or most basic and moving to the most difficult or complex. But some training may be better presented by working from the first step to the last, or from known to unknown. The sequence should also allow for variations in training pace and intensity. Malcolm Knowles[7] points out that there is a difference between a content plan and a process design. A process design is much more difficult. Further suggestions on the subjects of sequencing, pacing, and other lesson design ideas are found in Chapter 10.

Recognize that adults have short attention spans. Many researchers claim that adults have even shorter attention spans than children. Training works best when offered in "bite-sized chunks." A chunk is a key piece of information, a module, a natural unit of work in a task, or some logical subdivision of the whole to be

Figure 2-1   Stimulus-Response-Feedback Link

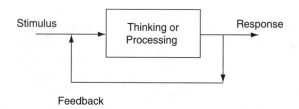

learned. Drawing on the work of behavioral psychologists, notably B. F. Skinner, many professional trainers use what are called "short S-R-F links." The letters refer to Stimulus (or Situation), Response, and Feedback. The trainer provides a stimulus—an idea, example, key point, question, demonstration of an action, etc. The trainee is given a brief time to process this information, then must respond by answering the question, performing an action, etc. The trainer then employs feedback to indicate whether the trainee's response was accurate. If it was not, the learning process is repeated, perhaps in some modified form, until the response is correct. Figure 2-1 depicts a Stimulus-Response-Feedback link. This process enables frequent shifts of activity, from receiving information to expressing information, on the part of the trainees. We will return to this topic in more depth, especially in Chapter 10.

Involve the learners. Learning is more rapid and efficient when the learner is a participant, rather than a spectator. Learning based on the trainee's past experience will be easier and more permanent than learning based on unrelated experience.

Have the learners do something or create something. Learning must be used in order to be retained. It should be applied immediately, hence the earlier suggestion for "just-in-time" training. A visible and tangible product that results from the learning process stimulates interest and accelerates learning. It also supports the learners who prefer a kinesthetic learning style.

Speak their language. Trainees want to feel that the trainer understands their situation. When trainees hear the trainer frequently speak in the abstract or use too many "textbook terms," they will be put off, and may question the trainer's credibility. Trainers must learn the jargon of and use examples from the workplace to which the trainees are or will be assigned; they also need to understand the typical style of operation in the workplace.

Use appropriate training techniques and support. Giving a lecture about art or music without also using some visuals or sound would be very poor training technique. The chosen training techniques must match the topic. Art is a visual medium; thus. it should usually be taught visually. Music is an aural medium; it requires sound to support effective understanding. Another reason to use various techniques is to engage more of the senses. Learners remember what they see longer than what they merely hear, and what they do longer than what they merely see. Using problem-solving methods and materials is conducive to heightened interest and, thus, learning.

Ask frequent questions. The trainer needs to find out how the trainees are doing, and such questioning involves them in the process much more actively. Be sure to use true S-R-F loops. Simply asking, "Are there any questions?" or "Do you understand?" does not meet the requirement of a true S-R-F loop. The question must require the learner to respond to some point that they have just learned. This is an important distinction, which will be addressed several more times in this book.

Promote concentration. Control the physical learning environment to the extent that you can, to help the learners focus on the task at hand. Control includes such things as requiring cell phones to be turned off and minimizing distractions, such as activity outside the windows or noise in the room. Vary the stimuli and pacing of the content and activities, and otherwise do what you can to help the learners focus. Hold the training off-site, if possible, or limit distractions and interruptions if the training is held on-site. Also, be sure to give breaks at appropriate times, before the trainees lose their concentration.

Tap into group dynamics, when possible. A number of people with common interests, working together, learn faster than the same persons working alone. Adults don't necessarily need the input or feedback of the trainer—they can learn from peers. The trainer's role may be simply to ensure that this learning occurs and is accurate. Besides, trainees often must work in teams when they get back to the job, and encouraging this structure during training may have the added benefit of building bonds and interpersonal skills.

What else would be useful to know?

Hundreds of other ideas and theories might be useful for a trainer. Some colleges offer education (and training) in adult education up to the Ph.D. level. Check the Psychology department (Human

Development and Learning), Workplace Learning and Development, or Adult Education departments of your local college or university for further suggestions about courses and materials. Learning is a very complex process, and no single book or text will make you an expert. Also see the list in the reference section at the end of this book.

Instructional systems design

Earlier in the chapter, a *model* was defined as a simplification of reality used to help us better understand the essential elements of that reality. In order to model a concept such as training, it must first be broken down into its component parts. Most processes that are as complex as training can be broken down in a variety of ways. Several training design models follow, each of which has its strengths and weaknesses; however, the rest of this book will build on the model shown in Figure 2-2, labeled "Vaughn's model." Before discussing specific models, however, the reader needs to understand some of the broader concepts.

Figure 2-2   Vaughn's Model of Instructional Systems Development

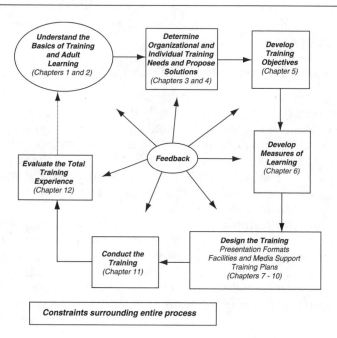

What is meant by "Instructional Systems Design"?

Instructional Systems Design (ISD) is a *systematic* approach to developing training programs to ensure that appropriate resources are created, evaluated, and modified until trainees attain the desired instructional goals. Glenn Snelbecker gives a nice historical summary of the origins and development of ISD.[8] He and many other writers on the subject of ISD advocate using an iterative process and doing what makes the most sense in individual circumstances. An *iterative process* means going back and adjusting a design, perhaps multiple times, in order to progress, because it's unlikely that a person will get through the exact series of steps in just one attempt. The reasons for this iterative approach are the complexity of training designs and the many variables operating in the organization in which the training is developed. For this reason, many ISD or systems models are shown with feedback loops between steps.

The iterative nature of ISD does not mean that "just any random approach" to training design will work. A plethora of models exist, and each varies from the next in sometimes insignificant ways. Some are designed as systems models, such as the one used in this book, while others are designed as checklists or merely step-by-step processes. The purpose of each is to provide some sort of structure to help the trainer move through a logical process of discovering what the trainees need to know, then designing a way to help them learn it.

What are some examples of ISD models?

Before going on to discuss the chosen model, this book will describe a few others that may help the reader to understand the ISD concept—or at least put a different perspective on it.

First, Richard Chang, a former national president of ASTD, has developed what he calls the High-IMPACT™ Training model.[9] His model is relatively simple, straightforward, and has a workable memory hook. "IMPACT" is an acronym for **I**dentify, **M**ap, **P**roduce, **A**pply, **C**alculate, and **T**rack.

Identify Training Needs. In this stage, the training designer gathers and analyzes appropriate information and prepares a description of the specific training needed to improve job performance.

Map the approach. Here the training designer defines what must be learned and chooses the appropriate training approach. The results of this stage are training objectives and a training plan.

Produce learning tools. The actual training materials, trainer's guides, handouts, job aids, media support, and so on are prepared during this third stage.

Apply training techniques. The training is delivered by appropriate means to the trainees.

Calculate measurable results. Find out whether the training has made a difference and communicate the results to the organization. Redesign it, if necessary.

Track ongoing follow-through. Ensure that the training continues to meet the organization's needs and make any other suggestions or take appropriate actions.

Another very useful description of an Instructional Systems Design process was created by the late Dugan Laird.[10] His fifteen-step model, outlined in Table 2-3, assigns training responsibilities to both the trainer and the line managers.

Notice that in Laird's model, as contrasted to Chang's, evaluation measures are considered early in the process. This point will be discussed more fully in Chapter 6.

Laird, Robert Mager, and many others stress that not all problems can be solved by training. If the workers already know how to do something but are not doing it, then training will not help. Motivation or other appropriate techniques are needed in such a case.

What is the ISD model used in this book?

This book is laid out to follow Vaughn's model of ISD. It is a relatively simple and straightforward model, and sufficiently comprehensive to meet the needs of most readers. It incorporates seven stages:

1. Understanding the basics of training and adult learning.
2. Determining organizational and individual training needs; proposing solutions.
3. Developing training objectives.
4. Developing measures of learning.
5. Designing the training.
6. Conducting the training.
7. Evaluating the training.

Table 2-3 Laird's Instructional Design Steps

STEP	ACTIVITY	SUPERVISOR'S RESPONSIBILITIES	TRAINING AND DEVELOPMENT STAFF RESPONSIBILITIES
1	Discover a problem	Usually begins the process, monitors, and must agree there's a problem.	Monitor management reports and other operating indices. Tactfully surface issues.
2	Check or establish performance standards	Agrees to or creates standards.	May be able to help create or document standards in a way to facilitate later training design.
3	Identify the deficiency causing the problem	Must admit that deficiency exists. (Often a painful admission.)	Help to objectify, define, specify, and measure the deficiency in ways to support possible training.
4	Cost the deficiency	Analyze all costs.	Estimate training costs to help in later cost-benefit analysis.
5	Identify causes for the deficiency	Must avoid a tendency to jump to solutions; may have unfounded preconceptions.	Should insist on following the process; may need to accept both short range and long range ideas.
6	Design and select solutions	Same as above.	Same as above; may be in difficult position as training specialist not willing to prescribe training.
7	Decide to go ahead with the best solution—Then, if it's training...	Must make the decision to continue, if training or other solution is recommended.	Can add perspective and prioritize the issue; can advise and recommend to client.

8	...establish behavioral (performance) objectives	Can check validity and make some decisions regarding objectives.	Has the expertise to do establish objectives. Can design appropriate objectives and ask about variable conditions.
9	Design the Training	Has neither skill nor reason to participate. Can be supportive.	Must do this, and establish evaluation mechanism now.
10	Select the trainers	Can recommend credible persons to do this. Should accept some responsibility for conduct of training.	Should encourage active role by management. Need to screen trainers for instructional and communications skills.
11	Upgrade the trainers	Supportive only.	Train the trainers in program content and training techniques.
12	Select the trainees	Must identify trainees, along with schedule needed. Communicate the importance of the training.	Support both line management and the trainees. Stress accountability for learning and job application.
13	Conduct the training	Active participation encouraged. May be best if line and staff can combine as a team to train.	Must rely on line for awareness of norms and climate of job. Must handle the learning dynamics.
14	Measure results	Reviews data for pre- and post-measures. Must understand the importance of this activity.	Provides feedback at all stages of training and must insist that measurements be done.
15	Evaluate results	Can and must confirm conclusions from data about the program's effectiveness. Can identify remaining or new problems.	Can help identify and quantify symptoms of success and failure. Can retrain employees or redesign curriculum to deal with any new or continuing problems.

Source: Excerpted from Laird, D. 1985 *Approaches to Training and Development*. Revised 2nd Edition, Reading, MA: Addison-Wesley pp. 35–39. Structure as shown here by Robert H. Vaughn.

These stages, indicated by the boxes in Figure 2-2, start from the earliest point that a trainer is likely to begin the process of training design.

Understanding the basics

These seven stages must operate within **constraints**, which are limitations on resources available. All kinds of resources may be constraints, including time, equipment, money, space, management and trainer skills, and human resources. These constraints must always be considered in the design of any training process. One of the most important constraints on training design is the degree of top management and supervisory buy-in. These concerns, represented by the first box in the model, are covered in Chapters 1 and 2.

Determining training needs; proposing solutions

Regardless of which of the many models of ISD is chosen, the process of developing a training program is begun by first defining what the organizational requirements are for performing certain jobs, then determining which of those skills, abilities, and knowledge the employees already have. The difference between these two lists—*the training gap*—defines the core skills, knowledge, and abilities that must be taught. Everything else in effective training design depends on clearly defining that gap. The identification and definition of the training gap, represented in the second box of the model, is covered in detail in Chapter 3.

At this point, it may be necessary to make a formal proposal in order to get funding and approval to develop and offer a training program to close that gap. Suggestions for creating and effectively selling a training proposal are detailed in Chapter 4. For complex training programs, information such as costs, time required, and so on, may not be finalized for until later, so subsequent proposals may be needed prior to implementation.

Developing training objectives

Next, the instructional designer or trainer must translate that gap into specific training objectives. These objectives must be designed in such a way that they can be measured and provide sufficient information to design the training. This step is shown in the model in the third box (top right) in the series and is discussed in Chapter 5.

Developing measures of learning

Once the objectives have been developed, the next step is to develop a plan for measuring whether or not they have been successfully achieved. This step, which is best done before the actual training is designed, is represented in the center-right box. Commonly known as "evaluation," it is further explained in Chapter 6, with some additional follow up in Chapter 12.

Designing the training

With the measurement plan in place, the ISD process next requires development of a training plan. Concurrently, the trainer must choose which delivery techniques to use and design or select facilities and media to support the delivery. These tasks are represented in the bottom right box and are covered in detail in Chapters 7 through 10.

Conducting the training

The trainer then provides the training to the organization's employees, clients, or customers This is where all the effort pays off. The trainer needs to deliver the training effectively, using a variety of techniques and involving all of the trainees. Everything possible must be done to encourage the trainees to actually take their new skills and knowledge back to their jobs and use them. Chapter 11 explains a number of techniques for doing this.

Evaluating the training

Finally, to the trainer must find out if the training was effective and sufficient in meeting the organization's needs. This stage is shown in the bottom left box of the model, and discussed in Chapter 12. If the training is sufficient, the process is finished; if not, the process begins again at square one.

Across all of these steps is a feedback loop from one stage to another, because, as discussed, the process is iterative. The feedback loop simply represents the possibility that it may be necessary to backtrack and re-enter the process.

Just how much back and forth is likely to happen during the ISD process?

Of course, the number of iterations will depend on how carefully and thoroughly each step is carried out, but it is also influenced by how complex and dynamic any given job is. Sivasailam Thia-garajan (who goes by "Thiagi") discusses the basic trade-offs that must be made in ISD.[11] He says the first is between design and delivery, and the second is among presentation, activities, and feedback. He offers ten strategies and twenty guidelines to balance these trade-offs. Chief among these guidelines is the basic premise that *any ISD model should be treated as a guide, not a commandment.* It may be appropriate to perform the design steps sequentially or concurrently, or to skip certain steps in some cases, use pre-packaged materials for certain steps, and so on. The trainer should mold the ISD process to meet the organization's needs, not the other way around.

The more carefully the analysis is done, the more likely it will be accurate and lead to training which is in synchronization with what is needed. However, an excessively thorough and careful analysis will probably take a lot longer and cost a lot more than can be justified. If the job or the trainees then change even slightly, that thorough analysis will become obsolete more quickly than a simpler one. It may be better to approximate the need and get on with the training, accepting the probable need for revisions. There is no infallible way to approach ISD, and it must be handled intuitively, with appropriate input from the stakeholders. Strong interpersonal and questioning skills are a big asset to the instructional designer.

This summary completes the discussion of the basic training or instructional systems design model. Subsequent chapters will develop each of the components more thoroughly and create explicit steps to follow or list a variety of things to consider. In large training departments, each of these training elements might be completed by a different person. For the typical trainer or training consultant, however, it will be important to possess at least a knowledge of and probably some skill in all of these aspects of training.

3 Determining Training Needs

*"Never try to teach a pig to sing.
It wastes your time and annoys the pig."*

—Anonymous

The professional trainer begins with the basics: discovering specifically what skills and knowledge the organization needs in order to accomplish its mission, then finding out which of those skills the current or potential employees already bring with them. The difference between these skill sets defines the organization's training need. This gap can best be identified by a systematic analysis, using various tools and techniques of the trade.

■ ■ ■

The opening quote for the chapter is one my uncle has hanging in a frame on his porch in Montana. I thought it was good advice. Although a singing pig might get you on *The Tonight Show with Jay Leno*, it's probably not something that the world really needs. The preferred role of training is to provide something that the organization paying for the training really needs. Unfortunately, what's needed and what's not is seldom as obvious as a singing pig.

What signals the need for training in the organization?

Many events might signal a training need. Some of them have to do with human resource actions. Perhaps the most obvious is a new hire. At a minimum, newly hired employees need an orientation. They may also need skills training and development, either immediately or eventually. New positions, transfers, or promotions are other flags to suggest some possible training requirements. Finally, poor employee performance appraisals, along with many other types of indicators, might also suggest a need for training. Or, they might not, because many different things can cause poor performance.

More extensive training requirements might be suggested by changes in the organization's products, equipment, standards, or policies. Internal and external reports and industry trends may also indicate a need for action by the training department.

Once the broad needs are identified, the trainer or the managers should set some priorities. Which training is most urgent? Typical criteria for priority setting would be: (1) how to do the most good for the most people (cost-effectiveness), (2) what is legally required, and (3) what organizational politics surround training. For now, here is a summary of the some of the key issues and processes an organization might be able to use to help determine its training needs.

What training programs should an organization offer?

Many training departments develop a regular schedule of "off-the-shelf" classes they intend to offer. These standardized courses have a place in organizations that have a sufficient group of trainees (employees or customers) from which to draw. Perhaps some information or skills development is so universal that many people in the organization will need it. Examples of this generic training would include new employee orientation, diversity, stress control, general supervisory skills, new software that will be used across the organization, safety, and certain types of government-mandated courses.

Given a large enough population, the training department might offer such programs through open enrollment, letting managers in the organization send anyone they believe needs the course. But there are some hazards to this approach of becoming the internal little red schoolhouse. For one thing, the training department may become so focused on the existing catalog of programs that some higher priority needs may never be identified and addressed. Sometimes, trainees view involuntary enrollment in training as a punishment or implied warning that they are doing poorly on the job. Other times, they may see it as a reward or expect a promotion once training is completed. A catalog of off-the-shelf offerings may also limit line managers' and employees' perspective of the training department. It may suggest that the department can't offer anything else. So beware! Offer this type of training when it makes sense, but don't overlook chances to discover and help solve other training needs, which might not be covered in a catalog of offerings.

How do we uncover specific training needs?

The rest of this chapter describes a process for two different analyses that must be performed in order to determine what the organization requires its employees to know or be able to do in a particular job, and what the current and potential employees actually know and can do. Because these analyses use similar tools, they are covered together in one chapter. In practice, however, these studies must be kept separate in order to get good information.

Many writers on this subject begin with an *organizational* analysis instead of a *job* analysis. Although an organizational analysis is not a bad idea, several factors usually mitigate against it: it has a high cost, it requires an extensive time commitment, and it requires a different set of skills than training. The role of trainers usually does not include "organizational analyst" at a macro level. Most people who have done professional training in organizations are delighted to even be given the opportunity to do a good job-level analysis. Unfortunately, the more common mode for starting training is for a boss to say, "My people can't seem to show up for work on time. You, with the training hat on—fix them!"

Our discussion of training needs analysis begins with the assumption (however unlikely) that jobs in the organization have been appropriately designed and adequately defined. This pragmatic approach avoids a lengthy digression into organizational analysis and theory as well as a variety of human resource techniques. Realistically, this assumption is where the trainer will usually begin when brought in to help solve a problem. If these assumptions are not met in a specific situation, we suggest that the trainer "partner" with an Organizational Development specialist before engaging in a needs analysis.

Who is responsible for determining what is required in a job? The answer to that question can vary considerably among organizations. It may be a line supervisor, an industrial engineer, a job design specialist, or sometimes even a trainer. Whoever it is, the question is not as simple to answer as one might think. It's important for the goals of training and the goals of the job (as determined by the organization) to be consistent on two points: (1) What is the content of the job? and (2) What is the level of skill or knowledge needed? It is expensive and time consuming to train employees to an expert level if the organization only needs apprentices. Further, it frustrates everyone—the learners, their supervisors, and the trainers—if the skill training given and the tasks in the job that will be done by the trainees don't match. So investing the up-front time necessary to do a good analysis will be well worth it in terms of both improved trainee performance and reduced frustration for everyone. Here's how to do it.

The nine-step training needs analysis process

The process of analyzing training needs can be summed up in nine discrete steps:

- *Step 1*—Gather data about a job within the organization.
- *Step 2*—Develop an understanding of the performance standards applied to that job.
- *Step 3*—Measure the performance that is occurring.
- *Step 4*—Determine differences between standards and performance.
- *Step 5*—Calculate the cost of that disparity. If it's low, stop. If it's substantial, go on.
- *Step 6*—Assess employee levels of skill and knowledge about the job.
- *Step 7*—Analyze the gap between job requirements and the current or potential employee's level of performance.
- *Step 8*—Propose training (or other) solutions appropriate to eliminating the differences between requirements and employee performance.
- *Step 9*—Implement the solution(s) and see if that solves the problems. If not, repeat the process.

Steps 1 through 5 help you to develop a clear picture of training needs as they relate to the organization, and Steps 6 through 9 address aspects of training that are related to individual needs. Each step is described in greater detail later in this chapter.

The sources of data for a good analysis include (1) key individuals within and sometimes outside the organization, (2) job descriptions, (3) quantitative data, again from inside or sometimes outside the organization, and (4) any information about impending changes that will require new skills and knowledge of the workers. Steadham lists nine major categories or tools of basic needs assessment techniques that can be used to gather the information needed. These nine techniques, along with an analysis of the environments in which they work best, are described in Table 3-1.

Table 3-1   Steadham's Basic Needs Assessment Techniques[1]

TECHNIQUE AND BRIEF DESCRIPTION	WHERE AND WHEN IT WORKS
Observation—Watching the work being done. Could be as simple as walking through the area, or as precise as time-motion studies.	Where work is observable (requires physical action), performed in a short enough time span, and consists of repeated sequences. Observer must be non-intrusive and skillful enough to understand all job aspects.
Questionnaires—Administering usually written questions to people who should know. Trainer should follow good data collection procedures.	Where employees are literate enough to read and answer. Can reach many people easily. Data is easily summarized and reported, as long as questionnaire was well designed. Up-front work is required to design effective questions.
Key Consultation—Getting information from people who don't do the work but have some knowledge of it, e.g., customers, professionals in the field, even competitors.	When different perspectives about a job are needed. It's relatively simple and inexpensive to conduct. May help improve lines of communication. Must be cautious of biases.
Print Media—Researching trade magazines, textbooks on the process, in-house publications, rate books, professional journals.	When a printed source is readily available and can provide an outsider's view of certain jobs.
Interviews—Talking with people who should know the answers to questions about job requirements and influences. Can be structured or unstructured.	When two-way interaction (unlike that with questionnaires, for example) is required to flesh out details more effectively. Requires skill in asking questions. Data can be more difficult to synthesize.
Group Discussion—Using several people to enrich the understanding or get different perspectives. Tools such as brainstorming may help.	When group dynamics may enhance information gathering. These same dynamics, when not properly handled, can inhibit data collection. Time consuming, and data may be difficult to synthesize.

(continued)

Table 3-1   Steadham's Basic Needs Assessment Techniques (*Continued*)

TECHNIQUE AND BRIEF DESCRIPTION	WHERE AND WHEN IT WORKS
Tests—Administering tests, either skill (performance) tests, such as a typing test, or knowledge tests used to determine understanding of job concepts.	When good data, which is quantifiable and comparable, is required. Can be intimidating, especially for incumbents. Effective tests may be difficult and time consuming to design and validate. Tests may fit only one specific situation.
Records, Reports—Using any data maintained about a job, such as scrap rates, minutes of meetings, turnover statistics, accident reports, budgets, etc.	When data must be collected with minimum interruption of work and effort on analyst's part. Can be an excellent clue to trouble spots, but frequently indicate symptoms or effects, rather than causes of problems. Reflect past data, not necessarily current situations.
Work Samples—Examining tangible outputs of the job (whether a physical product or a report) may help the analyst better understand the work to be done.	When a highly reliable source of information is required. Must be effectively analyzed. Again, may show effects and symptoms, but not causes of problems.

Several other sources of information, which aren't in Steadham's list, include trade and professional associations related to the specific field of work and the specific industry. Other resources may be available through broader-based organizations such as SHRM, ASTD, ISPI, and other organizational development, industrial engineering, and related groups.

What is the process for determining organizational performance needs?

Begin the process by defining a job that the organization needs done. Selling shoes? Running a lathe? Installing software? Managing a project? It doesn't even have to be a complete job. Perhaps just part of a job, or even a part-time job, must be studied.

Once you have defined the scope of the job, the next task is to determine the skills, attributes, knowledge, and abilities needed by *the employee* to perform that job. A key point here is to determine *exactly and only what has to happen in the job to meet the needs of the organization.* This stage of the analysis, which consists of steps 1 through 5, has nothing to do with the actual existing skills or knowledge of any specific present or future employees. If necessary, that analysis comes later. It consists of Steps 6 through 9, described later in this chapter.

Step 1: Gathering data about a job within an organization. Perhaps the best starting point for Step 1 is to look at the job description for the position, if one exists. Another technique is to simply ask various individuals who perform the job to list what they do. Supervisors and managers should also be asked for their input.

In very simple jobs, workers will list a step-by-step chronology of what they are required to do. In more complex jobs, the data that workers provided is usually very disorganized, and the trainer or analyst must make sense of it. These brainstorming sessions may produce simply a raw list of tasks. The tasks can then be sorted and categorized through outlining or other data organizing strategies, such as the fishbone technique, various kinds of flowcharting, or a job decomposition (Figure 3-1). To outline a job, list the major categories of work as first-level items, then, below each first-level item, list what second-level tasks must be done to accomplish the work named in the first-level category. In a third level, further break out the second-level tasks, and so on.

Job decomposition is a particularly helpful technique. An example of decomposing the job of a machine repair technician is shown in Figure 3-1. This process starts with the overall job title and breaks the duties of that job into major sub-parts, then divides each of those into minor elements, and so on. The net effect is the same as outlining, but it ends up with a visual aid that looks something like an organization chart. It is not only helpful in clarifying the job, but it often suggests areas that have been missed and may also be useful later while designing training objectives and the training plan.

To decompose a job, begin with the job title or a general description of how the job fits into the organization as a whole. In the example in Figure 3-1, the machine repair technician has several major duties to perform. One of them is to engage in preventive maintenance. Doing preventive maintenance requires

Figure 3-1 Job Decomposition

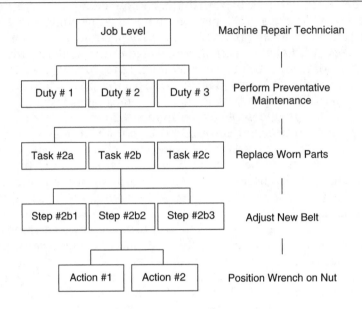

accomplishing a number of tasks, one of which is to replace worn parts. Among the steps in replacing worn parts is adjusting a new belt once it's installed. An action necessary to adjust the belt is to place the wrench on the nut of the bracket. Many jobs, including nearly all manual jobs, can be decomposed in this manner. Although this example shows five levels, some jobs may be easily described in two or three, while others might require nine or ten. Eventually the analyst or trainer gets down to the level that industrial engineers call "therbligs." Therbligs are basic movements such as reach, grasp, turn, etc. For purposes of a job improvement study, it may be appropriate to analyze a job at this level, but this much detail is seldom needed for training or lesson design purposes. *Decompose a job only to a level at which an effective training objective can be written.* It's unlikely that an individual will be trained how to reach and grasp, so there's no need to decompose a job to that level for training purposes. Training objectives will be discussed in depth in Chapter 5.

Which of Steadham's nine tools (Table 3-1) could be used in the process of decomposing the job of machine repair technician? At a minimum, observation, interviews, group discussion, and work records would all be helpful. Any of the tools could apply to certain types of machine repair jobs.

Some work, on the other hand, can't be "observed" in the normal sense of the word. Management, sales, advanced accounting, and engineering are all examples of mental work that can be accomplished in a variety of ways. None of those jobs can be reduced to "therbligs" or even to easily defined and measured pieces. An analyst would certainly need to use tools that go beyond simple observation to decompose these jobs, but many others are available. That's why having a varied toolkit, such as Steadham's list, is so useful. If your only tool is a hammer, all jobs begin to look like nails.

Step 2: Determine what standards apply to the job. You should now have a clear understanding and definition of the job. The next stage is to determine how well (i.e., to what level) that job must be performed. For example, knowing that a worker must use math is one thing, but it is also essential to understand whether "math" means simple arithmetic, algebra, or advanced calculus. Also, will the math be done manually or with the help of a calculator, cash register, or computer? Getting people to help with this stage is often difficult, and frequently, the bias is to set the standards too high.

In the maintenance example, the trainer might look for standards such as how many machines must be serviced each month, or how long it should take to service one, or what failure level (breakdown, despite periodic maintenance) is acceptable, etc. Again, some of Steadham's tools, such as group discussion, records, and key consultations, could be used for this analysis.

Such knowledge can help to prevent the trainer from teaching either too much or too little about a job. A clear description of the job is invaluable to help the training designer create objectives that have an appropriate level in terms of Bloom's Taxonomy (discussed in Chapter 5). It will also make training more cost efficient.

Step 3: Measure performance in that job against the standards. Is the job now being performed in a satisfactory manner by the current workers? If so, probably no skills training is needed for the current workforce on that particular job at this time. Of course, training may be needed as new people are hired to do that job, or if the nature of the job is going to change because of new technology, equipment, or materials. On the other hand, if the job is not currently being performed in a manner that meets the standards, training *may* be needed. But do not jump to that conclusion just yet. Many things in addition to (or instead of) a lack of training for workers may be the cause of not meeting standards.

Step 4: Determine the difference (if any) between the standard and actual performance. If the job is now being done in a way that does not meet the standards, the analyst or trainer needs to specify what is not happening that should, or what is happening that shouldn't. This discrepancy or "gap" must be defined as clearly as possible, because it may provide guidance in developing a training plan later. Put the differences into specific terms, such as:

■ "Workers need to complete installation and set up in 40 minutes; the average worker now requires 55 minutes."

■ "Employees should be able to complete 35% of cold sales calls; they are now completing about 20%."

■ "Operator needs to respond to all requests for information without reference source; does not yet understand the features of products a, b, and e and needs better recall of managers' names."

Step 5: Determine the cost of that deviation. How much is that failure to meet standards costing the organization? Costs come in many forms. A few examples could be:

■ lowered production

■ increased scrap and rework

■ customer dissatisfaction

■ returns

■ defection to competitors

■ employee turnover

■ accidents, including increased workers' compensation rates

As much as possible, these costs should be quantified as a dollar amount. If the cost is minor, and the deviation presents no serious danger—such as customers leaving or a machine exploding—ignoring the problem may be appropriate. All businesses ignore at least some problems, if those problems are minor. And it often makes sense to ignore them—this is not a perfect world. If fixing the problem will cost more than the problem is costing now, leave well enough alone. If organizational decision makers determine that the problem is something that must be fixed, move on to Step 6. This step takes the analyst or trainer to the next stage of the process: how to deal with the *individual*.

Step 6: Determine the workers' skills in relation to the job. Now that you have defined in adequate detail what is necessary to do the job, the next step is to find out if the employees actually know how to do the job correctly. Do they have the requisite skills, knowledge, abilities, and attitudes? Are they fast enough, accurate enough, and otherwise capable of meeting the standards required in the job? If not, this performance gap probably identifies a training need. If they do possess the knowledge and have all the skills, attitudes, and abilities to do the job, then no *training* need exists, and training will *not* remedy the problem. Instead, the solution could be improving logistics (getting the work to the workers), equipment (more of it, better, faster, etc.), management competence (lack of skills in motivation, scheduling, etc.), materials, or many other factors. Figure 3-2 represents this kind of needs analysis.

How does the trainer or analyst get the information to make this determination? As staff persons, they are required to determine which of the skills, abilities, knowledge, and attributes needed

Figure 3-2 Needs Analysis Model

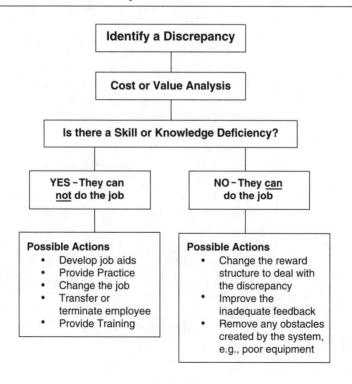

to perform the defined job are already part of the employees' or trainees' repertoire. The employees might be recently hired or transferred to a new job, or they could be employees who have been on the job for awhile but are not performing adequately. Further, they could be persons who will soon be doing a new or substantially changed job. To determine their training needs, the trainer or analyst must return again to Steadham's list of tools (Table 3-1). Any or all of the tools might be used to determine an individual's training needs.

How is a "gap analysis" performed?

Step 7: Analyze the gap between job requirements and current skills of the potential trainee. At a minimum, the trainer can simply ask people what they know and don't know, or how they perform a task. The "Supervisory Training Needs Analysis" form at the end of this chapter illustrates one format for asking these questions. The trainer can also ask the workers' supervisors or subordinates, or even customers, as is routinely done with customer complaint or feedback forms. This gap analysis can be accomplished through any of the techniques listed by Steadham (Table 3-1). These tools provide effective ways to gather opinions of individual training needs, but—beware!—as *opinions*, they may not be accurate or complete. Observations, work samples, records, and reports also might be used to give more direct indications of what knowledge and skills are not being used on the job.

A caution with these tools, as discussed earlier, is that there is no way to be sure the results actually indicate a lack of knowledge or skills on the part of the workers. Other factors—such as poor attitude, motivation, equipment, or materials—can result in poor performance, even if workers possess the necessary skills and knowledge.

Print media is probably the least useful of Steadham's tools for determining individual training needs. Testing may be one of the best, but it is perhaps most difficult to apply. Designing accurate, valid, and reliable tests is challenging. Entire courses on tests and measurements are offered in education and human psychology departments, which deal with nuances beyond the scope of this book. Sometimes it is possible to find pre-existing, even standardized tests that clearly apply to the job. Because of the important issues of **reliability** and **validity** (discussed in Chapter 6), tests should be used with caution when important human resource decisions are being based upon them. For a preexisting test, ensure that reliability and validity indices are explained in lay terminology to line managers, executives, and union personnel. Some jobs are sufficiently simple and well defined that either a customized or standardized test can be used fairly confidently to determine whether an individual has the knowledge or skills to perform a given job. Employment tests, for example, often are used to test applicants' ability to type, do math problems, follow directions, etc. Standardized tests of this nature are available from dozens of sources.[2]

In the case of a technology change—for example, when a new piece of equipment has been purchased or the organization is going through an upgrade in computer operating systems—it's fairly likely that most of the workforce involved will need training. But how about a less clear situation? What if just two or three salespeople out of twenty are not meeting their quotas? Should everyone be trained, or should poor performers be singled out for individual support? If they are singled out, how should they be trained? What if the organization is hiring just one or two new people? The answers to questions such as these depend on the organization's circumstances. Is a trainer available? How many people are affected by a change and thus require training?

A side benefit to effectively determining the workers' skill levels is that it establishes a benchmark. The trainer has, in effect, given them a pre-test for the training, if it occurs.

Step 8: Propose what is necessary to solve the problem. Once the analysis is complete, training needs will be evident in some cases, whereas in others, training may be obviously unnecessary (see Figure 3-2). Perhaps, however, even if the job is clear and the employees currently have the necessary knowledge and skills to perform it, some *emerging needs* will still require that training be developed. Emerging needs could include such things as: (1) new equipment or facilities, (2) additional employees needed for a job, or new hires replacing some current employees, (3) a new product or new activities to be added to an existing job, (4) an upgrade in technology, (5) new government regulations, or any number of other situations. In all of these cases, the training proposal must fit the situation. Chapter 4 provides a format for writing training proposals.

Step 9: Implement the solutions. The implementation process should, of course, be spelled out in the proposal and in the plan that evolves from discussing the proposal.

Once the organization's performance needs have been identified and the individual employee's level of skill or knowledge have been assessed, the training should reduce the difference between the two. This difference, earlier referred to as the ***training gap,*** can be expressed as a simple equation:

$$= \frac{\textit{Organization's required skills and knowledge} - \textit{Individual's existing skills and knowledge}}{\textit{Training needs for the individual}}$$

If one-on-one training will be used, this equation presents a basic plan of exactly what the individual needs to learn in order to do the job as defined. If group training is anticipated, a pattern of common needs must be developed. Decisions must be made as to how much training will be offered and how any shortfalls will be addressed. This outline covers the basic process of specifying what training is necessary, as described in the second box in Vaughn's model (Chapter 2). The next step is to create training objectives and measures in order to evaluate whether learning has occurred as a result of the training that will be developed. Note that, in accordance with the model, the objectives and measures both precede actual designing of the training itself.

What if we can't do an assessment of the job or the trainees?

Most people who have been in the training business for a time know that a trainer is often asked to design and perform a training program with a less than adequate study of either the job or the trainees.

Unfortunately, that's probably the norm. Trainers often walk into the training session not knowing for sure what objectives should be met or what pre-existing skill levels the trainees have. Of course, this situation requires reaching into the magic bag of tricks to dazzle trainees with showmanship, since one can't impress them with planning. In this instance, there is no substitute for experience and a repertoire of standby techniques, forms, and questions.

Admittedly, not having a decent needs analysis before training begins creates a tough situation, but here are a few hints. First, if possible, refuse to do the training. Insist that no one can do a good job unless he or she understands what the trainees' job requires and what the trainees already know and can do. If refusing is not possible, then try to at least talk ahead of time with some trainees, their supervisor, and anyone else who might give at least an informal assessment of the situation. Also, take the time to visit the work environment. This step can help considerably to get the feel of the operation. Ask questions, look at equipment being used, and consider products or customers being served. This interaction has the added benefit of involving workers, supervisors, and managers in the needs analysis stage (however briefly), increasing the chances they will support the training later on.

In a situation where either needs or skill levels are unclear, start the training program using a deductive mode in order to quickly get an idea of the trainees' level. The trainer who starts inductively in this situation risks rambling on for hours, not knowing whether the presentation is over their heads or boring them to tears. Come prepared to be flexible with the training. Some of your trainees will probably be willing to help you out. Apply the principles of adult learning discussed in Chapter 2, and *let them* help you. Begin by doing an in-class needs analysis— perhaps even decomposing the job (Figure 3-1), using a flip chart. A tool such as the need analysis questionnaire (Figure 3-3) might also help you to get a quick feel for the group. Ways to handle this situation are also covered in Chapter 11.

Figure 3-3   Example Needs Analysis Format

This is an example of a needs analysis that could be used for a Supervisory Skills course. Similar types of questions can be designed for many topics.

This is an excellent tool to use before a class or early in the training. To use this analysis questionnaire, trainees make a mark somewhere between the extremes on each line to indicate where they feel their current mode of operation as a supervisor falls on the continuum. The trainer can show a quick class summary by placing a transparency of the form over the top of each of the forms and making a mark on top of each of the trainees' marks. The resulting summary can be viewed on an overhead projector.

Trainees will likely express much agreement on some topics and much disagreement on others. If this analysis is done before training or early on in the program, such information can help in planning or adjusting the training. It can also be shared with the trainees, to show the diversity of approaches used by their classmates.

An even simpler variation of this format is to list on a questionnaire the topics that might be covered. Have the trainees indicate their need to learn each of the topics on some form of Likert scale (i.e., a "1 to 5" rating or a "none-low-some-high" type of scale.)

(*continued*)

Figure 3-3 Example Needs Analysis Format (*Continued*)

Advantage: This type of questionnaire is quick to design and easy to complete and compile. *Disadvantage*: It represents the respondents' opinions only; therefore, it may not be accurate. This type of questionnaire is certainly not a substitute for a needs analysis, but it can be a stopgap measure to provide at least some information about trainees' existing skills and knowledge. It can also be a good opening activity for the training.

SUPERVISORY TRAINING NEEDS

1. I am more comfortable if I am given:
   An end goal only ---------------------- Details and an exact process

2. I tend to make decisions:
   Quickly, then act
   on them ---------------------- After much study and thought

3. On the job, I am personally:
   Easygoing ---------------------- Uptight and hurried

4. I personally use my time so I:
   Get everything
   done easily ---------------------- Am always behind in work

5. I am most comfortable working on a project:
   By myself ---------------------- With a group

6. As a supervisor, I am most concerned about:
   Subordinates ---------------------- Assigned jobs

7. I would rather communicate with people by:
   Talking with them ---------------------- Sending them memos

8. I can deal more effectively with:
   Individuals ---------------------- Work groups

9. When training a new worker for
   a job I know, I'd rather:
   Do it myself ---------------------- Delegate it

10. Most of my subordinates will usually:
    Do a good job ---------------------- Goof off if they can

11. I discuss job performance with my
    subordinates:
    Daily, or more
    often if needed ---------------------- When the annual evaluation is due

12. I would personally prefer to get from
    a supervisory training program:
    Background to
    develop my own ---------------------- Direct, specific suggestions

©1985 by Arvon Management Services. Used by permission.

4

Developing Effective Training Proposals

"It is much more pleasant to make the decision than to justify it."

—*Malcolm Forbes*

Once you have determined what the organizational training needs are, you will often need to get approvals from the decision makers in order to proceed. The professional trainer approaches this task in a way that will optimize the chances of acceptance.

■ ■ ■

Successfully designing and presenting proposals for training requires careful thought. The process recommended here can apply to proposals that are created by external consultants or internal training and development departments (staff employees) or by individuals, supervisors, or managers (line employees). The presentation to the decision maker may be in written or oral form, and the decision maker may be an individual manager or a group, such as an executive committee. The suggested proposal format that follows can also be applied to nearly any type of subject matter. An example proposal, including nearly all of the elements that are suggested in the discussion, is included at the end of this chapter.

Many projects will require more than one proposal and approval. So far in this book, we've only come through the stage of determining what training appears to be necessary. A lot of the information that would support a good proposal may still be unknown until further along in the planning stages. Although discussing a training proposal seems to be appropriate here, recall from the ISD model used in this book that you may need to return to this stage again. Think of this process as first getting approval to *design* the training, after which you'll have more information to go back for approval to *implement* the training.

Why is a proposal necessary?

Managers require information to make decisions. This information can come from a variety of external or internal sources including staff, lower level managers, participative employee teams, or individual employees. Getting training recommendations implemented by management depends on making credible, effective proposals. Invariably, these proposals, whether they are in written or oral form, will include similar information.

Regardless of how the information is conveyed, movement to and acceptance of any training program comes only when the decision maker is convinced of a valid need. The focus of your presentation must be: *Why* is the training needed? If you can't sell the "why," the "how" is irrelevant.

How can I design a proposal that is likely to be accepted?

Training programs will result in new ideas and, probably, in changes in the organization. Organizations tend to resist changes for the same reasons that individuals resist most changes. These reasons include such concerns as cost of the changes, the fact that existing comfort levels and patterns are disrupted by change, and so on. Further, organizations often resist changes more than individuals do. One reason is the physics concept of inertia: A body at rest tends to stay at rest; a body in motion tends to stay in motion in the same direction at a constant speed. Changing either of those states takes energy, and the larger the body, the more energy it takes. Also, besides organizational inertia, there is something that might be called organizational immunization. In the biology of an organism, if something causes an unwanted change, the body will send defenses against it—white blood cells or whatever—to keep the change from happening. Organizations tend to do this, as well.

Although most proposals will encounter some resistance, that resistance can be reduced by thoughtful and appropriate design. In general, changes will be more easily accepted if they are:

- *as small as possible rather than radical.* This aspect suggests that a one-day training program that will solve 70% of the problem will be more readily adopted than a week long program that may solve 90%.
- *reversible rather than permanent at first.* Suggest a pilot program, rather than a permanent, long-term process.
- *the product of input from persons who have an interest in the subject.* See the following section for ideas.
- *timely.* Right after an announced budget cut is a good time to suggest ideas that will save costs, but not ideas that will add costs.
- *open to discussion rather than presented as ultimatums.*

Decision makers of all kinds usually respond better to ideas that aren't totally new to them. Before making any formal presentation or submission, the individual who is recommending the training should do some pre-selling. Pre-selling may come about naturally as the proposal is designed. Make a conscious effort to involve:

- persons who will be affected by the training.
- the decision makers.
- the evaluators, who may be different persons than the decision makers.

Also, it may be wise to discuss the training proposal with those who oppose it as well as those who favor it. The key to dealing with those who oppose it is to explain the proposal in generalities, but not in specifics. This discussion can provide needed feedback, yet the lack of details will make it difficult for opponents to obstruct the idea.

How detailed should the proposal be?

In-depth development of the proposal and implementation plan has some benefits. Yet, deciding which people should be trained first or exactly which shade of green to use for the handout folders has some hazards. Developing a complete proposal takes much longer than putting together a quick overview. It also commits the creator of the proposal to extensive efforts, which may be wasted if the decision is "No" or "Yes, but . . ." instead of just

"Yes." Also, extensive details may murky the waters if the decision maker is interested only in the results, not the process.

Under-developed ideas may be harder to sell, however, and they may also reduce the presenter's credibility in the eyes of the decision maker. They do, however, enable you to change them more easily and include improvements, as long as the decision maker is tolerant of less than completely developed plans. Get a decision on whether to develop training at all before getting into a discussion of how and who to train.

Be conservative in any estimates of the benefits. For example, if the training is estimated to save $10,000 a year, it might be proposed as, ". . . at least $7500." The lower figure may be more believable, thus less distracting to the flow of the presentation, and if it really saves $9,000, the individual who proposed it is a hero instead of having overestimated the benefit.

What are the key elements of an effective training proposal?

Design the proposal appropriately. The level of formality will vary among proposals. As mentioned in Chapter 3, the need for training might be identified in many ways. The proposal, as well, may take the form of a feasibility report, a suggestion system form, or an informal chat with the boss. The source of the issues that need training and the decision makers' general familiarity with those issues will influence how you approach and develop the proposal. Some of the first steps would be to:

Classify your audience. Begin designing the proposal by classifying the audience that will be evaluating the recommendations. A useful way to think about the audience is to consider whether this person or group could be classified as a/an:

- expert
- technician
- executive
- layman
- combined

The expert loves facts, will challenge any assumptions, and needs to be convinced on a theoretical level. The technician wants to know the mechanics and process of the proposal. The executive will look at the proposal from a management, cost/benefit, or "value" perspective. The layman will be interested in the big picture, but will rely on the proposal for details and information at a basic rather than technical level. The combined or unknown audience can best be addressed by compartmentalizing the proposal. This way, information of interest to each reader can be extracted without requiring complete review and understanding of the whole package.

Establish your credibility. This step is sometimes unnecessary and sometimes impossible. You should, however, consider including some information to suggest that the proposed training is appropriate and that you will handle it competently. If you or the individual or group that generated the idea for training are well-known to the decision makers, you are probably stuck with your existing reputation—at least in the short run. If the reputation is good, be sure to keep it that way. If it's not, you may want to use additional sources to support your idea. At least you will know that you need to carefully present and document your recommendations.

Credibility is, of course, in the eyes of the beholder. It always pays to scope out your audience and play to your strengths and their preferences as you design your proposal. Sometimes you can be more credible if you remind the decision maker of your MBA from Wharton; others may need to be reminded that you've done the job for five years and produced 120% of standard every quarter. Or, perhaps you can mention that your team's last three training programs were accepted and implemented at a savings of so many dollars. Sometimes showing that the training has worked elsewhere in similar circumstances (maybe for a competitor?) will establish that it might be worth trying.

Whatever process you use, the key point is to maneuver the decision makers into willingness to read about or listen *to* the idea. They have to believe that you may have something worthwhile to say.

Ensure focus on the idea. It has to be possible for the decision makers to get *to* the idea. One seldom finds jewelry in a rusted coffee can, though it can happen. One seldom expects, then, to find great ideas within sloppy presentations with coffee stains, misspelled words, or missing pages. On the other hand, an exquisitely produced, superbly printed, and graphically memorable training proposal that is shallow or unworkable will still not sell. Besides, if it's too slick, management will wonder why you spent so much time and money on the presentation instead of doing your job.

The objective of proposal packaging can be summed up by saying that it must be of "appropriate quality" for the situation at hand. Avoid distractions that will inhibit your message. This caveat applies to both written and oral presentations.

What categories should be included in a training proposal?

Not all of the categories suggested below are needed in each proposal. Depending on the topic and other circumstances, several of these ideas may be handled in a single sentence, while others may require pages or hours of discussion. The example proposal at the end of this chapter includes nearly all of these points and is still less than a page long.

Begin by expressing the need for training. State early and clearly *what* the proposal is and *why* it is needed. The only exception to this rule is when the proposal is so radical that stating the what and why up front will result in immediate rejection of the idea. In that situation, you will need to build up to the recommendation through discussion. Normally, though, that approach takes too much of the audience's time, so get right to the point.

Define the problem or opportunity that led to the proposal. What brought this training idea to mind? Remember, management frequently looks at problems or opportunities in terms of numbers. How much did it cost? How much more could be produced? How much time could be saved? The *"M resources"* might cue you to a way of defining the problem: What money, materials, methods, minutes, machinery, maintenance, management, markets, manpower, milieux, or manuscripts are doing less than they could?

Explain the background on the problem or opportunity. How did the underlying problem or opportunity develop? Has it always been there, or did some change occur that has caused it?

Emphasize the need for a solution. What will happen if no training is provided? Will the organization still be able to operate? This "down-side discussion" must be tied to specific dollar and time costs whenever possible.

Specify the benefits of adopting the proposal. What specific savings or improvements will occur as a result of implementing the training? Increased production, faster turnaround, reduced complaints, etc.? Once again, tying these items to defensible and clear numbers will be helpful for most decision makers. You need to be enthusiastic about the benefits, without coming across as a stereotypical used car salesman.

Note that the proposal details have still not been divulged. Presenting the benefits at this point is part of developing momentum. The intent is to get the decision maker into a receptive enough mood to listen to the details. Subsequent headings specify these details, but you first need to sell the benefits that will come out of the proposed training.

Define the nature and scope of the proposal. What training is being proposed, and where will it be implemented? Is it training for one person or one department, or is it a company wide possibility? How pervasive will the effects of the training be? What other areas of the organization will be affected in addition to the areas being trained? Who else, if anyone, needs to be involved?

Present a plan for implementation. What methods will be used in implementation? What tasks have to be done by whom? What facilities and equipment will be needed? When do these things need to happen? *Clarity* is the keyword in the implementation plan. Use analogy, example, simple graphics, and terms and formats comfortable to the audience. These formats might include charts, photographs, and tables.

The implementation plan, however, should include only the key points. Details can be included in an appendix for a written proposal, or in handouts or visuals to be used only if needed during an oral proposal. This arrangement allows the presenter to engage in an unobstructed overview yet drop to a deeper level, if necessary. The appropriate level depends on understanding the audience and knowing whether the decision maker will merely be involved with simple approval or disapproval, or with the actual process of implementation.

Provide support for the proposal. Do you personally have any experience relevant to the proposal? Can you cite examples of where it has been tried before? Who else in the organization (or outside) may have the background to help? Could you cite any articles, books, or other reference sources to support the ideas? Remember to include those people who helped to develop the original idea and others in the organization with whom the proposal has already been discussed.

Discuss the likelihood of success. No training program is perfect. Of course, your proposal should have more going for it than against it, but don't leave yourself open to criticism by ignoring potential problems. It is far better to bring them up yourself than to respond to them only when challenged by the decision maker. Disarm this situation by listing possible criticisms and problems, with either a valid response to each or a summation of the consequences if these problems do interfere.

Explain and justify the cost of the proposal. It is typical sales technique to leave discussion of the cost until the sale is made. Sooner or later, however, the issue of cost will come up. Be ready to present it accurately and in projected cost/benefit (value or return on investment [ROI]) terms. Remember, too, that total cost for training includes man-hours, materials, and many other things. In some organizations, the kind of cost may be as important as the amount of the cost. For example, a government agency may have budget for equipment but not for hiring people. In this type of situation, you may need to specify costs by category. Overall, do as much as possible to focus on the value created by the training.

Ask for a decision. Incredible as it may seem, salespeople sometimes lose the sale simply because they don't ask the customer to buy. You need to ask for a decision. It will help to recap the main points, ask for questions, or offer clarifications and follow-up data. Set a deadline by which you'd like (or must have) the decision. You may also need to say whether or not the proposal can be modified or accepted in part. That possibility is frequently, but not always, obvious.

Beware of too much pride of authorship. Decision makers often have information or agendas unknown to the persons who are proposing the training, so the questions and suggestions that come out of the presentation should be given serious consideration. Be willing to accept improvements and criticisms.

Include an appendix. The term "appendix" is frequently applied to written presentations and understood in those terms. It should include any supporting material that might be of interest to the decision maker, but which is so detailed that it would impede the flow of ideas. Examples of this kind of material could include charts, surveys, computations, input data, flow charts, articles, lists of personnel, etc. Ensure that similar information is on hand or available for review following an oral presentation. Give the decision maker some documentation for later review or as a reminder, to enable him or her to consider the proposal efficiently.

Be prepared to deal with the decision. The proposal will probably generate a "Yes," a "No," or a "Yes, but . . ." decision. Be sure you are ready to deal with any of these possible outcomes. Ask yourself what your next steps should be, and whether you should try again if you get a "No." Ask for and accept constructive feedback. Always continue to build your credibility. If the answer is "Yes," be sure to follow through and provide information on the results of the implementation. Remember, even the best ideas are useless without understanding and support from the decision makers.

Again, not all of the above categories will be needed for every proposal. Use this summary as a checklist when you develop the proposal and include each category only when it serves a purpose. Figure 4-1 is an example of a simple training proposal that incorporates most of these concepts.

Figure 4-1   A Sample Training Proposal

MEMO

TO: J. P. Sousa, Executive Director
FROM: R. Vaughn, Training Department
DATE: January 19th
TOPIC: Proposal for Training

Sousa Industries needs to arrange a training program to improve the skills of our forklift operators. This need has resulted from two sources: (1) an increasing accident rate, and (2) new standards imposed by government regulation in this area.

First, our safety records show that lost time injuries for our forklift operators have gone up in each of the past three years at a rate faster than the increase in hours worked by persons in that job classification. Although there may be various reasons for this increased accident rate, the supervisors report that at least part of the change is attributable to employee turnover during that period. Further, because this is apparently a statewide trend, forklift drivers who handle hazardous materials (ours occasionally do) must soon be certified by the state commerce department.

A training program will help reduce the accident rate and associated costs, including employee medical expenses, damaged equipment, merchandise, and insurance costs. It will also prepare our employees for the upcoming certification process so that we can comply quickly with no loss in productivity.

This program should be provided for all current personnel in this job classification, and for others in related classifications who may occasionally fill in for our primary workers. All plant locations except Gainsborough are affected.

(continued)

Figure 4-1 A Sample Training Proposal (*Continued*)

We propose using ACME Forklift Services as an external provider for this training. They have been in the business for six years and are certified by the appropriate agencies to be in compliance with all standards related to the upcoming certification. They already have materials and training plans developed and have provided excellent references from several companies in our industry.

The cost for this training will be approximately $280 per employee, plus mileage and any overtime incurred by their absence from the job. Training will be done off site at ACME's classroom in the Market Square area. This price includes all materials. If any of our employees who pass the ACME training do not pass the state certification, a free retraining session will be offered.

The total cost of approximately $6,400 will be charged against the operations budgets for each location.

We need your approval by the end of the month in order to set schedules for March. If you have any questions, contact me at my office (555-5432).

5 Developing Training Objectives

> *"Cheshire Puss, would you tell me, please, which way I ought to walk from here?"*
> *"That depends a good deal on where you want to get to," said the Cat.*
> *"I don't much care where—" said Alice.*
> *"Then it doesn't matter which way you walk," said the Cat.*
> *"—so long as I get somewhere," Alice added as an explanation.*
> *"Oh, you're sure to do that," said the Cat, "if only you walk long enough."*
> *—Lewis Carroll, Alice in Wonderland*

The professional trainer knows that developing a training program, like any major activity, requires knowing where you're going. Or, as Steven Covey puts it, you must "Begin with the end in mind." Once the training requirements have been identified, they must be refined into explicit objectives.

■ ■ ■

As Alice learned in talking with the Cheshire Cat, deciding where to go is an essential first step in planning anything, whether business or training. Otherwise, one may end up—as the Walrus did—speaking of many things, but lacking coherence ("cabbages and sealing wax"?). Developing good training objectives is essential, tedious, and a step you may be tempted to skip. Don't.

In *Basic Training for Trainers*, Gary Kroehnert[1] says that the chapter on objectives is the most important in his book. Certainly Robert Mager, who earned his reputation in the business of writing objectives for nearly 40 years, would agree.[2] Objectives may be variously referred to as "training," "instructional," "learning," "behavioral," "performance," or "criterion" objectives by different authors. Mager continues to use the term "instructional" objectives, though he specifies that they must be written in a form that describes what behavior or knowledge the learner should be able to demonstrate following training. Each perspective has its arguments to show that its name is the appropriate one, but all agree on the importance of objectives.

Why are training objectives needed?

Training objectives serve a variety of purposes. Among other things, they help improve training design, communications, evaluation, administration, conduct, and success. When they are effectively used, their benefits can also influence other Human Resource activities.

Effective objectives *help to design the training* precisely to fit the needs of trainees and the organization. Written objectives indicate that conscious decisions have been made about what skills, knowledge, and abilities to include in the training. If the organization requires the skills, knowledge, or abilities described in the objectives, based on the needs analysis process described earlier, they will be included. If they're not needed, the organization will not waste time or money by including them.

Objectives *provide a basis for clear communication* with all persons involved with the training—trainers, management, supervisors, and participants—and let them know what's expected. Ideally, objectives should be the result of collaboration among these groups.

Objectives are *key to evaluating the overall success of a training program*. The evaluation processes described later in this book are entirely dependent on stating clear objectives as a basis for measurement and evaluation.

Establishing training objectives can *help simplify training administration*. Well-done objectives facilitate such efficiencies as the use of multiple trainers; standardized tests; improved design of materials, content, and techniques; and so on.

Objectives *guide teaching* by providing a preview and summary of the training. Objectives provide excellent points for discussion at the opening and closing of the training program. They allow the trainer to say, "Here's where we're going," and "Here's where we've been." Objectives help students understand the plan and the roadmap—essential ingredients for most adult learners.

Written objectives *increase the likelihood of success* of the training that flows from them. Various studies on goal-setting, which suggest that setting objectives enhances the likelihood of reaching them, support this benefit.

Finally, effective objectives *influence other human resources activities* through a carry-over effect. Training objectives can be a catalyst that enables supervisors to establish and validate performance standards. These standards can then be used to perform effective employee reviews. Carefully analyzed training needs can be converted into job descriptions. They can also be used to help develop employment interview questions, and so on. These and other benefits that emerge from the training design process should be effectively integrated into all aspects of organizational operations. Defining training objectives is a key starting point.

What are the components of a training objective?

Each objective should describe exactly what results are expected from the training. It should be phrased parsimoniously and only in terms of *behavior the learner must exhibit* in order to be considered competent. Thus, objectives should *not* describe the process by which the training will occur, the experience the learner will have, the actions the trainer will use to present the material, the content of the lesson, or anything else that is a *means* rather than an *end result* of the training.

Objectives usually begin with the phrase:

"Upon completing the training, the learners will . . . [action verb] . . ."

A well-written training objective is *specific, measurable, singular, possible, and serves a purpose.* It also *may require specifying conditions.*

Specific—This condition means that the objective should detail *exactly* what the trainee is supposed to know or be able to do after the training has occurred. Ambiguity is anathema. *How* specific must it be? A simple guide is that it must be specific enough that if the knowledge or performance were to be measured by several different people, they would agree as to whether or not the specified standard was met.

Measurable—A measurable objective is one that enables effective evaluation of the trainee. It should be stated in terms that can be understood clearly as right or wrong, black or white, yes or no; or else, in a quantitative fashion that defines a standard expected outcome in terms of actual numbers or percentages. Sometimes the measurement is a physical specification. For example, a good objective might state that the trainee be: ". . . able to produce a part that is exactly one inch within a tolerance of three-thousandths." Sometimes measurement comes in the form of a count of something, such as: ". . . able to type sixty words a minute with fewer than three errors." Sometimes the measurement is more qualitative, such as: ". . . will wear appropriate safety gear on the job at all times." A supervisor who knows what "appropriate safety gear" is could, upon observation, determine whether or not the standard is being met.

Translating such an objective into a list of specific nouns would be tedious and generally unnecessary. If reasonable and qualified people would agree on the measurement, it is probably described explicitly enough.

Singular—Each objective should cover only one outcome and require only one measurement. This condition also means that the objective probably fits into only one category: skill, knowledge, and so on, as described below. The use of conjunctions or of multiple verbs or objects immediately makes a training objective suspect.

Possible—Although an objective should probably be challenging to the learner (in order to motivate), it must reflect an expected outcome that is based in reality. Specifically, any objective should be the result of a needs analysis, as described in Chapter 3, which means that the objective . . .

Serves a Purpose—Training objectives must be tied to specific organizational requirements or goals. Even if learning something seems like a good idea, that knowledge is not an appropriate objective unless there is a good reason for it to be learned. That reason may be because the job requires the trainee to have the knowledge or be able to perform actions based on that knowledge, or because someone with policy-making authority wants it included in the training. Nevertheless, some knowledge or skills that are not required to physically perform a job may still be relevant in training. Sexual harassment policies and safety issues are just two examples.

Specifies Conditions—Sometimes training objectives have to detail what type of support or external environment is required during training. As with the requirement that objectives be measurable, the "reasonable person" test should be applied here. Excessive detail—belaboring the obvious—is not appropriate, but on occasion, conditions may vary, and clarity would be well-served by a few extra words. Examples of conditions that might be specified include the tools and materials with which the learner must work, the setting in which the learner will be required to perform, information with which the learner will be provided, time limits for completing the task, and assistance or barriers relevant to the training.

Are all training objectives similar?

Like most concepts, objectives can be categorized in several ways. One method is to understand that *training objectives come in four levels: Attitude, Knowledge, Skill, and Job Behavior.* Each of these levels is evaluated using a different technique, as discussed in Chapter 6.

Attitude (or Awareness) objectives are the lowest level, though not necessarily the simplest. They specify that the training will result in a heightened awareness or changed attitude about a specific subject. An example of an attitude objective for a new employee orientation would be: *Upon completing the training, the participants will understand the role of our organization in the transportation industry.* The trainee is not expected to learn specific facts about the organization, and no specific skills will be learned as a result of this training. The trainee is expected to emerge with only a broad and general understanding about the organization and its role in the industry. Typical training modules using this level of objective would include parts of new employee orientations, training on teamwork, cultural diversity, etc.

Knowledge objectives specify that, at the end of the training, the trainees will know certain facts and be able to recognize or recall them at appropriate times. An example of a knowledge objective for a new employee orientation would be: *Upon completing the training, the participants will be able to list by name and position all individuals in their chain of command.* Even though the end result of training is that the trainees "know" something, using the word *know* as the action verb in an objective is not a good idea. How can you tell if someone knows something? You must have them list or describe or explain it to find out. Write the objective so it uses those words, which define actions that can be directly measured, not a word like "know," which can't be.

Skill objectives require that the training teach someone how to do something. This thing may be a physical or manual dexterity action or a cognitive or mental dexterity action. An example of a cognitive skill objective for a new employee orientation would be: *Upon completing the training, the participants will be able to calculate overtime pay, based on the current employee contract.* A manual skill objective for an orientation could specify: *Upon completing the training, the new employee will be able to operate the building security system using a pass card without setting off the alarm.*

Finally, **Job behavior objectives** relate to training that changes the way the trainees accomplish the jobs they actually do for the organization that sponsored the training. An example job behavior objective would be: *Upon completing the training, the participants will follow all rules specified in Section II of the employee handbook.*

One other important aspect of these levels of objectives must be considered: The four levels are not discrete; instead, they tend to be cumulative and hierarchical. Effectively dealing with knowledge objectives usually presupposes achievement of at least some attitude objectives. Likewise, most skills can't be performed without some knowledge, and an employee won't be able to achieve most job behavior objectives unless the prerequisite skills have been mastered. Don't just look at the highest level of objective needed in training; look at them all and include those that are appropriate. Typical training programs in a company are apt to have some of each type of objective. Write them out for each level, rather than just listing the most sophisticated objective. If it turns out that there are problems in the training program, having a comprehensive list of objectives will improve the analysis.

What is Bloom's Taxonomy?

The simplified, four level classification system for objectives discussed above applies mainly to the field of training. A similar, but more complex, system created by Benjamin Bloom may be familiar to persons who have a background in the field of education. Bloom[3] and his colleagues conducted an exhaustive study that resulted in a classification structure (a *taxonomy*) that uses three domains in which we can write objectives: affective, cognitive, and psychomotor.

- ■ *Affective or emotional objectives* emphasize a feeling, tone, emotion, or degree of acceptance or rejection. This type of objective is needed where there is *a lack of desire to use new knowledge or skills*. Bloom has identified five levels of affective objectives. Table 5-1 outlines these levels.

- ■ *Cognitive or mental objectives* relate to recall or recognition of knowledge and development of intellectual skills and abilities. This type of objective is needed *when the trainees don't know something*. Bloom's model includes six levels of cognitive objectives. Table 5-2 describes the levels of the cognitive domain.

- ■ *Psychomotor or behavioral objectives* have to do with neuromuscular or manual skills required to effectively perform a task. This type of objective is appropriate *when the trainee can't do something*. Bloom dealt extensively with the first two categories but found very little of the third used in secondary schools. Laird[4] points out that, while others have devised taxonomies for psychomotor objectives, ". . . this domain has never been the problem in organizational training. The manipulative skills very easily reveal observable actions and measurable criteria." For examples of psychomotor levels, see Dave,[5] Simpson,[6] or Harrow.[7] Table 5-3 outlines Dave's interpretation of this aspect of Bloom's model.

What is the value of Bloom's Taxonomy in training?

One requirement for a good training objective is that it will precisely define the organization's needs for the level of a particular knowledge or skill. In other words, how much does a person need to know to do a job, or how skilled must they be to meet organizational standards? Bloom's model allows much more precision in specifying details. Is an employee supposed to merely recognize a problem, or to identify its probable cause, or to fix it? Each of these actions would occupy a different category under Bloom's Taxonomy.

In many of the so-called "soft-skills" areas, this precision is difficult to accomplish. *Soft skills* areas are fields such as management, sales, communication, and others that are dependent

Table 5-1 Bloom's Taxonomy of Education: Affective Domain

LEVEL	DEFINITION	TRAINERS	LEARNERS	SAMPLE VERBS
Receiving	Recall, recognize, and process specific information	Provide information	Listen or watch attentively; Accept sensory input	Be aware of, Sense, Hear, See, Smell, Taste, Feel, etc.
Responding	Express willingness to react to stimuli	Ask questions; Set situations	Respond to questions	Restate, Discuss, Describe, Recognize, Explain, Express, etc.
Valuing	Sense worth; Commit; Conceptualize a value	Provide or propose standards; Suggest structure	Develop understanding and commitment	Apply, Use, Practice, Interpret, Demonstrate, etc.
Organization	Organize values into a system; Establish dominant values; Determine interrelationships	Provide framework; offer models; Act as catalyst or mentor	Create an intuitive or explicit structure for dealing with their emotions	Distinguish, Create, Structure, Test, Calculate, Criticize, Solve, Analyze, Construct, Design, etc.
Characterization	Foster reliable performance of individual's value system; Support individual's unique character	Support and encourage internal process	Develop and use a consistent behavior pattern	Compose, Propose, Assemble, Manage, Arrange, Create, Evaluate, Compare, Choose, Predict, Appraise, etc.

Source: B. Bloom, *ed.*, *Taxonomy of Educational Objectives, Handbook II: Affective Domain.* New York: David McKay, 1956. Structure of this table created by Robert H. Vaughn.

Table 5-2 Bloom's Taxonomy of Education: Cognitive Domain

LEVEL	DEFINITION	TRAINERS	LEARNERS	SAMPLE VERBS
Knowledge	Recall or recognize specific information	Direct, Tell, Show, Examine	Respond, Remember, Recognize	Define, Repeat, List, Relate, Name, Label, Recall, etc.
Comprehension	Understand information given	Demonstrate, Listen, Question, Compare, Contrast	Explain, Translate, Demonstrate	Restate, Discuss, Describe, Recognize, Explain, Express, etc.
Application	Use methods, concepts, principles, and theories in new situations	Show, Facilitate, Observe, Criticize	Solve problems; Demonstrate use of knowledge	Apply, Use, Practice, Interpret, Demonstrate, etc.
Analysis	Break information down into its constituent elements	Probe, Guide, Observe, Act as a resource	Discuss, List, Uncover, Dissect	Distinguish, Test, Calculate, Criticize, Solve, Analyze, etc.
Synthesis	Put together elements or parts to form a whole; Require original, creative thinking	Reflect, Extend, Analyze, Evaluate	Discuss, Compare, Generalize, Relate, Contrast, Abstract	Compose, Propose, Assemble, Construct, Manage, Design, Arrange, Create, etc.
Evaluation	Judge the value of ideas, materials, and methods; Develop and apply standards and criteria	Clarify, Accept, Harmonize, Guide	Judge, Dispute, Develop criteria	Evaluate, Compare, Score, Choose, Rate, Estimate, Predict, Appraise, etc.

Source: B. Bloom, *ed.*, *Taxonomy of Educational Objectives, Handbook I: Cognitive Domain.* New York: David McKay, 1956. Structure of this table created by Robert H. Vaughn.

Table 5-3   Dave's Model of Bloom's Psychomotor Domain Taxonomy

LEVEL	DEFINITION	POSSIBLE VERBS
Imitate	Observe a skill and attempt to repeat it, or see a finished product and attempt to replicate it while attending to an exemplar.	Attempt, Copy, Duplicate, Imitate, Mimic
Manipulate	Perform the skill or produce the product in a recognizable fashion by following general instructions rather than by observation.	Complete, Follow, Play, Perform, Produce
Precision	Independently perform the skill or produce the product, with accuracy, proportion, and exactness, at an expert level.	Achieve automatically, Excel expertly, Perform masterfully
Articulation	Modify the skill or product to fit new situations; combine more than one skill in sequence with harmony and consistency.	Adapt, Alter, Customize, Originate
Naturalization	Complete one or more skills with ease and make the skill automatic with limited mental or physical exertion.	Naturally, Perfectly

Source: Dave, R. (1967). *Psychomotor Domain.* Berlin: International Conference of Educational Testing.

on the individuals and situations involved, rather than a specific set of procedures that always works (as in computer training, for example).

Referring to Bloom's Taxonomy model can help to clarify the criteria for effective job performance when designing appropriate knowledge-level and some (soft) skills level training. Bloom's more refined structure enables the trainer or instructional designer to better specify the levels of training appropriate to the trainees and the organization. It also is a good head start toward designing a training evaluation.

Here's an example of Bloom's affective levels as they might relate to a safety training program. At the lowest level (receiving), there would have to be some indication that the trainee has heard the message. Perhaps a nod of the head or some other body language would be adequate to say that the objective of "receiving" had been met. If the objective requires that the trainee respond (second level), then something beyond a physical indication would be required. ("Yes, you have told me, and I have heard, that no open flames are permitted in the paint room.") If the objective is third level (valuing), then we want to know that the trainee now understands the importance of the lesson. ("The fumes in the paint room are flammable. That's good information. It is important for me to know that.") A fourth-level (organization) objective would require the trainee to integrate this knowledge into his or her existing crystallized intelligence and method of operating. ("If I light a cigarette while I'm working in the paint room, I may cause an explosion. I only have so many sick days, and I don't personally like pain.") Finally, the highest-level objective (characterization) is achieved when the trainee consciously acts on the knowledge because it is now part of their learned behavior.

Consider an example of cognitive objectives that could be part of a training session about ice skating. Starting with Bloom's lowest cognitive level, this is how you might adjust it to move up the hierarchy. The knowledge level (lowest) could be: Upon completing the training, the learners will be able to name three types of jumps that might be used in a performance. A second, or comprehension, objective could be to recognize each of three types of jumps when they are used in a performance. An application objective could be to clearly describe (or demonstrate) each of the three jumps; an analysis could be to explain how to approach, rotate, and land each of the three jumps. A synthesis objective could be to design an appropriate program, putting the jumps into a sequence that properly uses the skater's body momentum and position to allow effective execution. Finally, an evaluation-level cognitive objective could be: Upon completing the training, the student will be able to effectively serve as a professional judge in a pre-Olympic ice skating competition.

Again, the reason for bringing Bloom's model into the discussion is to help refine the four levels for training objectives described earlier in this chapter. Write the training objectives so that they represent not only the knowledge and skills that are required of the trainees, but also the level of sophistication required to effectively perform the job within the organization.

How do the traditional four levels of training objectives compare to Bloom's Taxonomy?

The two systems exist in somewhat parallel universes, and some overlap occurs in the margins between them. As explained in Chapter 1, the rules and roles vary rather substantially between training and education. Table 5-4 is an attempt to show how the different Bloom categories would match up with the four levels of training objectives.

How many objectives are required for a training program?

No specific number of objectives per hour or per program can be universally applied. The appropriate number of objectives is determined by what the trainees are expected to prove they know or can do. This proof will come through measurement *during or at the end of* the training, or—in the case of job behavior objectives—some time after the training is completed. The longer the program, the more objectives will probably be covered. Very complex objectives should be subdivided. Creating at least one objective per major task is probably appropriate for most situations.

Trying to encompass too large a part of the training, or too small, in one objective will result in difficulties in later stages of developing the training program. If you subsequently find, for example, that you must use several measurements to determine whether the objective has been achieved, then the objective is probably too large. If you find that your lesson plan can be completed in two minutes of instruction, then the objective is probably too narrow.

"*Upon completing the training, the learners shall know how to turn on their computer*" is probably too narrow. The lesson plan would read, "Move switch to 'on' position. Wait for image to appear on screen." Expand that lesson to include such things as logging on, opening certain programs, and so on, to make it a more reasonable objective.

Are there ways to evaluate the effectiveness of objectives?

You were cautioned at the start of this chapter that creating training objectives is a time-consuming process. But it's important to do it correctly. Shapiro[8] has created a fairly detailed point system for

Table 5-4   Comparison of the Traditional Four Levels of Training Objectives to Bloom's Taxonomy

TRAINING MODEL OF OBJECTIVE LEVELS	EXAMPLE: UPON COMPLETING THE TRAINING, THE TRAINEE WILL...	EXAMPLE MEASUREMENT	BLOOM'S TAXONOMY EQUIVALENT
(1) Attitude or Awareness	Be aware of the company's organization structure, products, and major competitors in the industry.	**Student surveys (also called "Smile sheets"):** "As a result of training, are you aware of the company's organization structure? ( ) Yes ( ) No"	**Cognitive:** Knowledge **Affective:** Receiving **Psychomotor:** No
(2) Knowledge	Be able to list the six steps in completing a Form 2101.	**Written or oral testing:** "List the six steps required to complete a Form 2101."	**Cognitive:** Comprehension, Application, Analysis; **Affective:** Responding **Psychomotor:** No

(continued)

Table 5-4 Comparison of the Traditional Four Levels of Training Objectives to Bloom's Taxonomy *(Continued)*

TRAINING MODEL OF OBJECTIVE LEVELS	EXAMPLE: UPON COMPLETING THE TRAINING, THE TRAINEE WILL…	EXAMPLE MEASUREMENT	BLOOM'S TAXONOMY EQUIVALENT
(3) *Skill* *Cognitive*	Be able to compute the correct interest rate for an application.	**Performance tests:** "Given five different credit applications, compute the interest rate to be charged with 100% accuracy." **Or:**	**Cognitive:** Application, Analysis, Synthesis, Evaluation; **Affective:** Organization; **Psychomotor:** No
Psychomotor	Given a standard tool kit, be able to remove and replace the hard drive in a PC.	"On the table you will find a PC, a standard tool kit, and a new hard drive. Remove the old hard drive and replace it with the new one so the computer boots and operates correctly. You will have 25 minutes."	**Cognitive:** Application, Analysis, Synthesis, Evaluation; **Affective:** Organization; Characterization **Psychomotor:** Yes
(4) *Job Performance*	Complete at least ten sales calls per week and close at least 30% of sales with a minimum of $5,000.	***Company records and data external to training:*** Weekly sales report from accounts receivable office, which reflect the standards established.	**Cognitive:** Application, Analysis, Synthesis, Evaluation; **Affective:** Valuing, Organization and Characterization; **Psychomotor:** Depends on job

rating objectives, but common sense is usually all that's needed. Simply take the time to think the process through carefully and write objectives that follow the criteria outlined in this chapter.

Here are some example objectives. Try evaluating them to see if they are specific, measurable, singular, possible, and purposeful, and whether conditions need to be specified.

The first is an objective for a sales training program. (The term *closing a sale* means that the customer agrees to buy as a result of the sales presentation.)

- "Upon completing the training, the participants will be able to substantially increase their rate of closing sales."

Here's another for a skilled trades training program.

- "Upon completing the training, the participants will be able to write a description of the steps involved in making, then copying, a blueprint."

Here's a third, this one relating to a sports activity.

- "Upon completing the training, the participants will, on a 15-yard range, be able to throw five standard game darts, hitting within ten inches of the target bull's eye with at least 80% consistency."

Do these examples meet the standards? Are they specific, measurable, and so on?

The first one needs some work. How "substantially?" What is the rate now, and what rate of sales should the trainees be closing? Will that rate still apply if the market changes? Should trainees be able to close the same percentage with all customers? A better version of this objective would read: ". . . to close at least 70% of all sales presentations to qualified customers." (A *qualified customer* is one who has the means and authority to buy.) That objective is more specific, clearly measurable, asks for a single action, and includes appropriate conditions. It also serves a clear purpose. Whether or not it is possible depends on the product and the market.

The second example violates the singular criterion. Besides, the trainees probably should know how to *do* it; their supervisors won't necessarily care if they can *write about* it. They could probably do the job in a rote fashion, even if they were illiterate. As for measurability, 100% accuracy is implied—which might or might not be possible or realistic. Also, the trainees' success at meeting the objective might be hampered by their writing skills, rather than their actual knowledge of a process gained from the training program. In that case, they would be measured on a skill (writing) that was not taught during the training, and only indirectly and ineffectively measured on what was taught, namely the required process.

The third example objective is effective. It includes appropriate conditions, namely the range and the style of darts, and is clearly measurable in terms of either yes or no, or a percentage.

As with most subjects of a cognitive nature, the foregoing discussion assumes more clarity than one may find in real life. It's common to find objectives that may not fall neatly into one of the four levels. It may also happen that an objective clearly violates one or more of the criteria listed in this chapter and still is reasonably effective. In general, following the suggestions of this chapter will lead to appropriate and effective objectives.

Writing training objectives takes some time and effort, but they will be very important in developing an effective training program. If the trainer is following the ISD model recommended in this book, a quick check on the effectiveness of objectives will happen as soon as the next step is begun. With a weak objective, writing an effective evaluation will be difficult. This difficulty will be a cue to take one step back and rework the objective before going on.

Once effective objectives are in place, the next issue is how to measure whether or not they have been achieved through training. Chapter 6 describes this process.

6 Evaluating Learning

"Evaluation of training is inevitable. You can not avoid it. All training is evaluated because people in the organization will form judgments about it."
—*Robert Brinkerhoff*

Setting objectives is important and necessary, but not sufficient unto itself. The professional trainer next needs to develop a means to determine whether or not those objectives have been achieved as a result of the training.

■ ■ ■

Evaluating training is an essential process to ensure that the organization's resources are being used wisely. This assessment is important to the organization, to the trainer, and to the trainees. Organizations will want to know: "Is the cost of training justified?" And, "Can these trainees safely be turned loose in our organization?" Trainers will want to know, "How successful have I been in doing my job?" Trainees, too, will want assurances that they have been successful in their learning efforts and will be able to perform effectively on their jobs.

The current literature indicates that the number of organizations that attempt to evaluate training is increasing every year. According to ASTD statistics,[1] evaluation activity is increasing fastest for training related to the more complex levels of objectives. This chapter describes how to approach this very important process of training evaluation.

What is the definition of evaluation?

Two different, yet quite interrelated, meanings are attached to the concept of evaluation as it relates to training. Trainers frequently confuse these two meanings without even recognizing the confusion.

- *First*, has the trainee **learned the content** according to the specified training objectives? This aspect is represented in the fourth box of Vaughn's model (Chapter 2, Fig. 2-2).

- *Then*, was the **process** by which that learning occurred effective and appropriate? This concern is specified in the seventh box of the model.

As used in this book, **learning evaluation** means the process of determining whether the trainee has learned what the trainer attempted to teach. When discussing the overall training experience, the term **program evaluation** is used. As you will soon see, these data frequently overlap. This chapter deals with both learning and program evaluations, because collecting some of these data separately is impossible. Chapter 12 will expand on the concept of program evaluation and offer additional suggestions.

What makes a good evaluation?

Evaluating both learning and the overall program should be an integral part of effective training. Good training begins with an accurate definition of training needs (Chapter 3), then proceeds through developing training objectives (Chapter 5), moves on to developing measures (this chapter), then focuses on the design and presentation of the training (Chapters 7 through 11), and ends with—one hopes—more effective job and organizational performance. The role of evaluation is to ensure that this improvement has happened.

A basic and generally effective model of learning evaluation was developed by Dr. Donald Kirkpatrick, formerly national president of ASTD and now retired from teaching at The University of Wisconsin. He uses four levels of evaluation[2], which roughly correspond to the four levels of objectives presented in Chapter 5. Although some criticize Kirkpatrick's model as being *too* simplified, most would agree that he provides a good starting point for the process. His four levels are:

- **Reaction**—which generally parallels *Attitude* objectives, as described in Chapter 5.

- **Learning**—which generally parallels *Knowledge* objectives.

- **Behavior**—which parallels *Skill* objectives.

- **Results**—which generally parallels *Job Behavior* objectives.

As with training objectives discussed in the Chapter 5, the various levels of evaluation are not mutually exclusive. Even if the training objectives are clearly written at the skill level, for example, it is also appropriate to evaluate the reaction and learning levels. Each of these evaluation levels requires different tools and techniques.

Various other writers in the field have added additional levels. Jack Phillips' fifth level[3] is return on investment (ROI). ROI is a common economic and management measure, which relates the value received for the training to the cost of the training. ASTD's annual report for 2003 mentions level 5/ROI, and indicates that further attention will be paid to it in the future.[4]

Reaction: level 1 evaluation

How do we evaluate learning at the reaction level?

Generally, trainers use an end-of-course evaluation form to obtain a rating of how the participants liked the program, what they gained most from it, and other information related to the training. These forms are often (and sometimes ironically) referred to in the industry as "smile sheets." This "attitude" level of evaluation is used with nearly any training, including many college courses. National surveys report a "90% plus" application of evaluations at this level.

The reaction-level evaluation can include questions about both content and process. In fact, at this lowest level, content and process may be somewhat difficult to separate. Because the only practical and immediate way to determine whether an attitude or awareness has changed is to simply ask the trainees, such assessments commonly request their opinions on both content and process at the same time. While such analysis is obviously open to substantial bias, it still can serve a valid purpose. More on that point later in this chapter.

Reaction-level evaluations can be done at any time during training, or long after it is over, not just at its conclusion. If intermediate changes might be made or remedial training is an option, daily or weekly feedback may help a trainer adjust the training to better meet the needs of the learners. This approach is especially useful when the training is conducted over a long time period.

To create an evaluation at the reaction level, a trainer should:

- *determine what sort of information is wanted*
- *design data collection so reactions can be tabulated and quantified*

- *obtain honest reactions by making the form anonymous*
- *encourage additional comments and feedback on the form*
- *keep it simple*

Determine what sort of information is wanted. Different purposes will call for different designs. Feedback may be wanted for the purposes of suggesting changes in the program for the future, or for some other purpose, such as reporting statistics to the trainer's or trainee's boss. If so, the questions suggested in the bullet list below may be helpful. Sometimes, the evaluation is used only to make the trainees feel that they have contributed and to provide a good way to close the session. Evaluation would be used in this way if the training is not going to be repeated, or the trainer is not open to changes. In such circumstances, the format and content of questions are irrelevant.

Design the data collection form so reactions can be tabulated and quantified. The evaluation should lend itself to easy summation. Using some form of quantitative rating or *Likert scale*[5] will allow the trainer to determine that the course scored, for example, a "3.2 on a 5-point scale." While certain classes of statistics are limited by use of this form, it's nearly always an efficient and reasonably effective way of getting the big picture. An example question in this format would be: "The class was well-organized. Agree (5). Somewhat agree (4). Neutral (3). Somewhat disagree (2). Disagree (1)."

Obtain honest reactions by making the form anonymous. Names or numbers perceived as linking answers to an individual may reduce the candidness with which trainees respond. Allow, but don't require, names on the evaluations.

Encourage additional comments and feedback on the form, if they are wanted. If not, limit the form to checkmarks or similar indicators. Research shows that the most useful information comes from the open-ended questions, not from the Likert scales, which lend themselves to positive bias. Although open-ended questions are more difficult to tabulate, they allow trainees to express themselves candidly and will highlight their perceptions of what was both good and bad about the training experience.

Keep it simple. Trainees usually resist completing extensive forms, especially when they are requested at the end of the program or after the fact. This resistance will lower response rates, and make it likely that only trainees who felt strongly one way or the other will bother. Hearing from the extremes and not the majority is not conducive to good evaluation. One page, if it is well designed, should be adequate for a reaction-level evaluation.

What sort of questions should be included on a reaction-level evaluation?

When you need to get the trainees' reaction as to whether they have learned the *content* presented in training, possible questions are:

- Was the purpose of the training made clear?
- Was the information understandable?
- Do you (the trainee) consider it to have been useful?
- Did you accomplish your reason for attending?
- How will you use it on the job?
- What other applications will you make of the information received?

The first four of these questions could be handled adequately using a Likert scale; the last two would require written responses.

Trainees' responses to these content questions will represent their opinions and perceptions only. At this level, however, it may be appropriate to assume that perception is reality. If they say the training wasn't clear, for example, then it probably wasn't. On the other hand, if they don't think it was useful, that perception may or may not be accurate. Opinion as to the usefulness of the training is more likely to be accurate when it comes from experienced employees than when it comes from trainees who are new hires and who don't yet know the job and organization.

Typically, the questions asked and responses offered at this level have more to do with process than content. Common questions dealing with program evaluation topics include queries such as:

- How effective was the trainer?
- How was the training room or environmental ambiance?
- How were the refreshments?
- Were the timing and location of the training convenient?
- Comment on the quality of the handouts and other audio-visual support.
- Was the training format appropriate (lecture vs. demonstration vs. hands-on time)?

- Was an appropriate amount of time allowed for training?
- What is your (the trainee's) overall rating of the program?

Again, some of these questions would best be formatted as a Likert scale, whereas others require written responses.

All of these may be appropriate questions, of course, and the responses may help to improve future training programs. Remember, the results will reflect only the trainees' perceptions, and that may be all that matters. The point is that *these questions have nothing to do with measuring learning*; they are all measures of *process*. Measuring process will be discussed more in chapter 12 on *program* assessment.

Another way to get feedback is to have trainees mark words that they feel apply to the training from a list of choices, with lists of opposites included. Such a list could include, for example, words like: "fun, overwhelming, inappropriate, well organized, tedious," etc. A final word on using smile sheets: organize them logically, so that all written responses are together and all Likert-scaled or checklist responses are together and all are sequenced logically. Several of the references listed at the end of this book can provide other ideas.

In many organizations, the training is all measured by a standard, generic evaluation, rather than creating a unique format for each program. Box 6-1 shows a sample Reaction-level evaluation form, with some additional comments.

Knowledge: level 2 evaluation

How do we evaluate learning at the knowledge level?

Knowledge-level assessment is typically done by either oral or written testing. The subject of knowledge testing is long and detailed, and this book covers only some of the highlights. Anyone reading this book is already familiar with the idea of tests. Most people have taken hundreds of tests in their lifetimes, and probably could deductively critique most testing formats.

Some definitions must be clarified first, in order to understand this discussion of knowledge testing. Tests can vary in their validity and reliability. A *valid* test is one that accurately measures whether or not the specific training objectives have been met within the organization's own context. This definition means that all questions should be tied to a training objective and to some part of the training experience; i.e., that the questions measure

Box 6-1 Example of Level 1 Evaluation

The first five questions have to do with learning evaluation: have the training objectives been met? The next ten have to do with program evaluation: were the conditions under which the training was given appropriate and well-handled? Even if people did meet the training objectives, could it have been done better, more efficiently, and so on? The final questions are open-ended, enabling more direct information to be collected from the trainees. As discussed in the text, this type of evaluation elicits trainees' opinions only. Whether or not these opinions are accurate requires more information than can be obtained with Level 1 evaluation techniques.

Evaluation of Project Training Session

Your candid comments will help us to:
- *provide appropriate follow up support to help ensure the success of your experience under this grant.*
- *improve the program for next year's participants.*

CIRCLE YOUR ANSWER

AS A RESULT OF TODAY'S PROGRAM I HAVE	DISAGREE	NEUTRAL	AGREE
1. *A good understanding of individual career planning requirements in today's economy.*	— –	0 +	++
2. *A good understanding of the changes in roles of organizations in internal career management.*	— –	0 +	++
3. *A good understanding of the Job Trees concept as it can be used in organizations.*	— –	0 +	++
4. *A reasonable comfort level regarding what I need to do within the organization to create Job Trees.*	— –	0 +	++
5. *An understanding of how to approach the organizational analysis survey to collect input data.*	— –	0 +	++

(continued)

Box 6-1   Example of Level 1 Evaluation (*Continued*)

PLEASE RATE THE FOLLOWING COMPONENTS	POOR		AVERAGE		EXCELLENT
1. *Instructor #1's knowledge of subject*	0	1	2	3	4
2. *Instructor #1's teaching ability*	0	1	2	3	4
3. *Instructor #2's knowledge of subject*	0	1	2	3	4
4. *Instructor #2's teaching ability*	0	1	2	3	4
5. *Effectiveness of the handout materials*	0	1	2	3	4
6. *Effectiveness of visuals*	0	1	2	3	4
7. *Effectiveness of the software demonstration*	0	1	2	3	4
8. *Comfort of the facilities*	0	1	2	3	4
9. *Adequacy of preliminary arrangements*	0	1	2	3	4
10. *Overall Evaluation of Training Program*	0	1	2	3	4

Please also answer the questions on the back of this form.

(*Page 2 of the Evaluation in this example had the following questions and space to answer*)

What two things were most beneficial to you, and why?
What was least beneficial to you, and why?
What improvements would you suggest in the workshop?
What concerns do you have about the project at this point?

Thank you, and best wishes for a great experience with the project!

---

what they were supposed to measure—the content of the training program. No one ever asks, "Where did that question come from?" if the test is valid and the trainee is actively participating.

A *reliable* test is one that accurately measures results on a consistent basis among all learners and over time. This criterion means that trainees who learned most of the material will receive higher scores than ones who learned less of it. It also means that test scores are not subject to variations arising from differences in such things as language skills of the trainees, cultural background, etc.

Discrimination in testing is essential. This term means that the right answer and the wrong answer are unambiguous; one can be clearly identified as different from the other. For example, a person who has "discriminating" taste can tell the difference between Pepsi and Coca-Cola. The differences may be subtle in a challenging test, but they must exist.

Some of the common knowledge-level evaluation options include: *true-false, matching, multiple choice, fill in, short answer,* and *essay* questions, along with variations in each. Any of these options could be given orally as well as in writing or by using a computer or some other interactive medium.

Other terms that apply to the subject of testing include objective versus subjective. *Objective* tests are tests that have only one correct answer for each question (e.g., multiple choice or matching tests), while *subjective* tests may allow answers stated in a variety of ways (e.g., short answer or essay tests).

What are some of the pros and cons of objective tests?

True-false tests present a statement related to a learning objective, and the trainee must indicate whether the statement is true or false. Advantages of this method include the relative simplicity of writing and grading the test and the ability to cover a large number of points and sub-points relative to the objectives in a brief time. Responses are objective (rather than subjective), and thus a score is easy to determine and quantify. Beyond these utility measures, the true-false form has very few advantages.

In fact, creating test statements that are "always" true or "always" false (i.e., questions with effective discrimination) is difficult, because most knowledge items have some areas of gray or some exceptions. Further, because of the binary nature of possible answers (either True or False), even a person who did not take the training has a statistical probability of obtaining a 50% score, simply by guessing. This fact means that a score of 75% may indicate that the trainee actually knows *half* of the material. (50% was known and answered correctly, while another 25% was guessed correctly, and 25% was guessed incorrectly.)

At their best, true-false tests verify an extremely low level of knowledge. In Bloom's Taxonomy terms, the true-false format works only for the lowest of his six levels. True-false items deal with recognition, not recall of facts, and thus might not be valid as indicators of successful transfer of training.

Some variations on the true-false theme include a penalty for wrong answers to discourage guessing—the score equals right answers minus one half of wrong answers, for example. Another is to employ the famous "if false, explain why" device, which really turns the test into more than just a true-false format and moves it up a level or two on Bloom's model.

Multiple choice tests present a statement or question followed by several options, from which the trainee must choose the most correct completion or best example of the statement. As with the true-false format, the advantages of multiple choice include simplicity of administering and grading, and easily quantified results. Multiple choice tests require more discrimination by the test taker than the true-false format does; thus, they are usually a more valid indicator of knowledge.

Even though this format is very commonly used, writing truly effective questions is challenging. Much research and information exists in the literature, and college courses in tests and measures (or psychometrics) can be found in most schools of education. The design of each question must support a clear picture of what is being tested. Otherwise, the test may merely measure the trainee's skill at taking a test, rather than his or her understanding of the training content. As just one example of many things that might undercut a test's validity or reliability, the person designing the test needs to create plausible choices that have no subtle grammatical indicators. For example, the use of "a" or "an," or plurals, might lead respondents to the correct answer, even if they otherwise would have no clue. As with true-false, multiple choice tests recognition, not recall, and usually does not require the learner to deal with anything higher than Bloom's first level. Guessing is also possible, so the results are less valid than those obtained by some other forms of testing.

Variations on this form include a penalty for guessing, such as having the score equal the number of right answers minus half the number missed. This penalty encourages people to not guess at, but instead leave unanswered, any questions to which they really don't know the answer. Another variation is to ask questions that may have no right answer among the choices (and therefore is to be left blank), or may have more than one right answer (all of which are to be marked). These techniques generally increase the validity of multiple choice testing.

Matching tests list a number of items or questions, with a number of possible responses, and ask the learner to identify which answer goes with which item. Matching tests are objective, easy to grade, and fairly easy to write. In general, they are subject to most of the same advantages and disadvantages as multiple choice tests: they test recognition, not recall; guessing can reduce validity; etc. A common use for matching tests is to determine understanding of vocabulary terms.

Variations in matching tests include listing more responses than items or questions, which reduces guessing among the final questions answered and also requires more discrimination on the learner's part. Allowing responses to be used more than once is another way to improve the validity and reliability of this kind of test.

What are some of the pros and cons of subjective tests?

Fill in the blank tests are the first form in the testing hierarchy that deal with recall and not just recognition, even though the recall may be context-bound. These tests are relatively easy to write. In the simplest form, the trainer can take a sentence directly from the training materials or lecture and leave out a key word or phrase, which the learner must insert. *Context-bound* means that the phrase or sentence surrounding the blank may provide more clues than appropriate, suggesting the correct answer when the trainee would otherwise not know it. These cues may be grammatical, such as use of the articles *a* or *an*, or plurals, but recall of the answer might also be triggered by influences other than the wording of the question or other than the training that led to the question.

Grading a fill-in test is a bit more difficult than grading the other forms mentioned so far. All other test forms could be scored by a machine, if the test is properly designed and the technology is available. Currently, fill-in tests must be manually scored (though computer scoring is becoming feasible through word recognition), and decisions must be made on such issues as whether or not synonyms or incorrect spellings for the expected answer are acceptable. Precise spellings, for example, may be extremely important in a pharmacology training program—being a letter or two off in spelling a drug name could end up killing the patient—but might be irrelevant in a program about composting.

Short answer tests enable evaluation at the highest level of Bloom's Taxonomy. This format is the first clearly subjective form of testing listed so far. If the training objectives require that the learners accomplish more than just *knowing* some facts (for example, if the objective is to "explain" or "develop" something), then either short answer questions or essays will be required to accurately evaluate the trainees' knowledge. Questions must be written or asked in a way that demands that the level of response meet the training objective. If the training objective is that trainees know how to "recognize" something, the question must be worded differently than if the objective is for the trainees to be able to "analyze" or "evaluate" that same thing.

Grading is more difficult for a short answer test than for any of the objective forms or for fill-in-the-blank tests. The trainer and the organization must have predetermined what is expected in the answer and to what level that expectation must be met. This requirement means that criteria should be established against which each response will be measured. Another commonly used word for these criteria is a *rubric*. A rubric is a pattern or structure used to compare trainee answers with expected answers and includes rules for scoring responses. Commonly, partial credit can be given, rather than the "all or nothing scores" associated with objective questions. A sample rubric is shownin Table 6-1.

The quality of the answers will be affected, sometimes considerably, by the language skills of the trainee. To the extent possible, the trainer should design the questions so that writing or oral skills have minimal effect, whether or not the test is given in the trainee's original language, if the trainee is bilingual. Methods of accomplishing this goal include not requiring complete sentences or proper spelling or grammar (unless those are part of the objective, as in a writing-skills course), encouraging lists of points, and even accepting or encouraging non-verbal (e.g., graphic, tabular, or mathematical) responses. The trainer must maintain an open mind to recognize answers that could be judged "correct," even though they do not conform to the expected pattern of responses. Some thought must also be given to handling a response from a trainee who misreads the question and answers accordingly. Should that misunderstanding result in absolute failure on that question, or can a reasonable accommodation be made, perhaps by assessing a penalty but still scoring the question that appeared to be answered instead of what was asked?

Essay tests work best for the highest levels of Bloom's Taxonomy, and thus are more common in education and seldom used for most organizational training. (Relatively little organizational training is designed for the highest levels of Bloom's Taxonomy.) Essay questions must be carefully constructed to direct the learner to properly develop an answer that will allow the trainer

Table 6-1 Sample Scoring Rubric for a Level 2 Subjective Question and a Level 3 Skill Performance Evaluation

QUESTION	POOR (1)	NEEDS IMPROVEMENT (2)	GOOD (3)	EXCELLENT (4)
[Level 2 objective measure] Describe three possible approaches to resolving issues with a dissatisfied customer.	Only one or two described, or some of the approaches would violate company policy or relevant laws.	Fewer than three described, and customer's feelings are not considered; pure mechanics of the operation.	Three reasonable suggestions are given, which meet all standards covered in the training.	Three (or more) good ideas are suggested, all of which are both technically correct and consider the emotional needs of the customer.
[Level 3 objective measure] Demonstrate the correct technique for transferring a call to another office.	Call is disconnected or trainee is rude in making the transfer.	The call transfer is successful, but either or both the caller and person to whom the call was transferred were not alerted to the action taken.	Caller is told that a transfer is necessary, the transfer was successful, and the third party was notified that the call is being transferred.	A brief explanation of the need to transfer is given to the caller, who is then asked to hold the line, and the other office receives an explanation of the needs of the caller before connection.

to evaluate whether the objectives have been met by the training. Because of the time required to respond, fewer essay questions can be used in a given period than any other type. This restriction means that each answer must be more comprehensive.

As with the short answer form, the trainer must begin grading with a clear picture of what a good answer will include. Waiting to see what or how the trainees answer, then deciding how to grade responses, is a mark of poor planning. Various techniques are available to help objectify a subjective answer. One method is to set up a scheme in which each question is graded on the basis of 0 to 3 points. Zero means that the question was missed completely; one means it was partly correct, but lacked real understanding; two means essentially correct, but missed at least one key point; and three that the question was fully answered. Most essay answers are long enough that the question can be divided into parts, and each part be scored. This process is easier if the question reads something like, "Name any three uses for . . ." or has specific countable points that must be included.

What else should be considered in testing for knowledge?

For the trainer, administering knowledge-based tests may entail two different objectives. One is to determine that, when training is completed, the trainees possess the knowledge that they're supposed to have. This objective is the purpose of learning evaluation. The other is to clearly indicate that the knowledge the trainees possess is the result of the training and does not stem from other, extraneous factors. This objective is part of the program evaluation. To reach it, the trainer must set up some *controls*.

Control procedures require two parts to ascertain whether the knowledge was acquired as a result of the training program and not by some other means. First, the trainees must be tested before the training occurs, to verify that they don't already have the knowledge. (If they do have it, everyone can go home early.) This is known as the *pre-test*. The second requirement is that another, similar group of employees who did not receive the training—called the "control group"—must also be tested at the start and end of training. In the case of the control group, they should not possess the knowledge either before or after the training, because they weren't trained. If the control group also gained the knowledge without going through the training, the trainees may also have learned it from some other outside source—or could have done so more cheaply. If it's a very brief program, perhaps just a day or two in length, using a control group may be superfluous. Pre- and post-testing of the trainees would be enough for most purposes to clarify that learning occurred during the program.

Trainees who are thinking in "academic" terms sometimes ask if they will be graded on a curve. Somehow, they think that this approach will be easier on them than if they were graded according to an absolute standard or on objective criteria. Grading on a curve (applied to a traditional educational letter grade system) means that there will be an approximately equal number of A's and F's, an equal and larger number of B's and D's, and a still larger number of C's. Grading on a curve may mean that a score of 95% correct is an F, if most trainees scored higher.

In most job-related training, the purpose is to produce workers who have specific knowledge and skills, and grades (as opposed to performance) are seldom an issue. Using a specific standard based on objective criteria is more appropriate than grading on a curve in this environment; it is certainly of paramount interest to the organization! In educational terms, most testing for training programs would be done on a "pass-fail" basis.

What about testing that allows the learner to use other resources, for example, "open book tests"? This approach may be appropriate if the intent is to test not the trainees' knowledge so much as their ability to function on a job where access to resources is expected. The way in which the objectives are worded would indicate whether or not such a test is appropriate. In fact, testing items should always be tied to specific learning objectives. This is another reason to design the learning evaluation (test questions) as soon as the objectives for the program have been written. Further, each person should be tested equally, and results of the tests should be quantifiable and supportable.

Behavioral: level 3 evaluation

How do we evaluate learning on a behavioral level?

Explaining the steps necessary to do a task (possessing the knowledge) is no guarantee that the learner can actually perform the task (possessing the skill). Behavioral evaluations are related to skill objectives and thus cannot usually be accomplished with paper and pencil. They require that the learner actually perform the skill, to demonstrate that it has been learned and can be applied. Of course, skills that can be demonstrated orally or with paper and pencil, such as creating an effective and grammatically correct sentence, are the exception.

The behavior level of evaluation requires a systematic appraisal of trainee skill, using specific criteria for each job objective or skill at the behavior level. Such an evaluation (depending on the subject) may be carried out by the trainer, the trainees' superiors, their subordinates, the trainees themselves, trainees' peers, or an external observer. These evaluations must define conditions of performance and acceptable standards and levels of performance. The evaluation may occur during the training, in the form of skill tests, or on-the-job, following training. In some cases, post-testing should be delayed, perhaps by as much as several months.

To ensure that any changes are actually the result of training, both pre-and post-training testing of the trainees is necessary. Further, a control group should also be tested before and after the training. Obviously, this form of evaluation becomes more costly than a second-level evaluation.

Here are some examples to show how a third-level (skill) objective might be stated and measured. These examples follow the proper design of objectives, discussed in Chapter 5.

- For a training program on repairing a model C-23 copier, the objective might read: "*Upon completing the training, the participant will be able to diagnose the most likely problem within ten minutes, given a fluxmeter and list of symptoms.*"

To evaluate whether or not the trainee has met the objective, what must the evaluator do? Take the trainee to a room that contains a model C-23 copier that isn't working correctly, tell her the symptoms, hand her a fluxmeter and start the clock. If she comes up with the correct diagnosis within ten minutes, she has met the standard. That's the only valid way to test her. It is not appropriate, for instance, to use a model D-22 with a dynamometer and no time limit.

- For a sales training program, an objective might be: "*Upon completing the training, the salesperson will be able to close 35% of contracts provided through in-house leads.*"

How can that objective be tested? First of all, it can't be tested *during* training. At some reasonable point after the training, data must be gathered on how many in-house leads have been given to the former trainee and how many of those leads have resulted in a sale. Divide the number of sales by the number of leads, and the result should be 0.35 or higher.

An item that could be tested during this sales training program is a related skill-level objective, such as: *"Upon completing the training, the salesperson will be able to correctly use three different trial closes appropriate to the customer."* A test could be constructed using role plays (Chapter 7) during the training. In the role play, the trainee salesperson is confronted with a known type of customer and must choose a closing approach and demonstrate how to use it.

■ For a technical-skills training program, an objective might be: *"Upon completing the training, the learner will be able to install and configure an additional computer drive within twenty-five minutes so that it works on the first boot-up."*

This learning objective can be tested during training. In this case, no conditions were listed, so they must be assumed. It would be appropriate that the computer be a model that has physical room for the drive, that the software on the computer be working, that any required screwdrivers and so on be made available, etc.

Robert Mager[6] makes the point that you can't always test a skill under the exact circumstances specified in the objective. Practical issues of safety, cost, location, or many other things may prevent it. One of his examples is testing a trainee's skill at defusing an atomic bomb. You probably don't want to use a live bomb, unless the trainee has been really, really annoying during the class. Mager's recommendation is that if you have a circumstance (conditions) in which the evaluation cannot exactly match the objective, you might approximate the circumstances, but you should never accept approximate performance. Applied to his example, this means use a dummy bomb, but require that all actions necessary to defuse it be done correctly.

Certainly, some objectives can be tested using their own inherent and obvious indicators of trainee success. If the sample objective (above) for installing a computer drive is tested, the computer will either boot up correctly, or it won't. Not all objectives support such self-measures. Sometimes the trainer needs to create a test process to evaluate a skill, in the same way that artistic merit is judged in certain sporting events (such as ice skating) or other contests (poetry or music or painting, for example). In such situations, the skills of the participants are seldom judged on just one criterion and seldom judged as simply "pass" or "fail." Instead, scoring sheets may resemble checklists. If the skill has many steps or stages in the process, each one is judged separately. Box 6-2 is an example of a simple skill objective evalua-

---

Box 6-2   Example of Level 3 (Skill/Performance) Objective and Test Criteria

---

Objective: Upon completion of the training, the trainee will be able to effectively use a 3M type I overhead projector.

Performance Measure: The trainee will be given a 3M type I overhead projector and a set of six overhead slides. In a classroom with a screen, the trainee must set up and present the six slides to the instructor.

Checklist: Passing requires at least eight of the following ten items to be completed correctly.

☐ Student checks for power (or plugs in unit).
☐ Unit is positioned correctly so the light image is square (not keystoned) and fills nearly all of the screen without overlapping its edges. If positioning options exist within the room, the projector is set as low as practical so as not to obstruct learners' view of screen.
☐ Room lights are dimmed and/or window shades are adjusted so learners can see the projected images.
☐ Student does not block learners' view while projecting.
☐ Minimal motion is made above slide deck, once the slide is positioned.
☐ Pointing to items on the slide during discussion is done by pointing on the projector deck, not on the screen.
☐ Slide text is projected as high as possible on the screen to improve visibility.
☐ Slides are placed on the deck in proper position (not upside down or inverse).
☐ Image is in proper focus.
☐ Unit is turned off but not unplugged at end of presentation; room lights are readjusted.

---

tion checklist that could be used following a training session on how to use an overhead projector. Compare the way this check-list is set up with the concepts demonstrated in Table 6-1.

　　If evaluations must be done on the job after the training is complete, an additional related caution is that the evaluator must be cognizant of any environmental effects of the workplace that might interfere with the evaluation. An obvious example would be if the trainee can't successfully accomplish the objective in the time limit because the phone keeps ringing. Less obvious factors abound. Another example would be using the 35% close rate specified in the sales objective (above). What if market conditions have changed since the training objective was written, and that percentage is now unreasonable? What if the supervisor doesn't like the techniques presented in training and insists that the salesperson use a different form? As you can see, learning evaluations conducted on the job—although perhaps more valid than evaluations tested in a non-work environment—are fraught with pitfalls, especially when time has elapsed since training.

These considerations lead to another important point and the fourth, "results," level of evaluation. Sometimes, even when the trainee has developed and used the skill on the job, it does not make any difference to the organization's bottom line. That's what Kirkpatrick's fourth level is designed to measure: Has the training made a difference to the organization?

Results: level 4 evaluation

How do we evaluate learning on a results level?

The only true purpose of training in an organization is to enhance results. Training happens because the organization needs the trainees to know or do something better, faster, or otherwise differently than they would have been able to do it without training. It seems incongruous, then, that even in the largest, most training-oriented organizations, fewer than one of every nine companies even attempt to measure training at this level.[7] Of course, not all training lends itself to specific level-four objectives, and various other reasons exist that companies don't invest the time and effort for specific follow up.

Results-level evaluations require a long-term involvement, because the results may not be apparent for weeks or even several years following training. They also require a set of skills that are not necessarily associated with the training profession. The evaluator may need to deal with financial records, market analyses, industrial engineering techniques, and sometimes even the psychological and cultural aspects of organizational operations.

To continue with the example of a sales training program, an objective may have been that: *"Within one year of completion and as a result of the training, organizational sales will increase no less than ten percent."* After all, that's the sort of thing the organization would probably like to have happen with training. But it's difficult to assess whether any changes over a year's period are really the result of training.

According to Rob Brinkerhoff, "The contribution of training to human performance and, therefore, to overall business performance, is always partial (necessary, but not sufficient) and often marginal (only a small contributor)."[8] It should be obvious that hundreds of other factors may have intervened during the year to change the organization's results. Any change could have to do with the product or service itself, the economy, competition, pricing, fashion, general maturity of the trainees (they're a year more experienced), and so on.

Further, so many kinds of data may be relevant. Donaldson and Scannell[9] list twenty types of evidence that might be influenced by training, including direct cost reductions, work quality, accident rates, absenteeism, profits, sales volume, turnover, customer complaints, new customers, and eleven more. Glaser[10] lists a number of ways in which these evidence types can be used to evaluate outcomes, such as volume of cases handled, index of employee satisfaction, ability to adhere to a schedule, and others.

How can the trainer deal with all of this information? The net result is that the organization must often settle for evidence, not proof. This complexity also is the major reason that relatively few organizations even attempt to measure fourth-level outcomes, and most companies that do measure them limit their efforts to a few of the more expensive, high visibility, high volume, frequently repeated programs that exhibit outcomes lending themselves to easier measurement. In many cases, such measurements are more art than science.

Although all trainers should be aware of the implications of the fourth-level evaluations, most are not going to be able to accomplish more than a cursory attempt at doing them. It is beyond the scope of this book to develop this level in detail. Various books and programs are available to help design such evaluations. A very readable book on the subject is *Return on Investment in Training and Performance Improvement Programs* by Jack Phillips.[11]

What else should a trainer know about evaluation?

A serious issue with Kirkpatrick's four-level model is that research on training demonstrates that little, if any, linkage exists among the levels. Liking training has little relationship to learning; learning has little relationship to using the training; and so forth. Therefore, all levels may have to be assessed independently.

Remember that most of what has been discussed in this chapter relates to whether the trainees have learned the content specified in the training objectives. The process portion, which will be further treated in Chapter 11, considers whether the training could have been more efficient. Even if trainees did learn, did they do so in the best way? Are there ways to improve the transfer of training?

Trainers should virtually always use a level-one evaluation of training, even though some strong evidence exists that the results are unreliable. Levels two and three are normally appropriate, as well, but level four is used only when a lot is riding on the training in terms of time, repetitions, cost, and so on. The fourth level usually requires expertise outside that of of the training department.

What evidence is there that level one evaluations are flawed?

In a study that crossed various types of training and various organizations, the statistically strong evidence showed that even well designed level-one evaluations tended to be very positively biased.[12] Whether trainees did well in the training turned out to be a non-issue. If the delivery of the training was at least adequate, high satisfaction and low dissatisfaction were assured. If delivery was not at least adequate, there was still a better than 50% chance that trainees would report high satisfaction and low dissatisfaction. These findings mean that student evaluations of training using Kirkpatrick's first level, represented by "smile sheets," are of negligible value. Their only certain purpose is to provide a means of bringing closure to the class—that is, students seem to expect and appreciate the chance to give feedback and would probably not believe how irrelevant it really is. Also, the narrative (subjective) comments may occasionally be useful, but they tell us nothing of what the student really learned and frequently tell us nothing about either the content or process of the training. Scale-based (objective) ratings are ephemeral and should not be viewed as a true measure of anything.

Satisfaction and dissatisfaction with training clearly are unrelated to either a student's success in the training or the content of the training. They are related only to the process by which the training occurred. Examples of "process" include such things as an appropriate and adequate variety of training styles (not just lecture, for example), support by appropriate learning aids (handouts, visuals, simulations, lab work), tests that seemed fair in context, comfortable facilities, and so on. True measures of the success of training must be made at Kirkpatrick's second, third, or fourth levels to be accurate.

So, if you want to ensure good student ratings, it pays to design and present the material in an interesting, entertaining manner. Effective design and presentation of the content will probably help trainees to actually learn, as well. To make sure they've learned, you need to go to the higher levels of measurement: test them during training at both the knowledge and skill level and work with people in the real world (supervisors, advisory committees, graduate surveys, etc.) to see if what they take to the job really gets applied and makes a difference to the organization.

7 Classical Techniques for Training

"We have a propensity to learn. We also have a propensity to teach. These combine to make the student teacher relationship a very satisfying one. That it often is not may very well be that ... what is primarily a social relationship has become a technical transaction."

—Lionel Tiger and Robin Fox

The professional trainer knows that one size doesn't fit all when it comes to getting the message across to the learner. Rather than being dazzled by the newest and greatest techniques available or being stuck with the tried and true, it pays to have a variety of different choices, and—more importantly—to know when and how much of each to use.

■ ■ ■

Now that what needs to be taught and how to evaluate it have been decided, the next big decision is how to teach it. This is an important and sometimes complex decision. This chapter presents a variety of options, discusses the pros and cons of each, and offers a framework within which to evaluate each of the options in relation to the needs for an individual situation. The following chapter will offer some additional, higher-tech options for presenting the training material.

In fact, the eight different categories that follow (and the ones in the next chapter) are somewhat arbitrary. Trainers always need to create taxonomies and structures in order to reduce complex ideas into bite-sized pieces that the trainees can absorb.

For discussion purposes, this book presents these eight techniques individually, yet it would be a rare training program that uses only one. They actually overlap and are used in tandem, and training certainly occurs in additional ways as well.

What training techniques or strategies are available?

The eight training options covered in this chapter are:

- simple lecture
- enhanced lecture
- demonstration
- discussion
- case study
- experiential simulation
- self-directed learning
- on the job (coaching)

Simple lecture. This technique is familiar to everyone. The trainer talks, and the learners listen and try to take in and understand what was said. It has, perhaps, been the most common method by which many of us have learned facts throughout our formal education. The simple lecture is nearly always inductive, and it works best for lower level training objectives. An example of a pure lecture would be listening to an audio cassette or CD. It has no visual support or kinesthetic component, such as writing answers to questions in a workbook. It is strictly auditory, passive learning.

Enhanced lecture. The enhanced lecture attempts to engage more than just the auditory sense of the learner by using visuals or props. Word visuals (e.g., overhead projector slides, writing on a whiteboard, etc.), pictures, a video, handouts, sounds, props such as equipment, and even tastes or smells could be used to supplement the basic lecture. This technique is also inductive and is most effective with the lower levels of training objectives.

Demonstration. Demonstrations can run the gamut from simple show and tell to more complex forms, including behavior modeling or guided fantasies. The intent is for the learner to vicariously—or sometimes physically—experience the process or concept being taught. This technique is usually inductive, though it can be handled deductively if the trainees have sufficient background. It is limited to attitude or knowledge-type objectives; it can support skill objectives, but to be effective for this use it must be supplemented with other techniques.

Discussion. Discussion enables the learner to interact with the trainer and perhaps with other trainees in a two-way communication. Besides the usual meaning of the word, "discussion" can take many forms, including critiqued written assignments, debates or panels, or chat rooms and threaded discussions on the Internet. It can also include brainstorming and even the Delphi technique (see the Glossary in Box 7-4, at the end of this chapter), though these two techniques are usually reserved for group decision making or problem solving. Discussion is the first of the deductive forms, but if used by itself it is generally limited to knowledge objectives.

Case study. Case studies require the learner to examine an historical or hypothetical situation relative to the objectives of the training and to analyze and make judgments on that situation. Simple cases may be a paragraph or two long, but many complex cases have been developed that are monograph (booklet) length, with multiple concepts included. Some cases are presented through open-ended dramatizations on video or by role players or actors. They may be from the trainees' own organization or from other similar operations. Case studies are a deductive technique, and typically are most useful for knowledge objectives, though some kinds of skills can be practiced and improved through case studies.

Experiential simulations. These techniques include traditional laboratory exercises, games, puzzles, problem solving scenarios, in-baskets, role plays, team task experiments, field trips, and many other hands-on forms. Each requires a high level of involvement by the learner and—when properly chosen or designed—provides a high level of relevance. Simulations are usually deductive and may work for both skill and knowledge objectives.

Self-directed learning. Most of what people learn occurs through self-direction, but here the term means a structured, planned training program that employs a variety of options and allows the learner choices in achieving the learning objectives. This technique is usually deductive and, when properly designed, works well for both knowledge and skills.

On-the-job training (coaching). Purists might argue that a distinction exists between OJT and coaching; in fact, complete books are available on both subjects. They're treated together in this chapter, because they have a great deal in common. Most readers will understand that this category of training is usually accomplished outside of the formal classroom, and often, but not always, handled in a one-on-one, trainer to learner environment. Another common perception is that OJT isn't planned or formal instruction—it just "happens." Unfortunately, in many cases, that's true. But it shouldn't be. Effective on-the-job training requires every bit as much planning and preliminary preparation as a classroom training program.

Many other training techniques exist, but most could either be classified as a subcategory of one or more of these eight or fall into the technology categories discussed in Chapter 8. Some of the techniques in this chapter allow training in groups, while others only work one-on-one. Some must be done only off- or only on-the-job, but others can apply to either situation. Some can be done only in-person, but others may permit training by distance learning. Yet another difference is whether the method is procedural and sequential or can be adapted to self-paced or competency-based training.

How do I decide which technique to use for training?

The decision of which training technique (or combination of techniques) to use is most substantially influenced by the objectives for the training. Table 7-2, at the end of this chapter, compares the eight training strategies across six different criteria for their use.

Normally, one training style should not be used exclusively, even for a very short training program of an hour or less. Lessons should be planned to include several techniques in order to vary the flow and intensity of training and accommodate different learning styles of the trainees. The most effective training methods are the ones that present information in the manner in which the trainee will encounter it in the job setting.

The first consideration is whether the subject matter works best with the given trainees as a deductive or inductive presentation. (As described in Chapter 2, the inductive method largely consists of telling the trainees something, whereas the deductive method attempts to draw information from the trainees.) If an inductive presentation will work best, then the first two or three techniques described above are obviously the most appropriate. Another consideration is the size of the group to be trained, ranging from one person to hundreds. For example, for only one trainee, a lecture is probably not appropriate. Yet another consideration is whether the training will be on- or off-the-job. The nature of the

Figure 7-1   The Training Styles Grid

Learner Involvement						
Make Decisions and Invest	High					
Manipulate						
Write or Respond						
Move Physically						
Listen and Watch						
Listen only	Low					High
	None	Minor	General	Good	Specific	Exact

Training is Content Specific to the Job

objectives (skill vs. knowledge, for example) is also important in choosing learning styles. A final consideration might be the preferred learning style, if that has been determined and is relatively consistent among the trainees.

A grid method for comparing training styles is shown in Figure 7-1.

The training styles grid. The training styles grid is a two dimensional representation that describes how a given training style rates along two dimensions. The horizontal dimension indicates how relevant the material is to the objectives, and the vertical dimension indicates how involved the learner is. Any particular style can be placed on the grid to indicate both criteria at once. For example, "Lecture" is relatively low in learner involvement (they must simply listen), but if it is well done and precisely related to the material to be learned, it is highly relevant. This particular training style would be located at the bottom right of the grid. Well-structured OJT would be at the top right of the grid. In general, the closer to the top right of the grid, the higher the retention rate, and the better the transfer of training is likely to be. Table 7-2 at the end of this chapter indicates an approximate placement on the grid for each of the eight techniques covered in this chapter.

When and how should I use the simple lecture?

The simple lecture is an exclusively inductive technique; therefore, it demands a passive learner. It tends to be trainer centered, not learner centered. On the training styles grid, it is somewhere near the bottom; whether to the left, middle, or right depends on how relevant the content is. Lecture is most effective with trainees who have an assimilator learning style, under Kolb's model, and an auditory learning style under the Visual-Auditory-Kinesthetic model (Chapter 2). Remember, the auditory learning style is by far the least common among adults, so the simple lecture is usually a poor technique for training, unless it is supported by others.

Simple lectures may be presented face to face or through audio or videotape, over a radio, television, phone line, or computer line. Using a computer, lectures may be presented in an audio, text, or video format, or in a combination of all three (a "multimedia" presentation). If any video is used, the simple lecture technique would apply only to the "talking head" format. Using more elaborate techniques would bump it up into the "enhanced lecture" technique.

Why is the simple lecture so popular? Besides relying upon tradition, a simple lecture is extremely easy to design. The trainer is in complete control when using a lecture style—time can be planned down to the minute. It also can work quite effectively for a variety of topics and circumstances, particularly in meeting the first two types of objectives: attitude and knowledge. It uses time and human resources efficiently. A lecture can reach one person or millions of people through television, audio tape, and CD-ROM. It's a good and common supplement to other training techniques.

On the downside—Because lecture is, by definition, one-way communication, it lacks feedback and multisensory input. Doing a simple lecture well is difficult. By their very nature, certain topics are difficult or impossible to communicate in a simple lecture. Examples of this kind of topic are art (without also using visuals), music (without also using sound), and so on. Developing skills in the learner through the lecture format is nearly impossible, and even imparting knowledge well takes skill on the part of the trainer. Giving a good lecture requires that the trainer have excellent presentation and voice skills. Such skills may be developed in many ways, such as taking public speaking classes, joining Toastmasters International, recording and studying video or audio tapes of oneself, and just by practicing with an audience that is willing to provide feedback.

The subject matter must be clearly thought out and presented in a manner that engages the learner and progresses logically through the subject being presented. Because getting feedback from the learners is difficult, lectures tend toward information overload.

Some key ideas for effective lectures include:

- *Be clear and organized* with the presentation. Organize it around a single theme or topic.

- *Try out and adjust any amplification equipment* ahead of time when possible.

- *Preview the topic* (using an opening summary) and use frequent interim summaries.

- *Use effective speaking skills.* These include appropriate clarity and volume, good grammar, appropriate pacing and pauses, no verbal distracters (using "you know," "and," or "uhmm"), no visual distracters (pacing the floor, poor hand gestures, not being dressed appropriately for the training, playing with a pointer or marker while talking), showing appropriate enthusiasm, and so on.

- *Begin with some form of motivation*—tell them why they need to know the material—or employ an appropriate icebreaker to ensure their attention. Even a simple visualization exercise, visual aid, or interesting anecdote helps, as long as it's related to the objectives.

- *Encourage note taking* ("You may want to write this down.") and use key words as subheadings or memory hooks to support taking notes.

- *Use a lesson plan* and employ key concepts to keep on track. However, never read a lecture, except for short quotes or excerpts. Tell it like a story, when that's appropriate.

- *Use comparison, contrast, analogies, similes, examples, and mnemonic aids* that are appropriate to the learners and will help them to understand and retain the material.

- *Limit the length of the lecture*—because adults have a limited attention span—most sources say no more than 20 to 30 minutes—confine each session to that limit. Much can be covered in that time.

When and how should I use the enhanced lecture?

The trainer can use an enhanced lecture for many subjects, including most attitude and knowledge objectives. Although this method is still only one-way communication, it moves vertically up the training styles grid, because it requires the learner to do more than just listen. Because sight may account for 75% of our mental input, and sound accounts for only about 13%, this added dimension is important. Certain topics almost require an enhanced lecture. As mentioned above, art, music, and many other subjects would be nearly impossible to cover with a simple lecture, but the enhanced lecture fits them well. In fact, any topic that does not consist of pure knowledge will probably benefit from using this style. As you have learned, many more adults have a visual learning style than have an auditory learning style. The enhanced lecture supports both of these styles.

On the downside—The major disadvantage of the enhanced lecture is that it doesn't work for skill or job behavior objectives. Also, the need for extra equipment (e.g., flipcharts, projectors and screens, tape players, etc.) complicates the use of this technique. Attributes such as room arrangements, lighting, seating, and so on become more important and restrictive when people must see as well as hear. Sometimes the enhancements can get in the way of the information. For example, students may spend time carefully writing down the details from a slide, while ignoring the lecture itself. A *PowerPoint*® presentation can be so fascinating that it distracts from the content. (You may have heard the remark that some people using this medium have way too much power and not enough point.) Of course, enhanced lectures also take more time to prepare. Further, the medium can put emotional distance between the trainer and the learners and discourage participation and interaction. The learners may be either intimidated or reluctant to interrupt the trainer with questions if she or he seems to be caught up in the presentation.

Some suggestions for using enhanced lectures include:

- *Apply all the suggestions for simple lectures*. In general, most simple lectures will be improved by some additional enhancements, but don't overdo them.

- *Practice using props* ahead of time. For example, you should know where light switches are and how the equipment works.

- *Allow additional time* in the schedule. Even things like passing out written examples add time and slow down your progress.

- *Keep it professional*. Poorly designed materials will detract, not enhance. Keep materials in a consistent format, use good taste, check spelling and grammar, and so on.

More suggestions related to lecture enhancements will be covered in Chapter 9.

When and how should I use demonstrations?

A demonstration adds increased realism to the training environment. It moves the learner from the conceptual state to an observed or experienced reality. Learners experience some demonstrations passively, but others actively involve them. Demonstrations appeal to multiple senses, adding visual to aural. The demonstration is often a necessary step on the way to either discussion or experiential learning techniques when teaching a skill. It can set the standard for performance, highlighting sequences and safety issues. When used alone, the demonstration may be sufficient to teach very simple skills, though the feedback element is still missing. Trainers need to use demonstration in small S-R-F links (Chapter 2), and frequently need to demonstrate skills at slower than normal speed as well as in real time.

On the downside—The lack of feedback already mentioned is a limitation in demonstrations. Of course, sometimes demonstrations will fail. Although a failed demonstration can be a learning experience for the trainer as well as the students, it is also embarrassing and wastes time. To minimize this possibility, make certain to practice the demonstration thoroughly, know the current equipment, techniques, or software (if applicable), and have on hand everything needed to carry out the demonstration properly. A demonstration takes more time to develop than the simple lecture and often requires more materials. Group size is often a practical limit in the use of demonstrations—large groups may not be able to observe some demonstrations. However, if the demonstration is for a single learner, such as in on-the-job training, it can be personalized to specifically meet his or her needs. Sometimes the trainer lacks the skill to carry out a true demonstration, and so must rely on other techniques, such as simulations. For example, a trainer working with an Olympic-class ice skating athlete might be able to describe a complex move but not actually perform it. Because only a world-class athlete could perform the move, the trainer would need to use some other technique to demonstrate the concept.

Some suggestions for using a demonstration effectively include:

- *Prepare thoroughly*.
- *Explain the goals* of the demonstration before you start and review at the end what the trainees should have noticed and learned.
- *Break long demonstrations into smaller pieces*, then perform one piece at a time. Explain what is being demonstrated and why, and do it in slow motion, if necessary.
- *Use questions* or other techniques to maintain trainee involvement.
- *Use equipment identical to the actual equipment* the trainees will use on the job, when it's available.
- *Include lecture, discussion, and other techniques* in the lesson plan, because it is usually not possible to complete training with only a demonstration.

When and how should I use the discussion?

Discussion is not merely "talking about" a topic; it must be developed around the learning objectives and expected outcomes. Discussion in a formal training program is usually a response to something presented using one of the forms already described, such as a lecture. Discussion may also be based on reading written materials or on trainee experiences. The give and take of discussion enables the learners to explore areas that are unclear and helps to guide the training in ways more meaningful to them. It also allows misconceptions to surface and be corrected. Discussion is also a means to enhance other skills in the trainee, such as participation in groups, critical thinking, negotiating, speaking, and so on.

This technique assumes that trainees have something to discuss and are able and willing to do so. Because discussion is a more deductive style than the rest of the styles described so far, the participants need to have some pre-existing background in the subject and some communication skills. Therefore, the quality of the discussion is limited by the participants.

Some discussions are between the trainer and individual students who ask or answer questions during a class. Another form of discussion occurs when students are grouped and handle the discussion within each individual group.

On the downside—Discussion is considerably limited by group size and can be time consuming and inefficient. It requires a permissive atmosphere. The trainer must work to keep the discussion moving and not let it deteriorate into a gripe session or digress into unrelated topics. Dominance by one or two individuals, and emergence of factions and subgroups, must be avoided.

One of the techniques for guiding a discussion is to offer interim summaries. This approach requires the trainer to interrupt the discussion occasionally to say things such as, "Here are the three main points I've heard so far: . . ." or "We've covered several ideas about *why* we should do this, but I've not heard any comments about *how* to do it."

Using open-ended questions that can be answered in a number of ways enables the group or individual respondents to set the agenda. It's up to the trainer to use questions that will elicit discussions to match the training objectives. Examples of an open-ended question are: "What key points do you recall about . . ." or "What would you do in this case?"

To get the discussion back on track, the trainer may need to inject some directive or closed-ended questions that require "yes" or "no" or otherwise specific answers. For example, a trainer might ask, "Would you use form 2016 or 2116 for this situation?" or "Does this example follow the company's standard of ethical behavior?" Incidentally, simply asking, "Do you understand?" is usually not a good idea. Although it is technically a closed question, learners frequently will answer "Yes," whether or not that's true, in order to avoid embarrassment and to keep the program moving. A better way to get to an honest answer on this question is to either make the question open-ended or to require a specific response, such as: "What is the first step in performing the periodic maintenance for this machine?"

When looking for more detail or to adjust a partially correct answer, one technique that may be used is the reflection, or neutral restatement by the trainer of a participant's comment. This technique invites expansion by that student or further input by others. An example of this would be: "So you feel that option C is the best one?" The trainer is neither agreeing nor disagreeing with what was said, but simply repeating it in a way that may cause the learner to rethink the answer or expand upon it. (Keep the restatement neutral. It won't work if you roll your eyes or try to suppress a snicker while doing it.)

Panel discussions use several people, often experts or students who have been assigned to research a specific topic, to present content and discuss it with each other or with trainees. This technique can present some diverse perspectives and allow some higher order thinking among trainees (see Bloom's Taxonomy, Chapter 5). On the other hand, this style may come across as similar to a lecture and tempt the non-panelist trainees to remain passive, so it must be designed to encourage involvement. The design must also avoid introducing confusion arising from different perspectives held by the panelists or from their varying abilities in presenting the information.

If the topic being discussed has a correct answer, the trainer needs to know that answer and be able to defend it. If the topic under discussion is simply a matter of opinion, or if several different answers could apply, the participants may need to agree to disagree. This solution is not always easy for people to accept, so the trainer must be alert to any problems and often must set the stage, through an introduction.

Additional suggestions for effective discussions include:

- *Make sure everyone has a chance* to participate; don't let the discussion become a dialogue with just one or two students.
- *Make sure all trainees can hear and understand* their peers' questions.
- *Keep discussion groups relatively small* (3 to 7 people).
- *Give clear assignments or questions* for discussion, which are related to the training objectives.
- *Don't get into extended discussion too early*; trainees need a knowledge base from which to discuss.
- *Let the groups function on their own*, but move from group to group to keep people on task.
- *Use interim summaries and questioning techniques*, described above, to keep the discussion moving. Ask for reports from the groups at least some of the time.
- *Use alternative means for generating questions*, such as having people write them on a flipchart or a sheet of paper to pass in. This provision enables anonymous questions, so that even self-conscious trainees can participate.
- *Have someone write key points* on a flipchart or whiteboard during the discussions, to be used for brainstorming or generating ideas.
- *Set time limits*, so trainees know when to wrap up and come to a decision or agreement.

When and how should I use the case study?

The graduate business school at Harvard University is widely known for using cases as a primary teaching technique. Case studies can be carried out either by individual learners or as group projects, depending on their complexity and objectives. Some case studies, which are based on real situations, include the actual outcome of the case and ask the trainees to validate that outcome or to suggest what might have worked better. Others are open ended, where the learners must develop their own options. Either style can lead to good debate. Usually there is no simple right answer to case studies, so the intent is often to get trainees to practice analytical skills. Case studies are available from many sources, including listings at the ends of chapters in many textbooks. Such studies may be used in class or as outside assignments.

Case studies must be realistic and provide enough data for discussion, without divulging any obvious answer. This training style is generally deductive, so it requires that the learners have sufficient knowledge and group skills to use the technique effectively. Case studies encourage discussion and critical thinking, both related to higher order knowledge in Bloom's Taxonomy.

On the downside—A negative facet relating to case studies is that the bridge from theory to real life doesn't necessarily develop. Like the discussion, the case study can be difficult for the trainer to control. Transfer of training may be relatively low, because the cases may be seen as somehow different than the way things "really are" in the organization. For this reason, carefully selecting or designing the materials is critical.

When using the case study technique, be sure to:

- *Use only cases that apply* to the training objectives and that will seem realistic to participants.
- *When possible, use cases from the actual organization or industry* in which the training is occurring.
- *Provide a list of specific questions* to be answered.
- *Make clear how much outside research is expected,* if any.
- *Use small groups* (3 to 7 people), with mixed expertise to increase their involvement.
- *Use fairly stringent time limits* to minimize digressions. Box 7-1 presents an example of a case study.

Box 7-1 Example Case Study—New Blood

This case was designed to be used as part of a training program for a Board of Directors retreat. The board was for a not-for-profit professional association and was primarily made up of volunteers.

The case:

Members of the group:

Chairperson: Brenda	Treasurer: Ed
Communications: Cindy	Member: Bill
Events: Jill	Member: Jack
Member: Gloria	Member: Jinny
Secretary: Tom	Business Manager/Non-voting member: Al
Community Service: Bob	Member: Zee

Al called the meeting to order, because Brenda was out of town. The purpose of the meeting, he stated, was to consider how to find mid-term replacements for Jill and Jinny, who were moving from the area because Jill and Jinny's husband had both found new jobs. Both were missing tonight, along with Zee and Brenda. It would be five months until the regular elections came up.

Bill said that Jinny had talked with someone named Jim who was interested in what the group did, and wanted her to place his name in nomination. No one else knew him. Cindy offered to put an announcement in the next newsletter, going out in three weeks, to see if anyone was interested in the vacancies. Gloria felt that the group could operate okay with two vacancies until the next election was held, but Jack and Bob immediately disagreed. Al said he could probably do without Jinny, but that Jill had a subcommittee and some responsibilities that weren't finished for the year, so he thought that she, at least, had to be replaced. No one knew what Brenda, Zee, or Jill thought. Ed started making a list of names he knew from the organization and Gloria looked over his shoulder, adding suggestions and commenting on his list. Others began talking with persons next to them as the discussion bogged down.

Box 7-1   Example Case Study—New Blood (*Continued*)

Questions for discussion:

1. What should Al do to get the meeting back on track?
2. What are the pros and cons of selecting Jim, if he really is interested?
3. What are the pros and cons of Cindy's approach? How about Gloria's?
4. What other suggestions do you have for the group?

Suggested responses to questions about the "New Blood" Case:

1. What should I do to get the meeting back on track?
Presuming none of the comments in 4 (below) change the situation, Al should:

- First: List the options presented: (a) operate with vacancy; (b) "hire" Jim, since he's interested; (c) solicit other applications through the newsletter; and (d) make a list of known people to consider.
- Then: Focus on one option at a time, discussing and either accepting or rejecting it.
- Then: Ask if any other options are available and discuss them.
- Finally: Put all accepted options up for a vote and pursue the one that seems best.

2. What are the pros and cons of selecting Jim, if he really is interested?

- **Pros:** He's actively expressed an interest. It's an easy option (probably 2nd easiest). As a new member, he's apt to bring new ideas and energy and want to prove himself.
- **Cons:** He's unknown. We don't know his skills, his motives, or what he would do to the established group dynamics. We may miss other, more qualified applicants.

3a. What are the pros and cons of Cindy's approach (sending out a newsletter announcement)?

- **Pros:** Opens the opportunity to all organization members, not just Jim or the ones known by the group members present.

(continued)

Box 7-1   Example Case Study—New Blood (*Continued*)

May be viewed by the organization as more open and less inbreeding of the leadership group.
- **Cons:** Delays action for several weeks and still doesn't establish a selection process. Deciding among multiple applicants will be more work, and there may be no more applicants, which will make the delay pointless.

3b. What are the pros and cons of Gloria's approach (having two fewer members until elections)?
- **Pros:** Eliminates the need for any immediate action—easiest option. Keeps the group dynamics status quo.
- **Cons:** Fewer people to share the work. Others may leave later, as well, which would make the problem even bigger and delay experience that new members could start getting immediately. It may mean more new people coming into the group at once. Making a quorum will be harder, and Jill's ongoing committee work still needs to be resolved.

4. What other suggestions do you have for the group?
- This issue should be covered in their by-laws or charter. Have they checked? If it's not, the group should be aware that whatever process they choose may set precedent and should probably be carefully thought out and incorporated into the governing document.
- Have they determined if this has happened before and how it was handled? Was it successful or not?
- The group should have a succession plan, whether or not it is part of the charter.
- Persons who are not present should have sent their opinions in to the group, especially Brenda (as chairperson) and the two who are leaving.
- A prime source for Jill's replacement should be from her subcommittee.

When and how should I use experiential simulations?

This broad category may include anything from lab exercises to field trips to games or in-baskets, and so on. Some experiential simulations focus on knowledge level objectives, but many can be used to teach skills as well. They permit practice and reinforcement, and may be adapted as either individual or team activities.

On the downside—Most of these approaches take more time, more equipment, and a higher trainer-to-trainee ratio than other techniques. They may be difficult to construct and often relate to a limited portion of the lesson. Digressions will occur if the learning objective is not made clear. Simulations may exhibit poor transfer of training qualities, and—of course—they may occasionally fail to work or make their point.

All experiential simulation techniques require some knowledge training before being used, and they require at least some post-exercise outbriefing and analysis. Just doing the simulation alone is not effective. As you saw in Chapter 2, nothing is so useful as a good theory, but people understand the theory only as they begin to apply it. This is the role of simulations: experiential simulations require the learners to apply complex skills or knowledge.

Some of the common forms of experiential simulations in training include the following:

Laboratory exercises are familiar to all of us from elementary and high school science classes. These exercises are particularly helpful for skill development. They can apply to any number of manual and intellectual skills, including topics related to computer skills, psychology, physics, and many others. They usually provide a controlled environment in which to test and apply learning. For example, flight simulators have long been used to test pilots without risking an actual plane crash.

Puzzles, Games, and Problem Solving Exercises can also be quite diverse, ranging from brain teasers and creativity puzzles to solving mysteries. Sometimes the format from TV game shows can be replicated, such as creating a version of *Jeopardy* for bank tellers, etc. These sessions may be short, requiring only a minute or two, or longer—played over weeks or even months. Although they may be fun for the trainees, their purpose should still be tied to appropriate training objectives. Some people find this style frustrating, and some will dislike it intensely, so it is best used sparingly until you have a sense of the trainees' reaction to it. Dozens of books with pre-designed training games are available.[1]

In-Baskets are a special case of problem solving, in which the learner is given a series of problems or issues, which must be prioritized and dealt with according to procedures explained in the training. In-Baskets are a popular tool in assessment centers, which some large organizations use to determine promotability of employees. This technique generally requires "right" and "wrong" answers, and doesn't work well for broader concepts.

Team Task Experiments are often presented as a technique to meet objectives related to team development or leadership. They may be *conceptual*, such as the popular *Lost at Sea* game in which group decision making is critical, or *physical*, such as outdoor or wilderness exercises in which team cooperation is necessary to achieve the goals. Prior training or skill in group behavior is essential. A number of publications are available with predesigned experiments. They can be found under the heading of team-building training programs, along with the series of "*Games Trainers Play*" books, by consulting some of the references listed in Chapter 1, such as the ASTD and ISPI websites.

Role Plays provide two or more learners with a script outlining, in a very limited fashion, the open-ended roles they will act out in a small drama. Role plays can be a fun way to help individuals gain confidence and learn to apply new concepts, such as interviewing skills. Although some trainees find them threatening, others will excel. They are nearly always used to train for interpersonal skills. The technique is subject to some problems. For example, adults may resist this approach, not play roles well, or focus so much on the theatrical that the content of the lesson is ignored or missed. Role plays are time consuming and difficult for the trainer to control, but they can be very effective when they work. As with most of the other experiential techniques, a post-session debriefing and analysis is necessary to reinforce ties to the training objective and ensure effective transfer of training. Role plays can be done by one set of students with everyone else watching, or in small groups, each with a designated observer who has a checklist of points to evaluate.

Box 7-2 provides a sample role play.

Specific suggestions for using experiential simulations include:

■ **All Kinds:** Tie the experience to the objectives and clarify the instructional purpose to the learners before they begin. Set up the experience and get information from the learners about what happened at the end; don't just expect them to "experience it" and magically understand.

Box 7-2 Example Role Play

This role play was designed to allow trainees in a supervisory training program the chance to practice effective questioning techniques to use during employee interviews and counseling. One person plays the boss role, the other the subordinate. Each gets only that paragraph of information. An observer (or the entire rest of the training group) gets both sides of the information and is instructed to watch whether the boss uses effective questions to draw out information from the subordinate.

The role play:

Boss

Your Subordinate has appeared to be gathering information and spending a lot of company time talking with other people about "supervision." You've had some family troubles lately, and you suspect that he's building a case to go over your head and talk to your boss about performance in your section. You know you haven't been concentrating on your job as much as you should, but no one else seems to have noticed except him.

He's a person with ambition; in fact, he may want your job. One way to protect yourself may be to transfer him to an opening in the sales department. You're not sure what his reaction will be, but you intend to encourage this move. Sales will mean that he'll be out of the office—in fact, out of town—two to four days a week.

His work is good enough that you could honestly recommend him for the position.

Subordinate

Your boss has called you into his office. At this point, you're not sure why. He usually talks to you out on the floor or at your desk, so this must be important. As far as you know, your work is up to requirements, you've been getting along with everyone and there don't appear to be any problems.

You've been taking a course in supervision at the community college over the past eight weeks. You've found it interesting, but your boss seems to do well even though he follows very few of the practices you've discussed in class. You decide that you're going to watch your boss carefully during this meeting to see how he handles the discussion. You often take notes during his meetings, anyhow, since he frequently dishes out more information than you can remember.

You like your present job and enjoy the freedom it allows you to pursue the college program you've started.

- *Role Plays:* Consider videotaping the role play to make critique easier. Keep the cast of characters small (2 or 3), and use strong, simple character descriptions for each role. Sometimes a spontaneous role play can arise out of a class discussion, if the trainer feels competent to handle such creativity. Another useful technique is to have role players reverse roles if they seem to have reached an impasse.

- *Laboratory Assignments or Simulations:* These activities must be realistic enough to draw in the trainees (they must have "psychological fidelity"). All simulations must evidence specific standards, actions, and outcomes, which can be monitored. A competency-based approach (see the Glossary at the end of this chapter) is best when it is at all possible to state desired behaviors or observations as outcomes.

- *Games, Puzzles, and Problem Solving:* These activities should not be too complex, unless they are central to the objectives. They should provide a change of pace, not be used as a major medium of content presentation. If multiple games are used, vary their intensity between serious and light fun. Don't let the competition get out of hand!

- *In-Baskets:* This is a fairly limited style of activity, and it should be used only when it clearly fits. One variation is to design it for multiple trainees so that they must get information from each other.

When and how should I use self-directed learning?

Most of what we know is probably the result of self-directed learning. How many people have really had formal training in gardening, taking snapshots, word processing, choosing clothes or a movie, buying groceries, or similar life skills? For nearly everyone, these things are learned based upon our observations of others or by trial and error—all examples of self-directed learning. But when self-directed learning is used in an organization, making it as efficient and effective as possible is important, so the trainer must carefully structure the techniques and programs for trainees to follow.

Self-directed learning includes a multitude of formats. Reading, correspondence classes, video lessons, and other formats, such as computer based training (discussed separately in Chapter 8) are included. Oftentimes OJT, if insufficiently structured, lends itself to self-directed learning, sometimes in the most negative sense.

Self-directed learning is a positive experience for motivated students. It enables them to progress at their own rates and to explore areas of interest to them. If learners are widely dispersed or arrive for training one at a time, this method should be considered. Like other techniques, it is seldom used in isolation. Access to a trainer for discussion and help—even by phone or e-mail—will probably enhance the experience, as will real life feedback. When properly designed, self-directed learning allows the learners multiple entry and exit points. Rylatt and Lohan[2] state that a training bias against self-directed learning is a major barrier to using it. But they also cite six good reasons for using the method. Self-directed learning:

- provides improved motivation for the trainees to learn.
- is fairly adaptabe to change.
- gives both the trainee and the organization a flexibility in learning.
- is better aligned with adult learning theory.
- makes it easier to identify the results of learning.
- for long term programs, provides an excellent cost effectiveness, compared to traditional methods.

On the downside—Self-directed learning will not work well for students without a sufficient elementary grasp of a topic. Likewise, unmotivated students do not do well with this technique. Some accountability must be built in by specifying deadlines, administering tests, and so on. Self-directed training often uses one-way communication, and therefore must be much more carefully designed and validated than other approaches. The initial design is expensive, but subsequent per use costs are low.

To develop an effective self-directed learning experience:

- *Begin, if possible, with testing* to determine whether the individual has the basic skills and motivation to deal with self-directed learning.
- *Be especially careful to test and validate the design of the program* before mass distribution.
- *Allow for competency-based training* when possible (see the Glossary, Box 7-4).

- *Arrange for regular and timely feedback* between the trainer and the trainees.
- *Build in accountability*—tests, deadlines, and so on—and enforce them.
- *Recognize that the trainer will play a non-traditional role*, one of designer and administrator. Practiced at its best, the role enables the trainer to work as a coach and consultant for the learners.

When and how should I use on-the-job training (OJT)?

On-the-job training is the most common of all training forms in business and other organizations. Although hard figures are difficult to come by, estimates are that companies spend at least three to six times as much on OJT as on formal, off-the-job training.[3] It is the "default" method of getting a new or transferred employee up to speed and functioning in a job. As already mentioned in this chapter, it's often actually handled by ineffective or at least inefficient means. Although it is often the only means used for training, *a certain amount of on-the-job training will probably be necessary even if formal, off-the-job training is provided.* Thus, it's important for trainers to understand some of the key principles.

OJT can be handled inductively or deductively, one-on-one or in small groups. It can be aimed at any level of learning objective, but—ultimately—is going to lead to a level four (job behavior) objective. Most often the "trainer" is either a more experienced peer of the trainee or a supervisor. Frequently, this individual has no formal training or even guidance in how to train.

On the downside—Typical problems that can result from OJT are that the employee:

- learns an incomplete or incorrect way of doing the job.
- doesn't learn all parts of the job.
- learns in an unnecessarily stressful environment.
- provides customers with poor products or service during training.
- slows down the operations and sometimes creates hazards or causes injuries.

With all of these problems, why do companies use OJT at all? Frequently, it's because no alternative exists.

Fortunately, even if OJT is the only practical method for training an employee, it can be structured and designed to minimize some of these above. If only one or a few people need training at any given time, a formal off-the-job training program may be impractical or impossible. If the job is so specialized that no trainer except a peer or supervisor can do training, or if the work environment is so unusual that it can't be easily simulated, then OJT is probably the best way to achieve the organization's purpose.

If OJT is the most appropriate technique:

- *Select trainers carefully*, considering not only their skill at the job, but also their personalities, organization skills, and interpersonal communication skills. Train them how to train, and help them feel that this is a prominent part of their jobs, not just an annoying additional duty. Evaluate them on how well the trainee does.

- *Start the trainee at the slowest time*, perhaps on a second shift or weekend. When possible, avoid peak volume periods.

- *Plan how the training is to proceed*, rather than just letting it "happen." Use the techniques from Chapters 3, 5, and 6 to analyze what needs to be taught and to what level, then write objectives and develop appropriate measurements for those objectives. Chapter 10 provides some further guidance on designing lesson plans for OJT.

- *Use the model in Box 7-3* to guide the process.

So how do I choose the best method?

Other things being equal, choose the simplest of the methods discussed in this chapter that will work, given the nature of the learners, the time available, and the specified objectives. Except for very short training programs, more than one method should probably be used in order to provide some variety, meet adult learning needs, and allow for individual learning style preferences.

Tables 7-1 and 7-2 highlight the major pros and cons of each of the eight techniques discussed in this chapter and compare each technique across half-a-dozen important criteria.

Box 7-3   Job Instruction Training*

Determining the Training Objectives and Preparing the Training Area

- Decide what the trainee must be taught so that he or she can do the job efficiently, safely, intelligently and economically.
- Provide the right tools, equipment, supplies, and material.
- Have the workplace properly arranged, just as the new employee will be expected to keep it.

Presenting the Instruction

- **Step 1:** Prepare the trainee
  1. Put the trainee at ease.
  2. Find out what the trainee already knows about the job.
  3. Get trainee interested in learning about the job.
- **Step 2:** Present the operations and knowledge
  1. Tell, show, illustrate, and question to put over [sic] the new knowledge and operations.
  2. Instruct slowly, clearly, completely, and patiently, one point at a time.
  3. Check, question, and repeat.
  4. Make sure the trainee understands.
- **Step 3:** Try out the trainee
  1. Test the trainee by having him or her perform the job.
  2. Ask questions beginning with why, how, when, and where.
  3. Observe performance, correct errors, and repeat instructions if necessary.
  4. Continue until the trainee is competent in the job.
- **Step 4:** Follow up
  1. Put the trainee on his or her own.
  2. Check frequently to be sure instructions are followed.
  3. Taper off extra supervision and follow up until the trainee is qualified to work with normal supervision.

**Source:* War Manpower Commission, 1945. It still works today!

Box 7-4 Glossary of Related Terms and Minor Techniques

Behavior modeling (a type of demonstration): the trainer or an experienced person demonstrates the correct technique for performance of a skill, and the trainee models his or her behavior after that example. It is often most successful if the behavior is demonstrated in small pieces, with feedback provided to the learners as they attempt to emulate the performance.

Brainstorming (a discussion technique) requires participants to suggest ideas in a stream-of-consciousness form; any critical thinking is withheld until a large number of suggestions have been developed. It is typically used in creativity and idea generation sessions.

Competency Based Training (abbreviated *CBT*, which has also come to mean—and therefore be confused with—computer based training) is concerned with attaining and demonstrating specific skills and knowledge ("competencies") necessary to perform a specific organizational role. In other words, *it's outcome, not process oriented.* This is sometimes also called *Mastery Learning*. If the required competencies can be demonstrated by an individual at the established minimum levels, no training is needed for this person. But, if the person doesn't have the required competencies, they are trained until they can meet the established standards, regardless of the time required.

Delphi Technique (a possible format for discussion): a process by which participants who are not in direct contact with each other provide answers or opinions to a succession of questions or respond to various scenarios. An example of this technique would be if five experts in different plants were asked to project sales estimates for a new product. Their inputs would be sent to one person who summarizes the data, then sends a composite back to all the experts who review and respond with additional ideas. This cycle may occur several times.

Distance Learning (a delivery approach) is a term applied to nearly any learning situation in which the trainer and trainees are not co-located. Some distance learning is done in real-time, such as Ford Motor Company's training programs, which are

(continued)

Box 7-4   Glossary of Related Terms and Minor Techniques
(*Continued*)

broadcast by satellite to dealerships around the world. Others
are as simple as traditional correspondence courses. Media for
delivery include audio and video tapes, CD-ROM, webcasting,
radio and television, and others. See Chapter 8.

Guided fantasies (a type of demonstration) are most
often used for creativity exercises, to enable trainees to create
their own scenario. For example, in a career-planning program,
the trainer might use a guided fantasy to help trainees visualize
where they will be and what kind of a job they'll be performing in
five years. This technique generally involves having trainees
close their eyes and get comfortable while visualizing things in
their minds as the trainer takes them through an open ended
script. The results are very personal to each trainee. Some people see it as hokey and resist participating, and others find it
uncomfortably close to certain therapies and may even be
traumatized by it.

Self-paced learning is a process by which each individual
works at his or her own speed through the training program. It
is easiest to do with self-directed or computer based training,
but it can also be done using modular lessons and also in on-
the-job training. The opposite of self-paced learning would be
"group paced" or "lock step," in which everyone takes the same
amount of time to complete each part of the training.

Table 7-1 Summary Comparison of Different Training Techniques

TECHNIQUE AND EXAMPLES	KEY ADVANTAGES	KEY DISADVANTAGES
Simple Lecture (Inductive)	■ Trainer is in control ■ Fast delivery of details ■ Great for large groups ■ Works for attitude and some knowledge objectives ■ Efficient use of time	■ Student is passive ■ Disregards learning differences ■ Requires excellent speaking and organizing skills ■ No feedback to trainer ■ Skills and some types of knowledge can't be covered
Enhanced Lecture (Inductive) Includes using slides, computer projection, video, sounds, props, etc., *with a lecture*	■ Multi-sensory ■ Good for medium to large group sizes ■ Better memory retention ■ Necessary for learning topics beyond aural (i.e., ones requiring other senses like sight, etc.) ■ Versatile	■ Requires extra equipment ■ Requires additional preparation ■ May limit group size or seating ■ Must be properly designed ■ Visuals may distract from content ■ Skills can't be covered
Demonstration (Usually inductive) May occur using equipment or personal skills (e.g., Behavior modeling)	■ Encourages attention and involvement, though passive ■ Good for small to medium groups ■ Sets standard; highlights sequence and safety issues ■ Increases realism for learner ■ Some very limited skills may be taught	■ Learner is usually passive ■ Most skills can't be covered ■ Risk of equipment or process failures ■ May limit group sizes ■ Doesn't apply to many topics

(continued)

Table 7-1   Summary Comparison of Different Training Techniques (*Continued*)

TECHNIQUE AND EXAMPLES	*KEY ADVANTAGES*	*KEY DISADVANTAGES*
Discussion (Deductive) Includes debates, panels, critiqued written assignments, brainstorming Delphi, etc.	■ Encourages active involvement of the trainees ■ Allows learner to clarify issues ■ Accommodates individual learner needs better than most other styles ■ Can be done in small groups or in class as a whole	■ Difficult to control ■ Can be dominated by some people while others do not join in ■ Limited by group size ■ Panel discussions may discourage involvement in the same way a lecture would
Case Study (Deductive) Individually or in group work	■ Learner directed; trainer acts only as a consultant ■ Realistic scenarios are possible and improve transfer of training ■ Higher level skills involved	■ Relevant cases are difficult to find or create ■ As with discussion, can be difficult to control ■ Time consuming ■ Must be preceded by other training forms and requires follow-up
Experiential Simulation (Deductive) Lab Exercises, Games, Puzzles, Problem Solving, Role Plays, In-Baskets, Field Trips, Team Task Experiments, Etc.	■ Can be fun and engaging ■ Provides real life situations without the personal risk ■ Many have precise applications and work very well for those specific areas ■ Works well with competency based training models	■ Dependent on trainee skills other than those in objectives ■ Usually can't stand alone: needs other techniques to be used, as well as immediate and clear feedback of results ■ Some trainees will resist ■ Time consuming ■ Transfer of training may be weak

Table 7-1 Summary Comparison of Different Training Techniques (*Continued*)

TECHNIQUE AND EXAMPLES	KEY ADVANTAGES	KEY DISADVANTAGES
Self-Directed Learning (Can be either; usually inductive) Video based, Readings, Correspondence, Most computer tutorials, OJT	■ Progresses without heavy trainer involvement (at least after the design stage) ■ Motivating to many learners ■ Efficient in use of learning time ■ Works well with small, irregular flow of trainees ■ Flexible; open to competency based training	■ Lack of effective controls ■ Expensive to design ■ Limited interaction with trainer; mostly one-way communication ■ Unmotivated learners will fail quickly
On-the-Job Training (Can be either) One-on-one or in small groups	■ Trainee actually produces work ■ Transfer of training problems minimized ■ No separate training facilities or trainer needed	■ Usually inefficient and haphazard ■ Disrupts workplace ■ Workers are slow and they slow down others ■ May be unsafe or lead to very costly errors ■ Difficult to evaluate

Table 7-2 Training Techniques Comparison Chart

CATEGORY	INDUCTIVE DEDUCTIVE	KNOWLEDGE SKILL	1-TO-1 GROUP	ON THE JOB OFF THE JOB	NON-TRADITIONAL	LEARNING STYLES	TRAINING STYLES GRID
Simple Lecture	Inductive	Knowledge	Group	Off	D	Asm	Lower
Enhanced Lecture	Inductive	Knowledge	Group	Off	D	Con, Asm	Mid-Low
Demonstration	Inductive	Knowledge	Either	Either	D, S, C	Div	Anywhere
Discussion	Deductive	Knowledge	Group	Either	D, S	Div, Asm	Mid-Right
Case Study	Deductive	Both	Either	Off	D, S, C	Div	Mid-Left
Experiential	Deductive	Both	Either	Either	D, S, C	Div, Acc	Upper-Mid
Self-Directed	Deductive	Both	Individual	Either	D, S, C	Con	Upper-Right
On-the-job Training	Either	Both	Individual	On	S, C	Div, Acc	Anywhere

Key—
Non-Traditional codes: D is Distance Learning; **S** is Self-Paced Instruction; **C** is Competency Based.
Learning Styles codes: Con is Converger; **Div** is Diverger; **Asm** is Assimilator; **Acc** is Accommodator (See Kolb in Chapter 2)

Training Styles Grid: see Figure 7-1.
All entries are approximations. This table is for general reference only; individual cases may vary.

8 Technology-Based Training

"The illiterate of the twenty-first century will be those who can not learn, unlearn, and relearn."

—*Alvin Toffler*

The professional trainer realizes that form follows function. It's important to first clearly define what knowledge and skills are needed by the employees, customers, or clients, and only then decide how best to get that information across. Technology can be a wonderful tool, but it's not the only approach and not always the most appropriate choice.

■ ■ ■

Chapter 7 introduced and discussed eight categories of classical training techniques. They range from simple lecture, in which the trainer relies entirely on oral skills, through a variety of interactive options. Many of those techniques can be automated through the use of technology. A simple lecture can be put into an MP3 file or on a CD or audiotape and heard by anyone, anytime, as long as they have the equipment necessary to reproduce the lecture. Demonstrations can be video, recorded and distributed on DVDs or over the web using streaming video. Discussions—of a kind— can occur in a "chat room" or using threaded discussion boards in cyberspace, or—more traditionally—in a videoconference.

Merely automating the content of training in order to provide an alternative delivery system seldom qualifies as effective training design. This approach may only perpetuate a weak training program or even make it worse. As discussed in Chapter 2, design is a complex and varied process, which must take into account the fact that different adults learn best in different ways. Later chapters will suggest ways to incorporate all these different elements.

This chapter suggests some additional options or building blocks that trainers may wish to use. It presents some key principles for technology-based training, in which a computer or another technology handles the primary delivery of content. At a minimum, trainers need to be aware of technology and the ways it can contribute to or hinder the process of training.

What is "technology-based training"?

Training magazine defines **technology-based training** as "Anything that involves using technology to deliver lessons. Examples include: Web-based training (Internet, intranet, extranet); computerized self study, including CD-ROM/DVD/diskette; satellite/broadcast TV; and videoconferencing, audio conferencing, and teleconferencing."[1]

ASTD, in its annual State of the Industry Report, distinguishes between **presentation methods** and **delivery methods** when discussing technology-based training.[2] "Presentation methods" means such things as, for example, using a video projector and PowerPoint® software to get your ideas across to trainees. "Delivery methods" include such media as CD-ROMs or the Internet as means to deliver that content to the trainees. Technology-based training *presentation methods* are discussed in Chapter 9, whereas this chapter focuses on the technology-based training *delivery methods*.

Computer-based training, sometimes abbreviated CBT (and, therefore, sometimes confused with *competency based training*—see Chapter 7) represents a delivery mode for technology-based training, in that the training is digitized, and the content lends itself to interactivity and modularization. Most technology-based training delivery systems require use of a computer in some form, though analog (video) methods such as television and others also qualify. Computer based training uses a pre-constructed learning program (which may be based on simple forms of artificial-intelligence software) to guide learners through a series of experiences in order to achieve (and usually assess understanding of) the learning objectives along the way. Some additional acronyms that are used in the literature to refer to computer-based training include CAI (computer-aided instruction), CAL (computer-aided learning), CBL (computer-based learning), CMI (computer-managed instruction), and others.

Technology-based training is not limited to training about subjects related to technology. Sales training, management training, and nearly any subject matter content can be delivered through technology-based training. Of course, most training about technology will probably incorporate that technology in some way, if it is properly designed. Technology-based training doesn't necessarily mean that technology supplants the trainer. A trainer may be extensively involved in the delivery and must be involved in the design. Technology-based training can also be used to supplement more traditional training methods, a technique sometimes referred to as "*blended training.*"

Finally, technology-based training is not always *distance learning*, another widely used term. Distance learning occurs when the learner and trainer are geographically separated, and special techniques of course design and communication are required.[3] Although distance learning implies that technology is being used, distance-learning techniques such as correspondence courses, which have been around for many years, are not technology-based. Likewise, technology-based training can be used in-house and on-site, so it may not qualify as distance learning.

When did technology-based delivery of training begin?

The historical antecedent of much of today's computer based training is *programmed instruction* (PI). PI is a self-instructional, manual training method that was popularized in the 1960s. The design allows learners who already know some of the material or those who learn it quickly to move along at their own pace. Persons who need concepts explained more thoroughly or need more practice can be referred to additional materials and lessons. This approach is motivating to good students, because they aren't held back by others, while those who learn more slowly are given appropriate support to achieve the learning objectives.

This "branching" is accomplished as the learners move through small instructional units (called "frames" in the PI jargon), each of which is followed by some active response by the student, such as answering a question. If the response is correct (indicating that the learning has occurred), learners are directed to new material; if not, they can be directed back for more review and another progress check. In paper-based PI, review was usually accomplished by scrambling page content and offering multiple choice progress checks at the end of each frame. Directions might then follow: "If you chose 'a,' turn to page 73; if you chose 'b,' turn to page 38; . . ." etc. Computer technology makes this branching both instantaneous and effective.

PI is based on a behavior analysis technique popularized by B. F. Skinner, which features *immediate feedback* to the learner in the optimum number of steps. This means that when the trainee has mastered the skill or knowledge at the level specified by the objective, they can move on. It is self-paced, standardized, efficient, and economical. On the other hand, it must be much more thoroughly designed than, for example, a lecture on the same topic. It has a high development cost in both time and effort, most of the time requiring a trained instructional designer and a programmer. The technique also lacks social interaction, which may matter more for certain topics than others.

In the late 1960s, the PI technique was adapted to computer delivery on specialized mainframe systems such as TICAT and PLATO. Instead of paper, the computer presented screens of information and guided the learner automatically, based on his or her responses. When personal computers became popular in the late 1970s, instructional technologists quickly adopted the new technology. Today's computer platforms let the designer add graphics, videos, and sound to the self-paced learning experience, providing the same contrast and increased learner involvement, compared with older versions of PI, as an enhanced lecture provides compared with a simple one (see Chapter 7).

What are some of the benefits of technology-based training?

Technology-based training can be used for either inductive or deductive learning approaches. It will usually support knowledge or computer-related skills objectives, but certain other skills objectives can also work when appropriately sophisticated simulation or artificial-intelligence programs are used. An example of sophisticated simulation is flight simulator training for pilots, which is computer based but designed to develop skills. The design of computer-based simulations is extremely complex, requiring highly specialized skills. In general, more sophisticated programs are required for deductive approaches and skill-level training objectives.

Technology-based training is **self-paced**, which allows the trainee to speed up when possible or slow down when necessary. With continuing improvements in streaming video, bandwidth, audio, and interactive response time, a wide variety of realistic scenarios can be presented. These advances mean that true multi-media training can be used. If videos are the most effective means to get an idea across, the training can incorporate them and allow time to be speeded up, slowed down, or even "freeze-framed" to make certain points more effectively. Likewise, audio (such as for training in languages or music) can be used when appropriate. Computer based language training may include such things as the ability to record trainees speaking and electronically compare their accuracy, showing the result as direct feedback using a meter or some other scale.

Some technology-based training is done without a trainer at all (beyond the creation stage), thus reducing costs. Other designs incorporate live trainers in a variety of forms. They may be available to answer questions by e-mail, phone, or during real or virtual office hours. They may moderate on-line chats, control content, or provide additional assistance in a number of ways.

All forms of graphics (photos, line drawings, etc.) can be used, and even the attachment of robotics is possible. For example, in a flight simulator, the physical environment in which the trainee sits can be hydraulically tipped and turned to simulate physical conditions caused by the trainee's actions. MIT developed a simulated arm that is used to teach nursing and phlebotomy students; other medical related examples abound, such as a "cyber-Annie" to aid cardio-pulmonary resuscitation (CPR) training.

Finally, technology-based training enables consistent training of all users, can support widely dispersed learners, and can keep detailed records of individual or multiple trainees' learning patterns both for trainee performance evaluation and to suggest ways of improving the training in the future. Management and record keeping of training can be automated, including such things as fully automatic test scoring, registration, documentation of time spent participating, and so on. Automation frees time and enables trainers to engage in the higher level tasks associated with the field or work on training programs that are not technology based.

Is there a downside to technology-based training?

Certainly. Ever since its inception, technology-based training has provided special challenges to the training field. The first use of television as a medium for delivering a training program was at the University of Iowa in 1932.[4] At that time, televisions were hand built and learners had to get them from the University in order to participate. Today, technology-based training is still fraught with myriad issues such as platform compatibility, bandwidth, user accessibility, and so on. These issues will become less important as the technology-based training industry matures and more standards are established.

Technology-based training is difficult to design and requires that the technology hardware—the equipment—work for both the training provider and the trainee. It requires that trainees have some technical competence and the appropriate equipment to handle the training as it was developed. Technology-based training works better for knowledge than skill objectives, unless the skill is something that provides its own feedback, such as creating a computer program, which either works or doesn't. Also, as with the language program, if evidence of the skill can be understood and compared to a standard by the computer, the computer can electronically provide feedback on that skill. Otherwise, the trainer needs to intervene ("mediate") and provide the feedback component. If one trainer is working with multiple trainees, each may be at a different point in the lesson or in different geographical locations, a possibility that makes the trainer's job more complex.

Technology-based training, if not mediated by the instructor, is also impersonal and lacks the substantial human interaction typical of most of the other training strategies listed in Chapter 7. Although trainees could interact with each other through either *chat room* type models or *discussion threads* on bulletin boards, some of the complications that might arise include comments that are inappropriate, incorrect, irrelevant, too lengthy, or otherwise problematic. In these cases, trainer mediation and intervention is needed. Still, the research suggests that student-to-student threaded discussion can be an important enhancement to the learners.

In its simpler forms, technology-based training risks becoming just a "technical transaction," as the opening quote for Chapter 7 suggests. Non-completion rates for technology-based training tend to be much higher than with traditional forms of training. The lack of human interaction is cited by many experts as well as trainees as a factor in this problem. Self-motivation is very important when no trainer is available to help motivate trainees; it's much easier to avoid watching a DVD than to avoid showing up at a training class.

Finally—and importantly—technology-based training is expensive to design and produce (Figure 8-1). The further the training design is located from the model's origin, the more expensive it will be. The "Level of Interactivity" between the trainee and

Figure 8-1   Cost Model for Technology-Based Training

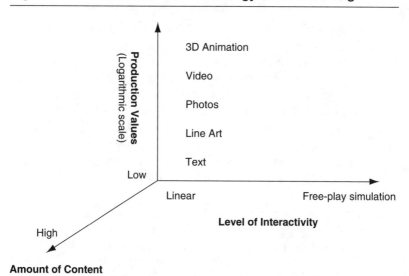

© Bergeron, C. 1999. "A model for estimating the development cost of e-learning models." Unpublished paper.

the technology-based training program can range from purely linear to a model that follows multiple and complex webs of thought and content. The "Amount of Content" reflects the volume and complexity of material to be covered in the training. "Production Values" indicates the means of representing the material to the learner. Note that this is a logarithmic scale, meaning that moving along this axis exponentially increases the cost.

Table 8-1, at the end of the chapter, summarizes the key advantages and disadvantages of technology-based training.

When is technology-based training appropriate?

A question that should be answered early is whether technology-based training is economically viable for a particular training need in an organization. Key factors in this decision should include the following points:

- Is the number of trainees adequate? If only a few people will ever need or want this training, more traditional methods would be preferred, because of the substantial up-front costs of technology-based training development and delivery.

- Is it practical to bring trainees to a central location for training? If trainees are geographically dispersed, technology-based training is more likely to be appropriate.

- Is the training to be done in a short time, or will the need for this training continue over a long period? If each new hire to the organization over the next year will need certain training, creating a single technology-based training program may be more practical than offering traditional training for just one or a few people at frequent intervals.

- Does the material change frequently? The counterpoint to the issue immediately above is that live classes can usually be altered more easily and deal with current issues more effectively.

- Is the skills component of the content substantial? As you'll recall, some skills can be handled by technology-based training, but many cannot. Including skills components in technology-based training usually increases both the cost and development time, as well as the complexity of delivery and evaluation. It works more effectively for knowledge types of objectives.

- If simulations are to be part of the training, is the task to be performed a difficult, expensive, or dangerous one to do "live?" For example, flight simulator training can, in the long run, be safer and more cost effective than using real planes to train pilots.

- Are the trainees effectively motivated? Self-motivation is best, but many trainees need some form of external motivation to complete a program.

- Is turnover in the job high? If so, the standardization and low per-unit delivery cost of technology-based training may be attractive, especially if OJT is not an option.

- What sort of validation of learning does the organization need? Knowledge testing can be handled in technology-based programs, but its security and validity can be more easily compromised than that of paper-based tests, and thus, its results are more suspect. Skill testing can be done for certain skills in which the results of performance can be in some way read, analyzed, and compared to a standard by the computer. Concerns about the validity and reliability of technology-based testing arise from such problems as the limited number of practical ways of verifying who is taking an on-line test or ensuring that they are not using inappropriate supports at the time of testing.

How does an organization begin to develop a technology-based training program?

The nine analytical steps detailed in Chapter 3 apply to all types of training programs, including technology-based. Likewise, the processes of developing objectives (Chapter 5) and evaluations (Chapter 6) also must be effectively handled. Some educational psychologists (*c.f.*, Robert Gagné, 1992) would add the stage of *event* planning, or planning the events of instruction, before actually selecting media. Gagné defines the events of instruction as, ". . . the bricks and mortar of an individual lesson. . . . A set of events (taking a variety of forms) which acts upon and involves the student."[5] Once those pieces are in place, you can begin to choose media to present the information to the trainees. More traditional media (such as overhead projection and video), which support classroom-based training, are covered in Chapter 9, and lesson plan design, which helps effectively integrate all the parts, is covered in Chapter 10.

After considering the various factors listed on the previous page, management in the organizational training department needs to make a decision on whether or not technology-based delivery of training makes sense from a cost-benefit point of view. No doubt organizations actually get into the process of developing and providing technology-based training in many different ways, but it might be instructive to look at the history of one company, ToolingU.com, as they approached the process.

How did ToolingU.com begin their operation?

A manufacturing company that provides technology-based training on topics generally regarded as "blue collar" jobs is Jergens, Inc., which created *ToolingU.com*. Jergens has for many years been in the business of building industrial products, such as fixturing used by other manufacturing companies. The initial concept of ToolingU was to help train their own customers on proper use of products they sold. As this program was implemented and well received by their customers, requests came to develop training for employees of the customers in a variety of shop floor basic skills. Over time, ToolingU has developed dozens of short "courses" in topics such as shop math, blueprint reading, CNC, metal cutting, quality, stamping, and extrusion, along with their original jigs and fixtures training programs. Each of these courses can be delivered in a variety of formats and can be taken by individuals or operated through an employer's training department.

Although hundreds of companies exist that develop technology-based training courses, ToolingU is unusual in several ways. The nature of their topics appeals to a demographic of trainees who may not be computer literate, and may or may not have traditional, academic educations. For this reason, ToolingU has chosen to make the training relatively linear in format. The term "linear" refers to a lesson that progresses directly from topic to topic, regardless of the learners' level of understanding. Non-linear forms could also be called "iterative" or branching (or several other terms), and these forms follow the pattern described earlier in this chapter, in which evidence of learning is required to progress. It can also mean that the trainee has a variety of different options or sequences by which to acquire the knowledge or skill.

Instead of using established distance-education delivery engines such as WebCT® or Blackboard®, ToolingU chose to create their own. Their courses have a number of features that are well suited to the adult training market. Vocabulary definitions will pop up when the cursor is hovered above a highlighted word, and a dictionary of relevant terms is available. Direct hyperlinks are provided to relevant articles in a wide variety of industrial periodicals. Discussion forums, FAQ's (frequently asked questions and their answers), calculators, and other tools are all part of the learning environment.

Although this format has proven successful for ToolingU, more academically oriented training programs, such as on-line college course offerings, probably will use more sophisticated and less purely linear forms of delivery. Some early providers developed their own platforms, but many now use one of the commercially available delivery engines, such as WebCT® or Blackboard®.

What do I need to know to develop technology-based training programs?

Using the content of an existing "traditional" training program and simply putting it on a DVD or an audio CD or on the web is not likely to result in the optimal use of such media. Certainly a lecture can be put onto an audio file or DVD, and so on, but to really be effective, technology must be used as an integral part of the overall instructional design from the beginning. Richard Clark tells us, ". . . the best current evidence is that media are mere vehicles that deliver instruction but do not influence student achievement any more than the truck that delivers our groceries causes changes in our nutrition. Basically, the choice of vehicle might influence the cost or extent of distributing instruction, but only the content of the vehicle can influence achievement."[6]

Therefore, creating an effective technology-based training program requires an individual or team with knowledge of the subject matter content, adult learning principles, interactive instructional design, and effective technology skills. Beyond that, here are some other points:

- *Outside help will be needed* unless the organization has or is willing to take the time to develop expertise in creating such programs. This is a complex field, not just because of the technology, but also because of the instructional psychology involved.

- *It must be carefully designed and thoroughly validated* before being distributed, as is true of all self-directed learning. Have a beta version (test version) and use people to try it out who have a similar background to the expected trainees.

- *The role of the trainer will be quite non-traditional*, in that the duties will be mainly administrative and will deal with exceptions and problems, rather than guiding learning and sharing knowledge.

- *Various software packages are available* to simplify the design and management processes, and several professional groups exist in this field. Computer based training requires a "platform," which is a software mechanism through which the training is provided. Think of this requirement as similar to needing a web browser to surf the Internet. Also, a number of learning management software packages are available to handle many of the "mechanics" of a training program, such as record keeping and related activities.

- *As with all training, consider the trainee.* Don't assume any pre-existing expertise unless entry standards actually exist for a program (prerequisites, for example). Trainees need to be able to learn it all and have access to the support they need throughout the program. This support includes not only the prerequisite content knowledge, but also the ability to use the computer and software that is providing the content.

■ *Consider the equipment that the trainee will have available.* If the program uses streaming video, for example, the trainees need to have equipment with a bandwidth that will handle that. As anyone who has worked much with computers will confirm, many compatibility issues must be considered. If trainees will provide their own technology, clear system requirements must be established by the organization providing the training.

■ *Design the program for usability.* Confine things to one screen at a time. Limit the number of mouse clicks it takes to get through the material. Maintain points of reference on each page (for example, use a consistent header and format throughout the program, etc.).

■ *It is not simple, and it is usually not cheap.* A basic, one-hour module with line-art graphics, a test with multiple-choice questions, and a low-level computer management interface can easily run $5,000 to $10,000 to develop. Sophisticated packages with simulators, extensive branching, video, and all the bells and whistles can cost $50,000 and up per hour of training to design.[7]

Besides computer-based, what other forms of technology-based training are available?

The *Training* magazine definition cited earlier includes such media as television (either real time live or in recorded form such as DVD or videotape), audio conferencing, and so on. Clearly, more and more training will be technology-based. Needless to say, the amount spent in this area is growing annually, as is the percentage of companies using at least some technology in delivering their training. Almost one-quarter of the companies in the *Training* magazine survey have a separate budget for technology-based training.[8] Trainers and organizations that plan to go this route must obtain competent counsel as they approach the design and delivery issues. Not all trainees will be comfortable or successful using technology-based media, nor will many traditional trainers find an easy transition.

Table 8-1 Summary of the Pros and Cons of Technology-Based Training

TECHNIQUE	KEY ADVANTAGES	KEY DISADVANTAGES
Technology-based Training (Can be either inductive or deductive)	■ Access to instruction without travel costs or time limitations ■ Highly standardized ■ Uses trainers' skills better (or at least differently), because learners only need to come to them for major questions or evaluation ■ Self-paced and works well with competency based training ■ Some trainees may prefer it	■ Numerous hardware problems and issues ■ Expensive to develop ■ More complex to maintain ■ Learners may be at varying points, causing extra work for trainers ■ Lack of interaction with trainer and any peers, except through chatrooms or bulletin boards ■ Difficult to validly assess some knowledge and most skill outcomes ■ Some trainees may not have enough technology skills to use this type of learning

It is beyond the scope of this book to give complete details on complex topics such as this. Chapter 9 discusses some general principles of using video and audio and other "low-tech" training support. The web sites and periodicals listed at the end of Chapter 1 lead to several good resources.

9 Facilities and Media Support

"The best plan you can have for using media support is to pretend you don't have any media support."

—*Gary Bunch*

The professional trainer wants learners to be comfortable and focused during the training. Therefore, the environment must be matched to the nature and content of the lessons. Because simple lectures are among the least effective means of training, the professional trainer's toolkit will include a variety of ways to support learning through media.

■ ■ ■

Good facilities design is a tremendous asset to effective training; poor facilities can really undermine an otherwise effective effort. Media enhancement can do wonderful things for training—such as dramatically increasing student recall during a simple lecture— when it works right and is properly designed. However, designing a training program that depends wholly or even significantly on media support technology is risky. The professional trainer knows that both facilities and support media are means to an end, and neither one is sufficient unto itself to make training what it should be. This chapter discusses these final two components of the training design, facilities and media, before putting it all together into a formal plan for training in Chapter 10.

Training facilities

What are things to consider when designing or choosing training facilities?

Most trainers would probably love to have the opportunity to design or at least have a choice from a variety of training environments in which to present their programs. More often than not, however, training is offered in whatever facility is available. Whether the trainer is simply choosing a location for training or participating in training design, a variety of considerations arise. These considerations include room size, seating configuration, lighting, media and equipment options, decor, amenities, and the physical location of the room.

Room Size is an obvious first factor. Training rooms must be of adequate size to accommodate the number of trainees who will attend, plus all necessary equipment for the training. They should not be too large—an auditorium for a group of five—or too small—a converted coat room for a group of fifty—but just right. Experts recommend at least 16 square feet per person for a classroom, and up to half again that in a conference room. Ten feet is the minimum ceiling height for a training room, but larger rooms need even more height, especially if projection screens are to be mounted.

Room Layout comes in many styles, such as traditional classrooms, conference rooms, auditoriums, and so on. Training considerations include such questions as where does the trainer stand and where do the students sit or stand to learn? Where are the doors and windows? Is the shape regular, such as a rectangle, or irregular, such as wedge-shaped? In an auditorium, is the floor flat, sloped, or tiered? And so on.

Rectangular rooms are certainly the most common. When possible, avoid long, narrow rooms with anything more than a 3:2 length-to-width ratio. Such rooms present difficulties in using most forms of visual media and increase logistical problems in everything from entering and getting seated to passing out and collecting materials. Sometimes, because of windows or other reasons, the room must be set up so that the focal point (trainer, projection screen, or whatever) is on the long side of the rectangle. Avoid this arrangement when possible, but otherwise, consider arcing or chevroning the student seating or not using the full room width. In this manner, the trainees can look straight at the trainer, and the trainer can maintain general eye contact without having to constantly look from side to side. In a wide room, leaving a center aisle might also be a good idea.

Doors are best located near the back of the room, or one front and one back. This placement enables trainees who must arrive late or leave early to do so with minimum disruption. Where possible, leave a back aisle instead of putting seats tight to the back wall. Windows are good to provide natural light, but there must be a means of controlling that light, such as blinds or draperies. In the best classrooms, windows are to the outside (not into the hallway), and high enough that students, when seated, cannot look out of them. Windows into a hallway should be non-existent or limited to just the door, or next to the door, so that persons walking by do not distract either the class or instructor.

The auditorium style environment is the only one that might have a sloped or tiered floor, rather than a flat one. Tiered floors serve a purpose in terms of construction, but also create problems for handicapped access, dealing with seating, and moving equipment in and out. Therefore, sloped floors (at least the aisle way portion) are preferable to tiered floors in auditorium settings where large numbers of seated persons need to have a good view of the front of the room.

Seating Arrangements vary and must be matched with the training style to be used. Some of the common formats are conference table, classroom, U-shaped, round table or cabaret, and auditorium.

The *conference* format (Figure 9-1) lets people see and interact with each other. It is limited to small groups, because the table quickly becomes inconvenient if people need to hand things across, move around the room, or be near a projection screen. It is a difficult layout to use for large group discussions. It also limits student movement around the room and access to equipment and materials. A conference "table" constructed of several adjoining rectangular tables with an open center is another option, but subject to the same general limitations.

The *classroom* format (Figure 9-2) typically uses rows and aisles but can also have arced or chevroned seating. This arrangement moves the visual focus to the front of the room and is appropriate for lectures and enhanced lectures. Any group work is limited to the dyad ("Turn to your neighbor and discuss. . . .") or requires moving the class or the furniture around. Of course movement is not all bad, because it allows some variety and

Figure 9-1 A Conference Room

© ericvaughphotography.com

Figure 9-2 A Classroom

© ericvaughphotography.com

Figure 9-3 A U-Shaped Format

© ericvaughphotography.com

stretch time, but should be planned and easy to do—not just an annoyance. If different arrangements are anticipated, furniture that is lightweight enough to move safely and easily should be chosen. Adults generally prefer tables at which two or three persons can sit, rather than individual student desks. Often student desks or fixed furniture do not allow for body size variations and moving chairs to more comfortable positions.

The *U-shaped* format (Figure 9-3) combines some of the benefits of the classroom and conference room layouts. The trainer can move into the throat of the U to work with individual students or check on work being done, yet all can see each other and interact as a group. This format is obviously limited by group size.

The *roundtable* (cabaret) arrangement (Figure 9-4) is good for small group work within a larger program. For example, if some of the training is lecture and some is case study or discussion, this form creates natural groups. Don't use tables that are too large, and especially don't place more chairs than fit comfortably around the table. On the downside, for training other than group work, this format provides no clear focal point in the room. This shortcoming means that at least some of the participants will have their backs to the trainer, video screen, or whatever.

Figure 9-4   A Round Table or Cabaret Format

© ericvaughphotography.com

And when they turn around to see the trainer, they will then have no writing surface. So this form should be used only when most of the training will be done through groups and group discussion, with the trainer moving among tables.

The ***auditorium*** format (Figure 9-5) limits interaction between or among participants and, in larger rooms, even discourages interaction between the trainer and trainees in general. The auditorium format works well for viewing videos, giving lectures, and other "formal" inductive training. Like the classroom arrangement, it reinforces the authority of the trainer. It also limits student access to and effective viewing of equipment and materials. Consider that even the name "***audi***torium" implies that this room is set up for listening, not for easy viewing or interaction. Unless the entire training program is inductive, consider arranging for several smaller break-out rooms in which trainees can meet in smaller groups to discuss the training and work on the interactive portion of the lessons.

Of course, dozens of other variations in room layout can be created. When flexible arrangements or multiple settings are needed, have them close together if possible; for example, an

Figure 9-5 An Auditorium

© ericvaughphotography.com

auditorium for lectures and videos, which is near small breakout rooms for individual group discussions.

If machinery or equipment is used as part of the training, consider whether the training should be exclusively in the room with the equipment or handled as a lecture, with a separate lab or work room. The former invites students to play with the equipment instead of participating in the training; the latter requires more careful structure and does not match certain learning styles. If the trainees are going to write anything (take notes, etc.), a writing space of at least 12″ by 27″ per person should be provided—and 18″ by 30″ is preferred. This requirement means that two people will fit at a five-foot table, but three will not fit at a six-foot table. Don't have more than one or two extra chairs in the room (stack them up in the corner). Classrooms tend to fill up from the back to the front. Often, those students who choose the back are ones who really need to be in the front to enable better interaction with the trainer.

Lighting in a classroom must be bright enough to effectively illuminate materials and enable the trainees to read and take notes comfortably. If any type of older audio-visual equipment is being used, the lights must be dimmable—at least in stages, if not as a continuous operation. Most new projectors have sufficient lumens to allow use in all but the brightest rooms. The *type* of lighting also matters. "Warm" (incandescent) or "cool" (fluorescent) lighting give different feels to the room. Florescent lights can tend to flicker as the ballast deteriorates in a way that is both distracting and even dangerous for people with certain kinds of medical problems. Lighting levels must be at least 70 foot-candles at desk level for writing, and 100 foot-candles for active visual tasks.

Media and Equipment considerations also influence room design. The need for such items as training equipment for student use can require all sorts of considerations including ventilation, power, plumbing, and so on. If video or computer projection will be used, screens and equipment space must be available and either the ceiling must be higher, or the floor must be sloped, in order to provide effective line of sight for all participants. Surge protected electrical connections must be available, preferably without stringing long extension cords. If a sound system will be used, the acoustics must be considered. Too much hard surface increases echoes and ambient noise, which makes understanding a speaker difficult. Too much soft surface (carpets, drapes, acoustical panels, etc.) makes it difficult to project sound effectively. Too little insulation between rooms, walls that don't reach the ceiling, or doors that don't close interfere with training.

Amenities include all the things that, if well done, usually are not even noticed. Specifically, such factors as the color of the walls (pastels are better for training than bright colors), the amount of natural light (with blinds or shades to reduce glare), the presence or absence of distractions such as windows onto hallways, artwork on the walls, and even the presence or absence of a clock can all influence how trainees "feel" about a room. So, too, do the room temperature (which should be between 68 and 75° F.), humidity (which should be kept at 30 to 60%), and air exchange (at least 12 to 25 cfpm). Handicap access is also a matter of concern as well as law.

The physical location of the room, ideally, should be near to building entrances, restrooms, break and snack facilities, and any other resources required for the training. It should also be "far" from the workplace—in emotional distance if not physical.

Taking the time to effectively scout out or plan for good training environments can pay dividends. Sometimes, however, there is no choice of location, and everything seems to conspire against effective training. Knowing the nature of the training facility is an important factor in designing the training plan, as you will see in Chapter 10.

What about the facilities for OJT environments?

Part of the big advantage of on-the-job training (OJT) is that the trainees are actually learning in the environment in which they will be working. Usually, the trainer has little or no choice about location and facilities. Even so, care should be taken to minimize distractions and maximize safety. A thorough job orientation should be accomplished before entering the work environment. If possible, begin the OJT of new workers during the slowest shift or on the slowest days or seasons of work. The trainer and supervisor should complete a thorough check of the equipment and area to ensure both safety and operational status of the equipment. Also, as stressed elsewhere in this text, the process of OJT requires structure and forethought. Just dropping a new worker into the job with directions to "watch what Joe does" is *NOT* effective OJT.

Training media

How can I use audio-visual support media most effectively?

Now that the physical environment for training has been established, the trainer needs to next consider the options of various kinds of media support. Hundreds of good reasons exist for using media to help support training efforts. The most obvious rationale comes from the adage that "a picture is worth a thousand words." People remember better that which engages more of their senses. Audio-visual supports can be used to focus the learners' attention, stimulate interest, explain, reinforce, simplify, and otherwise improve the effectiveness of training. Some training simply couldn't be accomplished without the use of media, due to the original form of the information to be communicated. As mentioned earlier, it would be virtually impossible to teach art or music by simply talking about examples. Likewise, many business topics can only be communicated in non-verbal forms, particularly when the objectives are at Kirkpatrick's third or fourth levels. It is doubtful that even an excellent trainer could effectively train a person to use word-processing software without the program itself on hand.

Remember, there are a variety of reasons *not* to use media, as well. Media should never be used just to impress trainees, nor should it be used to present simple ideas that can be easily stated verbally. It should not be a means of creating a barrier between the trainer and trainees. Finally, when it is used, there will be more expense, more complications during training, and much more pre-training preparation time. It's a tough job to design effective media support materials, often requiring the support of an outside expert. Dugan Laird[1] and others state that the choice of media should come fairly late in the lesson planning. In part, this timing is to make sure the media supports the objectives and is not chosen just because it's available. And just because a little media is good, don't assume that a lot is better. Keep it simple.

Finally, remember the caution in the opening quote at the beginning of this chapter: effective training should be able to stand on its own in terms of overall design, just in case the media support breaks down.

This chapter deals with training presentation, or "audio-visual" technology. Training delivery technology was discussed in the previous chapter. Audio-visual media is a very broad topic and is covered here in subcategories. The first subcategories include the simplest technology form of support media: handouts and readings. The next subcategories discuss written presentation aids such as whiteboards, chalkboards, and flip charts, followed by the overhead projector, computer projector, and videotape. The remaining subcategories include a number of other potential alternatives.

How do I design and use effective handout materials?

Handouts can greatly enhance a training session, but—when improperly used—can undermine it, as well. Like any other visual aid, handouts can be applied many ways and should be tailored to the particular lesson and the training and learning styles of the participants. For example, even deciding when to distribute the hand-outs takes some thought. Should the distribution come before, during, or after the training? It all depends.

If the trainees are expected to take notes, having the handouts ahead of time might discourage them from doing so, unless the handouts are specifically designed to encourage note taking. They may pay less attention, assuming the information is all down on paper, anyhow. Some of the better students, however, will use the handouts as a means to take notes and follow the lesson. If materials are distributed as they are needed (the just-in-time method), the interruption can distract from the flow of the lesson as the trainer walks around the room and people must turn around to pass things on. Distributing handouts at the end has the advantage that the trainees won't be reading and shuffling with them during the presentation, but it has the disadvantage that they might have expected more content (or less), thus taken "too many" or not enough notes.

As a general rule, do not provide handouts that simply and completely replicate a classroom presentation. If the material is complex or if it contains specific procedures or a list of sources that students will need to reference later, then handouts are a good idea. Handouts are also a good option for material that is already familiar to most of your trainees. Handouts allow material to be skimmed quickly by those who know it or read in detail by others who don't. This approach is more efficient than including such information as part of the training program.

Like other media support materials, the appearance of handouts should reflect quality and professionalism in the training. Use a consistent style of layout for the materials. Make sure there are no spelling or grammatical errors and that the ideas flow well. Use a good copy quality and package materials for the trainee's convenience by using a three hole punch, staples, binders or folders, and other techniques appropriate to the situation.

How do I use whiteboards and similar tools effectively?

In this category are such visual aids as **whiteboards** and their predecessors—**chalkboards**, **flip charts**, and even **posters**. These visual aids have been around for ages. It seems so simple to use them, but much can be said about such a seemingly mundane topic.

Writing on the board is not as simple as it seems. First of all, trainers need to practice in order to use these tools well. Here are a few perhaps obvious but frequently violated rules:

- Write large enough. Go into the training room when no one is around and write your name on the board or flip chart. Then go to the back of the room and see if it can be read. If not, why? Is it too small? Too sloppy? Not dark or contrasted enough? Too low to the floor (especially when you imagine a tall person sitting in front of you)? Be your own worst critic if you're going to use the medium.
- Write clearly—or print. You might have to slow down. If your writing actually *is* terrible, then use some other media

such as transparencies or typed handouts. Flip charts can, of course, be written on ahead of time and simply uncovered as the session proceeds.

■ Writing and talking simultaneously is difficult, even with years of experience. And many people find it difficult to spell correctly as they write on a board.

■ Another problem is inadequate contrast, caused by chalkboards that haven't been erased cleanly or by whiteboard or flipchart markers that are too light colored, too faded, or too thin for the background and viewing distance.

■ Don't write too much—leave some white space and use only key points, as would be included on an overhead. Plan the layout and spacing before beginning.

■ Don't erase too quickly. Give trainees a chance to write down the points; ask if they are ready before you erase.

■ Use several colors if they are available and if it makes sense—not just for the novelty of it. Multiple colors make sense when the trainer needs to group certain points by category—for example, putting all positive ideas in one color and all negative ones in a different color. Another reason to use colors is to clearly differentiate points in a column by alternating colors so the trainees can see where one idea ends and the next begins.

■ Be sure to cap markers between use. Some will dry out in just minutes.

■ Don't lean against the board. It erases your points and ruins your clothing.

■ Be sure to use the markers made for whiteboards (usually labeled as dry erase), because others can permanently ruin whiteboards.

■ Never talk to the board. Write, then turn and talk to the audience.

More elaborate training environments may have "smartboards," which are whiteboards that not only display writing, but can serve as a computer input, enabling the data on the board to be replicated in a file, stored, printed, broadcast in streaming video over a network or the worldwide web, or projected using video projection equipment. Some smartboards have a built-in memory chip or hard copy printer, which enables ideas to be saved before the board is erased for further use.

Flip Charts (large pads of paper, usually mounted on stands or wall hangers) can be used to support key points. Unlike white or chalk boards, they can prepared ahead of time and uncovered point by point. Otherwise, most of the same ideas from above apply to them. You might need to leave a blank sheet between ones on which you have written to reduce bleed through or revealing points before you are ready. Be wary of the stands flip charts are mounted on. Some stands are flimsy and will buckle beneath the weight of your charts or pressure when you write. Also, when planning to use the sheets other than on the tablet—for example by putting them on the walls for people to review or comment upon—be sure to bring the necessary supplies such as masking tape and additional markers. Be aware that many walls have been ruined in this process by tape that sticks too well or markers that bleed through the paper. If someone is going to later transcribe the points written on flip chart paper, it will be helpful to have some rubber bands along to roll them up so they can be handled more easily.

How can I design effective overhead transparencies?

Overhead slide projections help improve training in a variety of ways. Although slides are less versatile than computer projection systems, they are far cheaper and less subject to technical problems. The use of overhead projection slides can: (1) Augment the message (because oral and visual is better recalled than oral alone), (2) Provide a focus of attention for the audience, (3) Clarify the subject—some subjects simply require visuals when words won't suffice, and (4) Provide a reference point, enabling the trainer to keep to a lesson plan while moving away from the desk and notes. To be effective, each visual must be properly designed. Here are some points to consider:

Include a title at the top of each slide. This title provides a reference for the students, as well as the trainer. Logistically, it also helps you to sort and organize the slides. You might also want to include a footer reference and or sequence number in small print at the bottom.

Only one major point should be covered per visual. Use no more than seven lines total per slide and no more than seven words per line for readability. Don't crowd the slide—leave some "white space" for easier viewing. Each sub-point should be highlighted by a bullet point, especially if the sub-point wraps onto a second or third line.

If color is used, dark letters on a light field is best. In years of experiments on color perception, black type on a white or light blue background tested highest; purple on yellow tested worst. Another caution regarding colors is to avoid combinations that color-blind individuals cannot distinguish. These combinations include green and red, black and red, green and magenta, and cyan and brown. Negative, or "drop-out," images (light characters on a dark background) are difficult to see and can darken the room more than necessary, making note-taking more difficult.

The text must be of adequate size and appropriate style. For most projection equipment, using a black on white (clear) acetate with block letters, the rules of thumb in Figure 9–6 apply:

Figure 9-6   Typographical Rules of Thumb for Overhead Projectors

Type font actual size	*Typical distance**
72 pt.	(1") can be seen at 50 feet.
36 pt.	(1/2") can be seen at 20 feet
18 pt.	(1/4") can be seen at 8 feet.
12 pt. - Typical typewriter print	Too small for slide projection

* Actual viewable distance varies with a number of factors discussed in the text. These are guidelines only.

Font (typeface) styles also influence readability. See the examples below. Serifs are the added feet or end caps—the fine lines that project from the ends of a letter in some print styles.

- **Block (sans-serif) styles are best.**

- **Serif styles are better for written text, but not visuals.**

- **Bold, condensed styles are more difficult to see**

- *Script is extremely difficult to read on a slide.*

Strive for continuity in a series of slides by using the same font, layout, and colors for all slides. Use cardboard or plastic frames to make otherwise flimsy slides easier to handle. Keep the audience in mind when designing the slides. Different types of visuals work for different audiences. For example, people with a financial background are usually comfortable with pie charts, whereas many engineers find them less understandable. As a general rule, try to present information in the same style as the trainees are apt to encounter it on the job. Keep data orderly: chronological, alphabetical, small to large, or some such organization. When using charts and tables, avoid the use of keys and scales—keep the illustrations as simple as possible to enhance understanding. Follow cultural traditions— e.g., numbers grow left to right; height of an object is shown vertically; and so on.

Finally, remember this medium is not limited to just textual information. Graphics of all kinds, cartoons, diagrams, modified blueprints, photographs, and many other concepts can be used with overheads. If a concept can be reduced to something printed on paper, it can be made into an overhead projection transparency. As previously discussed, words may not be the best technique to get certain ideas across, so be creative.

What are the guidelines for using the overhead projector?

Once the visual training information is organized and ready to share with the trainees, make sure it doesn't get lost in the delivery process. The following suggestions are divided into three categories: *Room setup, Equipment operation, and Showtime.*

Room setup requires some thought. An overhead projector requires space to position the projector and electrical power to reach that space. Also, a projection screen must be located an appropriate distance from the projector and preferably against a wall near the middle of the training area.

- Use a low cart or table for the projector so it doesn't obstruct the trainees' line of sight, but don't get it so low that the image "keystones" (turns into a trapezoid) on the screen, due to the severe projection angle. This problem can be reduced by slanting the screen away from the projector at the bottom.
- Test the projector and locate it so that, once focused, it nearly fills but doesn't overlap the edge of the screen.
- The screen should be large enough that the distance to the last row of seats does not exceed six times the screen width. The front seats should be no closer than twice the screen width.
- In general, the screen should be positioned as high as reasonably practical. In a large auditorium, the bottom of the screen should be at least four feet from the floor, unless the floor is sloped to accommodate line of sight.
- If the screen is tripod mounted, it might be necessary to set it on a table to get it high enough.
- If the same classroom will be used regularly, mark on the floor where the projector should be positioned by using tape or small marker lines. That way, if it gets moved, it can quickly be re-set.
- Room lighting must be controllable. The trainer must know how and where to find the switch. Also, will windows cause a problem with glare? Be sure to check the lighting at various times of day during which training will be offered.

Equipment operation is the next consideration. Projectors come in different quality levels and with different bulb wattages and focal lengths. Some have lenses that enable them to be quite close to the screen. If the image is distorted or not bright enough, the problem could be the:

- projector (poor quality or low wattage bulb)
- screen (too small or reflectivity quality is poor), or
- room set up (too much light, audience too far away, or their eyesight is poor).

Keep a spare bulb or spare projector in the room. Some projectors come with two bulbs, which can be switched with a lever, but make sure both are good at the start.

Showtime. Once the program begins, the professional trainer needs to consider how the projector is being used.

- The trainer needs to be in a position to operate the equipment, but not blocking the view of the screen for any trainees. Sometimes proper positioning even requires sitting down or kneeling next to the projector.

- Don't read the slides to audience. Paraphrase or make only a passing reference to them.

- As each slide is put up on the screen, pause to enable the audience to read and maybe copy details from a slide. They're not going to listen at first, anyhow. Somehow, what's on the slide always seems more important than what the trainer has to say. This fact, however, speaks volumes as to why slides should be used.

- When using a slide with several points to be made, consider uncovering one point at a time by laying a piece of paper over the slide and moving it down one point at a time. Hint: If paper rather than a cardboard mask is used, the entire slide will be visible on the projector, but not on the screen. If cardboard is used, the trainer doesn't have that "cue" about what's coming up next until it is moved.

- Use the top part of the screen as much as possible, because more people can see it more easily. Doing so may require repositioning the slide or tipping the lens head on the machine when showing the last one or two points.

- Be cautious of the air stream created by the projector fan. Don't lay slides or notes where they will be blown away when the fan starts up.

- Switch off the projector when it's not being used to reduce the fan noise and visual distraction of either a blank screen or material that's not being referenced.

- Make as little motion above the slide table as possible to avoid making shadows with your hand. Some trainers even tape a piece of cardboard to the projector head, which can be flipped down, covering the upper lens so no movement shows on the screen as slides are being replaced.

- When pointing to an item on a slide, it's usually better to point on the projector table using a pencil or similar pointer, rather than standing next to the screen to point. The exception to this rule is when using a laser pointer. These pointers sell for less than $20 and enable the trainer to move freely around the room and still point to the slide from anywhere.

- If a solid or collapsible pointer is used, be sure not to fiddle with it during a lecture. It becomes a distraction to the trainees.

Much of what has been said about overhead slide design and operation also applies to other, similar forms of media support including computer projection and 35 mm slides. However, enough important differences exist when using a computer projector that it warrants specific discussion.

How do I design effective computer projection programs?

Multimedia presentation software helps focus attention on the topic and is more flexible than transparencies. It presents a consistently professional appearance, and research has shown that multimedia presentations engage the learner more actively than other formats and might, in fact, enhance learning. Improperly used, however, they can reduce the effectiveness of a training program.

Computer projection programs, such as Microsoft's Power-Point®, have many advantages over simple overhead transparencies. They provide great potential for dramatic and versatile multimedia presentations that include not only the key points of the lesson, but also sound, motion, video, effective on-line demonstration of working programs, accessibility to resources, interactive options, and more. Electronic key points can be changed when necessary—even on the spot—rather than being permanent, as slides are. The programs offer such options as timed presentations and printing of handouts directly from electronic files in a variety of formats. Unlike overhead transparency projectors, computer projectors can actually be hung from the ceiling, where they are out of the way and pre-positioned for correct focusing.

If the training concerns computers or software programs, the illustrated lecture points can be multi-tasked (switched) to the software itself for an on-line demonstration. Graphics-based computer screens are complex and difficult to describe, but using computer projection enables trainees to observe and discuss results of various keystrokes and mouse clicks. Sets of data showing different situations and simulations can be created and stored before the demonstration. Various programs can be stored on the computer and accessed individually or in combination, and computers offer the potential to connect to network resources or the Internet. For group projects such as brainstorming, the computer can be used to record ideas instead of using a flip chart or whiteboard. Ideas can then be sorted, stored, and printed. Programs or documents can be created or edited with input from whole group.

The many advantages of computer projection, however, come with certain disadvantages. These disadvantages include potential problems with physical equipment, the extra time needed for equipment setup and testing, and occasional difficulties with room lighting.

The equipment must be available, an appropriate room size and layout are needed for good projection, carts and cords should not get in the way of the speaker, furniture might have to be moved, and equipment might fail. Contingency plans must be created in case a bulb burns out or the hard drive crashes, leaving you with an entire training program based upon files that are now lost. Too much room light makes the projection difficult to see, whereas too little room light can make note-taking impossible. Some rooms have "all or nothing" lighting or uncovered windows. And, of course, projection equipment varies in intensity and clarity.

Some general tips on using computer projection training can minimize problems.

- Most of the rules given earlier for designing and using overhead transparencies also apply to this medium, such as not putting too much information on any single slide.
- Talk to the trainees, not to the visuals.
- Position yourself and the screen so that everyone can see both the trainer and the screen.
- Both the equipment and the software should be tested before starting a presentation.
- Arrange to sit at a table for lessons that require much typing at the computer.
- Laser pointers are good for indicating ideas on the screen from a distance. The mouse arrow also provides a means of pointing.

- A small light to illuminate the computer keyboard can be helpful in a very dark room, although a completely dark room is undesirable for several reasons, not least because the trainees will have problems taking notes (and staying awake).
- Use a light background in any slide presentation design.
- Fade out earlier points so the current point being discussed is highlighted.
- Conduct a trial run on the actual classroom computer and projector to identify and correct problems before they occur in front of the trainees. A trial run is especially important if the program was created on one version of the presentation software and is being presented on another. Possible issues are that the projector might show fewer colors or have a lower resolution than expected. Different versions of the software don't always support the same fonts, bullets, and background designs. It's awkward and embarrassing when a program that was created with much careful thought looks very badly planned because of technology issues.
- If the lesson plan includes connecting to the Internet or to internal organizational network resources, be certain the system is set up to accommodate these needs. The computer must have an IP address, a permission path into the correct server, adequate processor speed, and so on. Keep in mind the possibility that the network will go down or that the web site's server at the other end will be slow or out of commission. Once again, a trial run is highly recommended, and an alternative plan is a necessity (see the chapter-opening quotation).

How can I use video programs most effectively in training?

Using training videos for a class has several advantages—if they are *properly* used. Many people are effectively tuned in to television as an information source and will therefore be very attentive to ideas presented over that medium. Well-done training videos can bring drama into the classroom, presenting ideas visually as well as through the spoken or written word. Through video, the class can "visit" various departments or company locations and hear from executives. They can witness chemical and biological events that would be impossible to demonstrate in a classroom and even on the job, in some cases. They can see time compressed or slowed, and many other things that can't "happen" in real life classrooms. Well-done videos clearly present ideas and support them in a way that helps students to better learn and remember the material, especially trainees in their twenties and thirties, who were weaned on video and multimedia presentations.

Conversely, everyone has a video camera these days. Many so-called "training videos" are poorly produced or do not make their points clearly. They can also present ideas in ways that vary significantly from course materials or from the company's or the trainer's perspective. Out-of-date videos almost automatically lack credibility with viewers, and they can also be misleading, obsolete, or even dangerous, especially in fast-changing fields.

Externally produced training videos are available for either rent or purchase for use in training programs. Large training organizations usually have procedures in place to help arrange renting or borrowing video programs. Typical rental costs are $50 to $300 for a 3–5 day period, and the typical purchase price for a commercially produced video is $595 to $4,000. Some production companies give quantity discounts or licensing agreements, and some videos might be available through public libraries. Nearly all commercially produced videos are copyrighted, and the copyright is zealously enforced. Organizations take a serious financial risk if they violate it. A complete listing of commercially available training videos can be obtained from directories such as *Gale's or Bowkar's*, which are in the reference sections of larger libraries, or through various on-line resources. Various video providers such as CRM Learning (www.crmlearning.com) and many more can be found through the website references at the end of Chapter 1.

Original production of a video can be extremely expensive (running up to $1,500 per minute of final production), if quality is a consideration. However, home-grown videos can be used in small doses to highlight or demonstrate specific points of a training program. Video clips can also be inserted in PowerPoint® presentations and used in distance learning programs. Remember, though, that production quality is a *very big* factor in the "watchability" of a video, partially due to high expectations created by commercially produced programs.

Some large companies have created their own digital networks. Ford, for example, has a satellite system to broadcast training programs for mechanics and the sales staff to every

North American dealership. Many universities, notably the University of Chicago, have broadcast credit and not-for-credit television or video-based courses for years.

Obviously, the cost involved and additional logistical problems complicate the use of videos in the classroom. Besides the cost of renting or buying or producing the video, extra equipment is needed, as are facilities that accommodate using it. There is also some loss of flexibility. Therefore, the video should do more for the class than just fill time or entertain.

Trainers should never show a video that hasn't been pre-screened. Plan how to use the video to present or support the objectives of the training. Set the stage before starting the video and have some questions ready to ask the trainees at the end. Some videos come with instructor manuals, which will help with this process. It also helps to focus the trainees' attention if they expect some test questions to come out of the video. Finally, make sure you know how to operate the equipment and room lighting, that the equipment is working, and that the video is available when needed.

What other audio visual media might support my training?

Some older types of media are seldom used any more, such as *slidestrips* and *8 mm* or *16 mm film*. If such media are needed for the training, the reason for choosing them will be obvious, for example when nothing more current is available on a topic.

Others, such as *audio recordings*, have always been limited to certain applications. Because no visual stimulus supports the audio, they are usually applied only in training situations where the main subject content is aural—for example, learning a language or music. Recording lectures to play back for students (perhaps someone who missed a lesson or needs to hear it again) might be a good idea. If you record lectures often, consider a tape recorder—player that has speech compression technology, which allows the listener to hear a lecture in a shorter time. Research shows that learning is greatly enhanced by this process.

Opaque projectors are another "old" technology that, though pretty much obsolete in its original form, is now making a comeback in a computerized form. The ELMO® is a blend of opaque projector and overhead projector: it uses a mounted video camera to show whatever is placed on the platform below it, whether opaque or transparent and whether two- or three-dimensional.

This equipment enables the trainer to project onto a screen such materials as books, newspapers, student papers, and so on, without needing to convert them to transparencies or computer files. The same general rules apply to materials for projection as were discussed with the overhead transparency slides.

Finally, *video cameras* can be an excellent training tool for providing feedback to learners in certain situations, such as interview techniques, sales presentations, employee counseling, and train-the-trainer courses. Like the other tools described, it takes some skill and practice to use them effectively, so don't pick one off the shelf and expect to look professional the first day. Many books and magazine articles and several professional associations and continuing education programs are available to help those interested in improving their use of this technology.

What else should I consider in terms of audio-visual support for training?

Besides the equipment for presenting information, probably the most important equipment to use for *skill* training (either on or off the job) is the actual work-related equipment for the trainees to practice with during training. If making the job-related equipment available for training is not possible or practical, at least provide models or "mock-ups" of real equipment for simulation. Recall from earlier chapters that skill training must be hands-on and designed to ensure effective transfer of training.

Finally, as the opening quote to this chapter suggested, always have a back-up plan. Obviously, the more sophisticated the technology in use, the greater the risk of problems. Not much goes wrong with flip charts, except for the collapsible stand and the dried-out markers. The satellite-downloaded video training in the computer room to show how to use the software upgrade installed the night before has far greater potential for catastrophe. Check, double check, then have a "Plan B" ready, even if that plan is to come back the next day.

The following table provides a quick summary of the important advantages and disadvantages of major pieces of media support equipment discussed in this chapter.

Table 9-1 Comparison of Audio-Visual Media

AV MEDIA	MOST USEFUL	ADVANTAGES	DISADVANTAGES
Handouts and Readings	Pre-study; support of detailed information.	Good for self-paced, no equipment required	If properly used, none. They must be well-done and relevant. Be alert to any language or literacy issues among the trainees.
Whiteboards, Flipcharts, etc. Includes "Smartboards"	Support discussion, enable participation.	Available almost anywhere, very flexible, minimal pre-work needed, can be colorful.	Difficult to write clearly; can be messy. Markers not yet equipped with "spell check."
Overhead Projection and ELMOs	Reinforce key ideas, show still pictures.	Widely available, easy to use, color enhancements.	Arrangements*, set-up, less flexibility.
Computer Projection	Reinforce key ideas, demonstrate programs, access network resources (Internet, etc.).	Professional appearance, use of color, sound, and motion, flexible. Utilize various learning modalities.	Arrangements*, set up, preparation, and risk of technology failure.
Video players Including VCRs, DVDs, and CD-ROMs	Demonstrate visual concepts, add drama and realism; reach dispersed audiences.	Videos can be professionally produced; brings in otherwise inaccessible concepts; action and color.	Quality is expensive; less flexible; cost of equipment.
Audio players Including tape, CD, MP3, etc.	Aural only situations such as language, music, etc.	Very portable, widely available, easy to use, adds variety and reinforcement.	Quality is difficult to develop; single sensory input is limited.
35mm Slide Projection	Show still pictures.	Flexible, easily updated.	Arrangements*.

*The term *Arrangements* refers to the need for electrical power, control over room lighting, cost of equipment and screens, seating limitations, etc.

10 Developing the Training Plan

"Whenever you set out to do something, something else must be done first."
— *Murphy's Law, Corollary 6*

A professional trainer knows that "just winging it" is never the best way to achieve the training objectives. An effective plan is the key to being successful and to feeling prepared and comfortable when working with trainees in the organization. Developing a plan is a time-consuming but rewarding part of the job.

■ ■ ■

Previous chapters have covered how to identify training needs, write objectives, measure achievement of those objectives, select training processes, and choose facilities and support equipment. Now it is time to organize all the different thoughts and materials into a systematic plan. The purpose of a training plan is to guide the trainer and trainee through the learning process in the most effective fashion. Like any plan, it begins with goals and strategies, specifies resources required, lists steps and activities necessary, and provides a basis for control and evaluation.

Why is a training plan important?

A trainer can't show up at the appointed time and ask, "What shall we talk about today?" any more than a supervisor could show up in an office or on the shop floor and say, "What shall we make today?" Both need to plan. Both need to control and give feedback, regardless of whether performance evaluations are expected. Trainees will be more involved in learning if they feel the trainer is putting forth her or his best efforts. This perception requires a plan that will:

- Ensure the training objectives are met.
- Keep training on schedule and on budget.
- Provide a reference for the trainer during the instruction ("notes").
- Document training for organization.
- Enable multiple trainers to teach one program.

Where do I begin?

The important process of designing an effective training plan takes time to do properly. You need to answer a number of questions and think through your training strategies. A good place to begin is with the questions in the Figure 10-1 survey.

What are some important considerations in developing a training plan?

The model in Figure 10-2 indicates that the training plan must consider the trainer, the trainee, and the materials. It must also be developed considering the environmental factors surrounding the training, such as the number of people, equipment, facilities, time available, organizational culture and dynamics, and so on.

In the middle of the model are the three main components. First, the *content and objectives* strongly influence the design of the training plan, which in turn defines the type of training to be given. For example, training content might detail how to work with the latest version of Microsoft Excel® or how to operate the Model T-317 Modulating Action Lathe. These topics would require very specific content. On the other hand, how to deal with stress or the weekly safety meeting will be open to a variety of approaches and content. As explained in Chapter 5, the objectives should specify how thoroughly the content is to be learned by the trainees. Training people to an awareness level of a given subject is much different and requires different methods of training than training people to acquire a detailed operational knowledge survey in Figure 10-1.

The *trainer* influences the design due to his or her skills, abilities, and preferred mode of operating. Some trainers are excellent lecturers; others have the trainees dozing off before they get their names written on the whiteboard. A central issue is whether the trainers are subject matter experts, technicians who can do the

Figure 10-1   Preplanning Checklist for Training Program
(Use additional sheets as necessary)

Name of Trainer _____   Date _____
Training Program _____

Training Design Issues

The title of the job-related training session you will conduct
_____

This training is needed because
_____

The person (or department) who requested this training is
_____

The trainees are expected to have this level of knowledge or skill
base when they begin
_____

The objective(s) of the training is/are
_____

The benefits the trainees will receive if they learn and apply the
training include
_____

The main points that will be covered are
_____

Information that must be visualized (demonstration, A-V, etc.) or
practiced (hands-on exercises) to be understood and retained
includes
_____

Points that must be made in concluding the training include
_____

The manager is expecting the following to happen as a
result of this training
_____

This group of participants was chosen because
_____

(continued)

Figure 10-1 Preplanning Checklist for Training Program (*Continued*)

If a similar or related training program was previously conducted, the result was

_____

The following offices and individuals can help in preparing for this training

_____

The level of success of the program will be determined by

_____

Training Logistics Issues

The date(s), starting and ending times for the training will be

_____

The location for the training program is

_____

The number and types of participants in the training session will include

_____

The attendees will be informed how, when, and by whom

_____

The following equipment, supplies, materials, samples, handouts, visuals, etc., will be needed

_____

The deadline dates for each of the following stages are

Obtaining information	_____
Organizing outline	_____
Preparing visuals	_____
Practicing	_____
Previewing for management	_____
Finalizing	_____
Evaluating	_____

Other significant items to consider include

_____

Figure 10-2   Influences on Training Plans

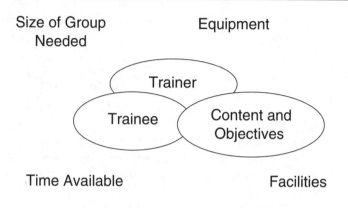

Size of Group Needed   Equipment

Trainer

Trainee   Content and Objectives

Time Available   Facilities

Organizational Culture Etc.

work but lack a theoretical base, or trainers who possess training skills but limited subject matter experience. Some trainers can handle deductive methods quite well, but are not organized enough for effective inductive training. Sometimes a trainer must work outside his or her range of comfort, but it's nice to accommodate the trainers' preferences when possible. Often trainers can create their own lesson plans, but it might be necessary to standardize the training plan when (1) multiple trainers will be required to use it; (2) it is controlled by some outside authority such as a government agency or regulation; or (3) when certification from a professional association (e.g., ISO training) or a specific manufacturer (e.g., Cisco) is expected.

The *trainees* will probably have different learning styles, different backgrounds, and perhaps even different motivations for attending the training. It's often hard to find a simple way to describe an entire group of trainees. One way of defining the target trainee population is to look at any prior analyses that were done. Another is to consider what attitudes and perceptions they bring to the training. Do they want to be there, or not? If not, the trainer has to start with a focus on motivation. Do they see the relevance of the training? If not, it is important to be very explicit on this point. Do they have confidence in you as a trainer? Why should they? Do they have confidence in themselves? Do they have effective backgrounds and sufficient mental and physical abilities to learn the materials? If not, why are they there?

Beyond the three central components, a variety of other factors influence the design of an effective training plan. All of these factors have some probably self-evident influences on the design of the training plan, and each should be considered by the instructor or training designer. Consider the:

- *Size of the group.* Is it one person or eighty? Group size affects the training plan in many ways. For instance, the larger the group, the more important it is to build in subgroups to ensure individual learning.

- *Equipment needed* or available for training. How much, how big, what power or maintenance or supplies will be needed, is it exactly the same as the trainees have on the job? And so on.

- *Time available* for the training. The shorter the time, the greater the need to use inductive training, though that usually reduces learning. Is the time all in one block or spread out? See comments in Chapter 11 about transfer of training.

- *Facilities* in which the training will be conducted. Is it going to be conducted on-site where you will have access to your office for copying or other administrative needs, or off-site? Is it going to be where you can have access to the equipment the trainees will actually be using, or do you need to create mock-ups or other alternative means to provide hands-on experience?

- *Culture and politics of the organization* in which the training is conducted and the trainees will be returning to work. Will the trainees be excited or threatened about having to go to training? Will their supervisors expect them to interrupt their learning to solve issues back at the job? How much transfer of training do you need to plan for, or will it happen naturally?

- *Structure of the planned training.* Will it be lock step (everyone doing the same thing at the same time), or competency based? Will it be on or off the job? And so on.

What makes a good training plan design?

Written to provide both content and direction. The training plan must tell *what* is to be covered, along with *how* the coverage is planned. This organization requires reminders of what questions to ask, a list of expected answers (in case the trainees can't come up with any), specific citations for information (references to handouts or readings), even "stage directions" in the sense of when to distribute handouts or take breaks, and so on.

Written as a guide, not a script. Don't try to memorize a training plan like a role in a play and don't make it overly detailed. The more often a trainer teaches a subject, the less detail he or she probably needs to include, because much of the content and flow becomes internalized. However, even experienced trainers should have a training plan—just in case the automatic pilot fails or someone else needs to take over. Overly detailed plans tend to encourage reading from the notes and too much focus on what's written down; plans that are too sketchy increase the chance of skimming the material too quickly and omitting key points of the content.

Whatever works for the individual. Of course, some organizations may require specific formats. But, in general, the trainer needs to be comfortable with the form of the plan. The form shown in Figure 10-3 is only one example.

In a convenient form. One suggestion is to use full-sized sheets of paper in a ring binder, so it lies flat. If the training plan is short, use full sheets of paper stapled in a corner to keep them in order. Note cards are usually a bad idea. They can be difficult to read and manipulate, and they can easily get out of sequence.

Large enough to easily read. The training plan must be printed clearly enough—don't rely on handwriting. Leave plenty of white space to (a) enable you to scan the plan, to help you stay on track and (b) write notes to yourself. Keep it simple and straightforward. Don't get too "cute"—for example, avoid using color codes, unless the organization requires you to do so and you are comfortable with their meanings.

What are the common stages of a typical skill training plan?

Most training plans are composed of one or more modules. A module could be one or a collection of stimulus-response-feedback ("S-R-F") cycles on one key point, or perhaps on one objective. In general, each module goes through a predictable sequence of activities. The following stages are usually found in effective training plans, oftentimes in repeated sequences:

1. *Anticipation/attention step/"set" (as in ready, set, go).* This portion of the training plan is designed to capture the attention of the trainees, motivate them, and interest them.

It should create anticipation about the training to come by displaying visual aids, outlines, artifacts, and so on. A multisensory approach is better than engaging only one sense. Using music, stories, show and tell, pictures, icebreakers, and even drama might all be appropriate to begin certain training, reconvene it after a break, or transition to the next topic. The trainer should be aware of and try to meet the needs of the different "audiences" that are present. People come to training with different needs, and one type of anticipatory set may not work for everyone. Another purpose of anticipation is to put the trainees at ease and make them feel they can handle the material. It should be supportive and never intimidating.

2. *Objectives.* Clarify the training objectives and relevance of the lesson to the trainees. Let the trainees know where they are headed. Learners benefit from a mental framework, or *schema*, upon which to structure their development of new information. What will be taught, how they will use it, and how they will be evaluated should all be clear. Don't make them overly dependent on the trainer. Adults want to participate and learn more easily when they do. As the training program first begins, the overall objectives and schedule should be explained. As training moves from one topic or sub-point to another, a brief recap and refocus is appropriate. For example, "We've just finished discussing how to remove the carburetor from the block, and we're now going to talk about how to start the process of reconditioning it. You'll learn about cleaning, adjusting, and replacing parts in the carburetor, before we move on to reinstalling it."

3. *Information.* Information is the content of the lesson. It should follow the objective and be composed of clearly defined parts. Use a variety of inductive and deductive methods (or both) in the presentation in order to accommodate different learning styles. Tell, show, illustrate, and ask questions of the trainees in order to help them develop the knowledge or skill being taught and make certain they understand.

4. *Demonstration/model/examples/applications.* If the objective is a *skill*, the trainees should observe the desired behavior. Observation might require a video or visit to the work

center. Break the content down into discrete steps and present them in the correct order. Demonstrate what a person who has the skill is able to do. For *knowledge or concept* types of training, focus on learner understanding of processes and structures. Use analogies and example cases to improve the relevance of the material. Explain how this information will be important to the trainees in their work for the organization using specific company incidents when possible.

5. *Checking.* Check for understanding; make certain the learners both heard and understood the material presented. Are they now ready to apply it? Did they reach the appropriate level of understanding, according to the objectives? To find out, use appropriate forms of the stimulus-response-feedback (S-R-F) process. Ask specific questions about the content just presented and demonstrated (stimulus). See if the trainees give the correct responses (response). Then, tell them whether the response is correct, and—if not—help them to learn what the correct response should have been.

6. *Practice.* Practice often requires direct instructor feedback, though some skill training provides its own feedback. For example, if the learner enters the wrong command for a computer, feedback from the program will normally indicate that it was wrong. Examples of guided practice include hands-on practice with the real equipment, lab work with simulations (*e.g.*, flight training), studio time, and even writing or doing exercises in class (*e.g.*, complete this purchase order correctly). As the trainees demonstrate their appropriate knowledge or progress in a skill, the trainer can become less involved and let the trainees continue to practice through review questions (tests) at the end of lessons or other assignments. Instructor feedback such as comments or even numerical ratings or ranking might be necessary to maintain student interest and focus upon learning.

7. *Perform a formal evaluation and either (a) release the trainees to go to their jobs or (b) move on to the next part of training.* Once the individual practice is complete, the trainees are ready to begin or return to their jobs, unless additional skills or knowledge are part of the training plan. Use the appropriate evaluation techniques as

discussed earlier. These techniques include performance tests and written or oral questions. The performance tests apply to skill objectives and can include such techniques as projects, role-playing, group work, and case studies. Once all the training has been completed, be sure to include assessments of the program as a whole.

What specific items should be included in a training plan?

An effective training plan design includes five main components: *Content, Administration, Method, Pacing, and Support*. For a memory hook, think of these components as *training CAMPS*.

    Content is, of course, probably the most important. If your lesson plan has nothing else, it must have this. Content comes out of the training objectives and includes the facts, processes, and concepts that the trainees need to learn as a result of the training. As detailed in Chapter 5, training objectives are a result of studying what the organization's needs are for specific skills, knowledge, abilities, and attitudes. Key points must be included in the plan, based on the training needs analysis. Material supporting or illustrating these points must either be developed or obtained from existing sources. An appropriate sequence must be chosen, as discussed elsewhere in this chapter.

    Administration refers to the mechanics, detail, and structure of the training. The training plan must specify who is giving the training and when, who is receiving it, and where it will be conducted. It should also specify what prerequisite skills are necessary and what time frame will be available for the training.

    The *method* is the choice of training techniques to be employed. These options were discussed in earlier chapters and should be selected to provide variety and match the needs of adult trainees. If the method is simple lecture, then not much has to be included here, except—perhaps—stage directions of when to change pace, change inflection for emphasis, or the like. If any of the more sophisticated techniques are used, consider including such items as appropriate questions to ask of the participants, examples to use, citations that support the examples, stage directions such as when to hand out materials, which exercise to use, and so forth.

    Pacing means that you must integrate the content into the appropriate or at least the available time and ensure that an appropriate progression and mix of content and methods are used to take advantage of adult learning styles. Projected time requirements for each part of the training must be considered and might even be specified in the plan itself as cues regarding whether you are on schedule. It's also a good idea to have a cushion for each part so you can expand or reduce certain things to maintain the proper pace.

Finally, *support* includes all the media options and delivery mechanisms that will be used to enhance and facilitate the learning for the trainees. You should include a list of required materials, such as handouts, slides, tests, tape, outlines, and software, as well as a list of any equipment you will use, including projectors, flipcharts, pointers, models, samples, audio equipment, and so on. This is your checklist of what to take with you to the training, and other things you need to confirm are in place before you begin.

What different options are available for sequencing training materials?

Most topics can be presented in a variety of ways. How would you describe your home? Some people would start with an overview of the city, then the street, then the exterior. Some would begin at the front door, whereas others might start with their most commonly used rooms. A compulsive person might describe it alphabetically, starting with the attic, then basement, bathrooms, bedrooms, dining rooms, and so on, ending with the utility closet. While all of these approaches might ultimately describe the home, some might be more clear than others. Certain topics have an obvious sequence to them, but many could be equally well handled in a number of different approaches. Here are some frequently used options, with suggestions as to when they best apply.

Start with the most interesting parts. This approach helps get the learner's attention and build enthusiasm for the training. Even if starting with the most interesting topic is not practical, avoid starting with the least interesting. Don't lose the trainees as soon as they begin.

Start with the simplest material. Sometimes the training material is cumulative, and you have no choice but to start from the bottom of a skill hierarchy. For example, trainees must know how to add before they can subtract, how to add and subtract before they can multiply, and how to multiply before they learn to divide. Many subjects, however, are not developed in increments, so this is not always an important consideration.

Start with the first step. For many topics, especially sequential procedures, it is easiest for the trainees to follow when training starts at the beginning of a process and finishes at the end. This sequence is not a given, however, because some topics might actually work best by starting at the end and working backwards.

Start with the big picture. A lesson that begins, "Pick up the hammer," might lead to a house being built or torn down. With some topics, trainees first need an overview in order to put the complex details into perspective. Consider using visuals to help clarify points. Other topics may be so complex that trainees must first understand each detail in depth before they can synthesize them into a coherent whole.

Start with the subordinate skills. Learning notes before chords, letters before words, and words before sentences makes sense. If the final set of skills or knowledge being taught are complex, the best place to start is probably with one easily acquired concept.

Start with the familiar. If some or all trainees already know how to do part of the task, or if they've seen part of the task done but not all of it, then this technique might make sense. It will help them relax and put the training in a more relevant context. It enables the trainer to use comparison and contrast in explaining new things, and it works best with the so-called crystallized knowledge common to adult learners.

Start with how to, then why, then exceptions. If the final objective of training is at some level higher than the first level of Bloom's Taxonomy, it might be appropriate to sequence the training material with the lowest level objectives first. Get the trainees through the mechanics of the process before taking them into the esoterics of it. Exceptions should be handled only after the foundation is established.

Start with one source of information. If the training content comes from a variety of sources (different manuals, different theories, different departments of the organization, etc.), dealing with one source at a time might be best. Recognize natural divisions. For example, an orientation session about the company might cover everything about the marketing department before discussing anything about finance. A technical training program might cover the entire installation manual before dealing with the service manual.

Intermix challenging and easy components. If the tasks being trained include a mix of skills or levels, vary the sequence so that the trainee doesn't spend all of a day on very difficult or very easy parts of the job to learn. On jobs that require substantial physical activity or repeated motion, mix them around to avoid undue fatigue.

However the presentation of content is sequenced, make sure the trainees know the structure and understand it. Adults easily become frustrated if they can't make sense of the sequence.

What does a good training plan look like?

The actual training plan can take any number of physical forms. A two column format is shown in Figure 10-3, but dozens of variations exist. Some individuals or organizations prefer a simple outline format, whereas others might require filling in a pre-printed form. Visual presentation programs such as Microsoft's PowerPoint®, include printing options that show each slide of the content in either an outline or single slide plus notes (serving as a training plan for that slide) on one page. Experts agree that whatever the physical form, it should include more than just a list of items to cover, although even that is better than no plan at all.

Here is one technique to prepare the physical training plan for a class. The example training plan (Figure 10-3) was developed using this process.

- Draw a line down the center of a sheet of paper. On the left side, list all the key points you want to present. If you have page number references or other materials you're bringing in, list those below the key points. This practice provides your list of *what* to teach.

- On the right side, make notes of examples, stories, overhead transparencies, films, handouts, exercises, questions you want to throw out for class discussion, and so forth. Now you have your list of *how* to teach your key points.

- At the top or on a separate cover sheet, list the details such as time, location, things you need to take to the training, and so on.

The example training plan below incorporates all the information suggested earlier, including:

- administrative information—when, where, who, and so on.
- the training objectives (referenced, in this case)
- lists of materials and equipment needed
- projected time requirements for each part of the training

Figure 10-3   Example Training Plan

Note: This training plan was for use by an experienced trainer who knew the subject well, so less detail is shown than would be appropriate for a first time trainer or for an experienced trainer who is planning for the first time with an unfamiliar subject. For example, in this plan, certain slides are referenced. If the presentation were to be done without slides, say using just a whiteboard, then it would be necessary to spell out what is on those slides.

Team Development and Management Class

Dates / Time: June 23 and July 9—8:00 a.m. to 4:45 p.m.

Location: CBI Classroom

Participants: 9 to12 per day—supervisory level (some have college experience)

Materials Needed: handout set; slides (see list); laser pointer; transparency marker

Objectives: Specified on Slide #1.

Welcome	*Logistics*
	■ *Rest rooms, vending machines, etc.*
	Brief self-introduction
	■ *Experience with the company as consultant*
	■ *Experience with the topic*
	Overview of day
	■ *Refer to handout set*
	SLIDE #1 OBJECTIVES
	Questions?
8:10	*Ask: Who was Frederick Taylor?*
	What does he have to do with today's topic?
Lecture on History of management in 5 minutes	
Management of anything requires planning and control	
Steps in Planning	*SLIDE #2 on PLANNING*
	Discussion of steps with usual examples
	■ *Determine need for plan*
	■ *Establish goals and objectives*

(continued)

Figure 10-3   Example Training Plan (*Continued*)

	■ *Determine limits (resources available)*
	■ *Develop options (creativity)*
	■ *Evaluate options (analysis)*
	■ *Choose best and implement*
Steps in control	**SLIDE #3 on CONTROL**
	Discussion of steps with usual examples
	■ *Establish standards*
	■ *Measure performance*
	■ *Compare results to standards*
	■ *Determine what corrective action needed*
Examples of planning and control tools: Gantt, PERT, Budgets, Control charts	**SLIDES #4 and 5 on Gantt and PERT**
9:10	Hand out Exercise #1, as time permits [or later]
Decision making process	**Brainstorm problems they have to solve**
	Distribute HANDOUT #1
	■ *Have them complete page 10 on handout*
	■ *Discuss implications*
Setting priorities	**SLIDES #6–8 on STEPS IN DECISION MAKING**
(ref. their book, p. 47 and 48)	**usual discussion**
	■ *Compare to planning*
	■ *How are priorities set?*
	Ask: What is the difference between decisions and problems?
Problem solving process	**SLIDE #9 on DIFFERENCE**
	(Answer to question)
	Relate to answers given by group
	■ *Characteristics of problem*
	■ *Characteristics of decision*
9:45—Break—10:00	**SLIDES # 10–12: STEPS IN PROBLEM SOLVING**
	....continued.

(Only the first two hours are shown as the example.)

- the points to cover in proper sequence
- training methods and audio-visual media to be used during the training
- questions to ask of the participants
- examples to use and references for these examples; stage directions such as which materials to hand out, which exercise to use, and so on.

What types of training plans are needed for on-the-job training?

In general, on-the-job training should have just as detailed a lesson plan as off-the-job training, especially if there are more than just a few trainees. The checklist provided below (Figure 10-4) can be used for developing an on-the-job training plan.

In terms of the *CAMPS* acronym, an OJT training plan should include:

Content—Plan to train the new employee on all the skills and knowledge that a new employee should exhibit. The trainer (peer, supervisor, or whomever) will need to deductively discover which of these skills the trainee already brings to the job. A sequence of learning experiences should be planned out.

Administration—A general schedule or time frame for the training. If more than one on-the-job trainee is working, some form of record keeping must be developed. Does the trainee need to change departments or shifts in order to get a better overview of the job or a chance to perform it on certain equipment or at a more comfortable pace? How will the employee learn work that is irregular, such as work that only happens twice a year or only happens in crises?

Methodologies—Is it best to demonstrate by showing the job to the employee or having them watch a colleague, or should just throwing them into the water (experiential) be the primary method? Simple lecture (aside from just description and direction) will seldom be used. Consideration must be given to issues such as dangerous parts of the job, cost of scrap, cost of lost customers, and other circumstances where the trainee could be a hazard to themselves, other employees, or organizational interests.

Pacing—How quickly should the trainee be expected to progress? When will close supervision be reduced to casual or as-needed supervision?

Support—What tools will be needed for the employee to adequately learn the job? Possible items include actual hand

Figure 10-4   OJT Training Plan Checklist

Supervisor / Trainer _____ Date Prepared _____

Trainee Name(s) _____ Department _____

Comments: _____

Note: The on-the-job trainer can use this checklist to provide a *structure* for the training, but all of the *job-specific* content must be developed individually to meet the needs of a given training situation. *As designed, this checklist is self-contained and starts with the assumption that we do not yet know the trainees' skills.* The items are in a logical sequence for most situations.

___ ***Trainee Orientation*** (Orientation may or may not be your responsibility; check with HR.)
- Cover the basic policies and procedures related to the job and training.
- Introduce other employees, supervisor, etc.
- Describe general facility layout, including restrooms, break area, emergency equipment, parking, etc.

___ ***Overview of Specific Job***
- Explain the product or result or work the trainee will be learning. Show actual examples, using multisensory examples when possible.
- Define the skills necessary to perform job (from job description, code sheets, etc.).

___ ***Determine Trainee's Existing Skill Level***
- Ask questions such as: Have you worked on this type of machine before? What do you know about this type of operation? Etc.
- Have employee demonstrate skills. Be aware of any concerns about scrap, safety, cost of materials, etc., and plan accordingly. Do not put employees or assets in position of risk.

___ ***Specify the Training Objective(s)***
- Training objectives come in four types: (a) awareness or attitude, (b) knowledge of specific facts, (c) skill, or (d) job behavior.
- Objectives should be (a) specific, (b) measurable, (c) cover just one thing at a time, (d) achievable, and (e) at the right level—not too big or too small.
- Objectives are usually stated in the form: "Upon completing the training, the individual will be able to [verb]...." The verb may be to do, list, explain, operate, demonstrate, etc.
- Objectives specify what must be done, any quantity, quality, or time standards, or other measurable criteria.

___ ***Give the Trainee(s) an Overview of the Training Process***

Note: Repeat this step for each of the objectives in the training plan.

Figure 10-4 OJT Training Plan Checklist (*Continued*)

- Present the key points in a logical order. Possible sequences include general to specific, specific to general, last step to first, first step to last, easiest to most difficult, etc.
- Follow these presentation guidelines:
  1. Build interest and introduce new ideas before getting into details.
  2. Vary the difficulty of activities—not all easy or all challenging.
  3. Teach easier concepts before more difficult ones and lower level skills before complex ones.
  4. Close each part of the training with discussions of reasons for and problems with that part.

___ *Demonstrate the Job*

Note: Demonstrate just one part of the job at a time.

- Be sure to break it into small enough pieces.
- Use "S-R-F" by starting with a Stimulus (show or tell trainee what to do)—Response (have the trainee answer questions or try it out)—Feedback (trainer confirms accuracy or makes corrections).

___ *Check for Understanding by Trainee(s)*

- Ask: did the trainees hear you? Understand you? How well did they understand? Ask questions about the process or have the trainee demonstrate it again or in a different sequence.

___ *Guided Practice*

- Observe while the trainee performs the job, having them first state each step before they do it.
- Let trainees learn from mistakes when possible.
- Do not be too quick to correct or hand-hold trainee.

___ *Feedback and Fine Tuning*

- Sometimes the process itself provides the feedback.
- Use feedback in such a way that it is:
  1. Clear, so the trainees understand exactly what was said.
  2. Specific, rather than general.
  3. Related to something the trainee has the power to correct.
  4. Descriptive rather than evaluative.
  5. Well-timed, meaning given when the employee is ready to hear and deal with it.
- Tie standards explicitly to objectives: Does the trainee produce "x" units of acceptable quality in "y" amount of time? Etc.
- If the trainee is not progressing, break the training into smaller elements (S-R-F links). Also, check for and correct communication barriers that might interfere with the trainee's understanding.

(continued)

Figure 10-4   OJT Training Plan Checklist (*Continued*)

___ *Individual Practice*
- Trainee performs the job (or part of the job), with support only as requested.
- Trainer should check back frequently, but not constantly.
- Frequency of checking can be reduced over time.
- Be aware of plateaus in the learning curve. Improvement will not necessarily be at a constant rate.

___ *Final Evaluation*
- This step confirms that the trainee is now at least minimally competent to perform the job on his or her own.
- Should probably involve someone other than the trainer, such as a supervisor or quality control.

tools, manuals, checklists, samples, employee handbook, names of people to contact with questions, and so on.

Now that the lesson has been effectively planned, it's time to move on to the next chapter and the important topic of how to actually conduct the training session.

11 Conducting Training

"Plans are only good intentions unless they immediately degenerate into hard work."
—Peter Drucker

Everything that has been developed so far is for naught unless the training is delivered effectively and the trainees take it back to the workplace and use it. Although the professional trainer attempts to do all stages of the process well, the actual delivery of the training is the culmination of all the effort. It is the most visible, challenging, rewarding, and—most trainers would say—the most fun part of the job.

■ ■ ■

This chapter deals with both delivering the training and improving transfer of training. Although an exhaustive treatment of these topics is beyond its scope, it distills some key points for the trainer and suggests a few practical references for those who need more detail.

Training delivery

Chapter 10 presents a number of suggestions for designing the training plan. As the opening quote for this chapter suggests, the next step is to put that plan into practice. Here are a few specific suggestions that can help you prepare to do that.

Where do I start?

Make sure everything is ready ahead of time. Have proper arrangements been made for the training location, and has everyone been notified of the place, time, and other requirements? Are refreshments, if any, arranged? Do you have all the handouts and materials for each trainee? Will you want nametags or name tents (placards) for participants? How about any equipment and supplies you will need? (If you're using equipment, see the additional suggestions on room set up and equipment use in Chapter 9.) Do you plan to use music as people gather and on breaks? Do you have your training plan, videos, pointer, board or flipchart markers, business cards, and everything else? Is the room unlocked, and do you know where light switches and the thermostat are located?

Make a good first impression. Be in the training area before the trainees arrive and have things in place so you can comfortably greet people as they arrive. You need to have materials laid out for the participants, the furniture arranged as you want it, with the media equipment in place, booted up, and focused correctly on the screen, and so on. Make a checklist for yourself or—as suggested in Chapter 9—make that list the first item in your training plan. Dress appropriately for the training that will be given; you don't want to be significantly overdressed or more casual than the participants will probably be. If you choose to use an icebreaker of any sort, make sure it's both relevant and appropriate to the audience. Keep in mind that if it's a short program, the icebreaker also must be short—or should be omitted entirely. Be sure to start on time. Doing so sets a good example that you take the training seriously and expect them to as well. The reputation of the training department tends to flow from the experience of the learners. If they've had bad experiences before, you may need to work extra hard to gain their confidence. If they've had good experiences, be sure not to disappoint them.

At the very start of training, you will probably want to deal with housekeeping issues, such as letting people know a general schedule (including when breaks will probably happen), where the restrooms are located, any rules on interruptions (cell phones, pagers, knocks at the door), any rules on food and drink in the training room, and so on.

Establish your credibility early on. Trainees need to know why you are the trainer and to feel confident that they can learn something from you. In business training, just having academic credentials is seldom enough. Trainees want to hear what you've done that relates to the training. It's even better if you've done it in their company or at least know about their company. Of course, now and then, trainers are put into situations in which they are required to train on something they don't know all that well. If you find yourself in this situation, here are a couple of suggestions. There must be some reason why you have been designated as the trainer, and that can be explained. Maybe it's because you are their supervisor or have some position of authority in the organization. Maybe it's because you have some special knowledge of the topic, even if you don't have experience. Without being self-depreciating, you might go around the class and ask what experience the trainees bring. If it's more extensive than yours, point out how much they can add to the program and emphasize your role as more of a facilitator than a subject matter expert. Also, you might begin with some relevant stories from inside or outside the organization, which will get them involved in the subject and indirectly indicate that you have planned effectively to cover the topic. You should not exaggerate your experience, but also never undermine your credibility by drawing attention to your inexperience. If you have planned an effective lesson, you should have the confidence to carry it off well.

Above all, don't exaggerate or try to bluff your way through. If you are asked questions you can't answer, tell the trainees that you'll get back to them with answers—and then do it. Exaggerating your experience or guessing at an answer will undercut your credibility quickly, and it can't be regained.

Determine the motivations of your trainees. People come to training programs for a variety of reasons. Some volunteer to come, while others are directed to come. Some are excited about learning new things, while others are concerned about keeping their jobs. Some will be filling a square and are attending only because they must. Although it's not good to let those people off the hook too easily, you should be wary of letting them drag down the rest of the group or take too much of your energy. If everyone else is engrossed in and enthusiastic about the training, they might come along; if not, just accept that you can't force a horse to drink (or a trainee to think).

An effective trainer analyzes how the material to be presented can help the trainees satisfy their job requirements. Will it help them increase efficiency, reduce costs, improve services, quality, or teamwork? Use the *benefits* to help "sell" the trainees at the start of the program. Sometimes just the experience of training can provide benefits. For example, employees who are motivated to be leaders or to increase their status among their peers could perhaps be allowed to exercise that inclination during training through work in groups.

Plan to use your students' backgrounds. Learn about individual trainees' strengths and weaknesses in order to structure the learning experience for them, either with or without their help. First, determine if the group is homogeneous or heterogeneous, in which students are at several different levels.

A group that is either all experienced or all inexperienced can be easier to deal with from a training plan point of view, because they all need the same information. But the mixed group can also provide some benefits for the trainer. These benefits come from using the skills and experience of those trainees who have knowledge or skills to help teach the less experienced. Adult students learn better when they teach others, and the novices gain the benefit of their classmates' experience as well as the trainer's own background in presenting the class material.

If the group consists of all novices, the trainer will have to rely more on personal experiences, plus any case studies, readings, exercises, and other materials selected to help bring home the points. Frequently, course topics can be related to some phenomenon that even novices have experienced.

If the class is all "old hands" at the subject, it is important to guard against the "I-know-it-all-already" syndrome, especially if you are seen as either their peer or as an "academic" who's not been on the firing line as they have. Sometimes a pre-test can do this, by helping trainees to realize that they have gaps in their understanding. Perhaps you could also point out that changes in the workplace require that everyone needs to keep current, even if they do understand and perform their present job very well. The fact is, bad habits creep in, and training is one way to help people get back on track.

Mixed groups of trainees present the biggest challenge to the trainer. As mentioned above, allowing the more skilled to help train is one option, if they're willing and able. You can enable them to do so by creating teams in which skilled and unskilled trainees work together on various activities. Another technique is to vary the training style and use different exercises so that even the experienced students are actively engaged. Sometimes it is possible to modularize the training and enable more skilled people to test out of any portions they already have mastered. Perhaps the training can be designed to provide some basic skills as pre-training assignments or homework (see Competency-Based Training in Chapter 7). Groups always contain faster and slower students, so try to make lesson plans as flexible as possible, while remembering that all the trainees ultimately must meet the same training objectives.

Involve the trainees in the course structure when possible. Trainers who are comfortable with a participative (deductive) style might want to allow trainees to determine which parts of the training should be emphasized. All objectives must still be met, but if some flexibility exists, it will help the trainees to feel some sense of control. Plan a variety of exercises and small group work so trainees get to know each other and practice group skills, especially if they will be working as a group on the job. If there was pre-work assigned, be sure to use it; otherwise trainees will feel like they wasted their time in preparing.

Be sure to treat students as adults. As discussed early in the book, adults learn differently than children. They often come into a class feeling they should know it all already. In this case, they are defensive and reluctant to admit their weaknesses. They also need to see a clear purpose and application for their learning— it has to be practical. Be sure to tie in examples with their own experiences. Talk *with* them, not *at* them. They can contribute in the classroom and would probably prefer to participate rather than just listen to a lecture.

What else can I do to improve the learning climate?

Use a consistent training style. The way you handle a program should be predictable and comfortable to the trainees. And, if more than one trainer is involved in presenting the program, they should consciously discuss and strive for handling their individual parts of the program in as similar a manner as practicable.

The beginning of the training is the time to set the learning climate. Whatever patterns are established in the first session will usually be expected by the trainees in subsequent sessions. The trainer is primarily responsible for setting these patterns, although they will be influenced by such other factors as the physical environment, personalities of the participants, and the organizational climate of the company within which the program is presented. Before stepping into the classroom or other training area the first time, consider these two important issues: what degree of formality is expected and how to focus on material.

Degree of Formality. Will the training method be formal lectures to the students, informal question and answer, or group interaction? Will the trainees be expected to have already read certain materials and be ready to respond to questions? Will the role of the trainer be closest to a guru, a coach, or just "one of the guys"? Are deadlines going to be strictly enforced, or will some reasonable latitude be permitted?

Focus on Material. Will the training tightly follow very specific content and assignments, or will trainees be permitted to spontaneously discuss timely issues of interest? If the latter, what will ensure that the required material is covered?

When more than one trainer is being used, consistency becomes an even greater issue. Multiple trainers must agree on their approach. Trainees can certainly learn to deal with two or more training styles, but doing so simply complicates learning.

Ensure a focus on learning. Another aspect of the learning climate has to do with how sacrosanct the training time will be. Can the trainees be interrupted or removed from training to deal with problems back at the workplace (usually a bad idea), or does training come first, except in a true emergency? Will cell phones, pagers, or messages be permitted, or must the trainees come with a clear understanding that someone else has to make the decisions in their absence? How important is it to return from breaks promptly, read pre-training assignments, or do any assigned homework?

What else can I do to make the content understandable?

Keep the S-R-F Links Short. Design the lesson so that the material is grouped into bite sized chunks. Don't just lecture for half an hour and then ask for questions. Trainees should go through one S-R-F cycle every five to eight minutes. The "*S*" is stimulus: anything that the trainer presents to the learner. It can be oral information, a visual, or anything that affects one or more of the senses of the learner. The purpose of a stimulus is to cause a fact, procedure, or concept to be acquired and understood by the trainees. To find out if learning has occurred, you need to in some way elicit a response. The "*R*" is the response to the stimulus. Response is the only short-term way we know if the trainee is learning. It serves three main purposes: (1) to give the trainer feedback on how well the trainee understands; (2) to give the trainee a chance to see how well he or she understands or can apply the material; and (3) to improve retention and transfer of the stimulus. The very act of responding forces the learner to manipulate and internalize new skills and knowledge. The "*F*" is feedback, which the trainee receives either from the trainer or from hands-on exercises and which confirms or denies that the knowledge or skill was learned correctly.

Use variety in the training design. Have the learners move around occasionally, talk with each other, try an experiment or exercise, or work on equipment. Use more than one form of presenting the material. Chapters 7 and 8 describe a variety of choices. Although using all of them in a half day session is probably not appropriate or necessary, three or four different approaches—perhaps some lecture, discussion, a video, and an exercise—will be more likely to keep adults involved and learning.

Read any material the students must read, but don't read to them. It's very frustrating, and usually quite obvious to the trainees, if the trainer doesn't know what the course material includes. However, the trainer's role is to highlight, extract, exemplify, personalize, and reinforce the material from the handouts, manuals, and other resources. Trainees, hopefully, can read the materials themselves; the trainer is not paid to read it to them. If reading level is an issue, the trainer may choose to present the material in the readings in a different way. If the trainer chooses to bring in additional materials, the trainees must be made aware when the class examples vary from any printed information, because they will probably be studying from the program materials.

Overplan. First time trainers are frequently surprised when their planned one-hour presentation is completed in only fourteen minutes. Worse yet, sometimes it's not completed in ninety minutes. Even experienced trainers agree that it pays to over-prepare. Practicing new training programs in a dry run with a tape recorder and timer is usually a good idea, but—especially if the training plan is deductive or interactive—have some contingency plans. Know what can be skimmed over or skipped completely if the training is running longer than planned; keep an eye on the clock when time is a concern. Have some extra material or additional exercises available if training runs short—or just let class out early, if doing so is appropriate *and* if the training objectives have been met. As a side note, many organizations and regulatory agencies still consider seat time as the only criterion for meeting a standard. So, if it's not possible to let people leave when they have actually met the knowledge or skill requirements, it's best to have planned some additional activities to keep them engaged.

Be willing to ask for help. A number of sources inside and outside your organization might be able to suggest ideas to improve the training. Talk with other people who have taught similar programs. Good professional contacts can be found in such organizations as the local chapter of ASTD, The National Society for Performance Improvement, or others. Depending on the subject of the training, related professional associations might be able to suggest some topic-specific ideas for training. Even the trainees may be willing to lend a hand during certain parts of the training in which they have personal experience.

How do I encourage participation in training sessions?

Unless you are intentionally teaching inductively with a lecture or some other one-way process, it's good to encourage participation among the trainees. (See Chapter 2). There's a difference between a challenging and a threatening training program. Adults usually don't mind training that is challenging, but they don't like to be embarrassed among their peers. Trainees learn more if they are involved. Here are some suggestions to get response and involvement from your trainees:

- *Use small groups.* People will participate more in small groups than in large classes. See the following section for more information about groups and group dynamics.

- *Ask questions that can be answered by everyone.* Especially short answer ones. You can also ask for a show of hands on some issues.

- *Use discussion, case study, experiential exercises* and other higher levels of training techniques. See earlier suggestions on the effective use of each style in Chapter 7.

- *Use written exercises.* Having everyone write down an answer to questions enables you to go around the room and see if people are learning. Discuss any misconceptions or gaps in knowledge that show up as a result of these exercises.

- *Call on people.* Ask direct questions of individuals. You can also just ask general or even rhetorical questions and see who answers. It's good practice to not take the first hand that goes up all the time. Distribute the responsibility of answering among all the participants. Wait a while (ten to fifteen seconds) before choosing who to call on so people continue the thinking process. If you're pushed for time and want to find out if people know specific facts or procedures, ask closed questions that have only one correct answer. If you want more discussion to see whether the trainees understand concepts, ask open ended questions that invite longer answers and can go in a number of different directions.

- **Give feedback to trainees.** Let them know how they're doing, or what they need to do more or less of. Positive feedback is always appreciated, but not always possible. If you must give negative feedback, try to consider the sensitivity of the individual involved. Some people will accept "you're wrong," better than others who need to hear, "that's not quite right."

- **Ask others in the group what they think.** Adults learn from others and from their peers, and critiques or support from them can be more important than agreement from the trainer.

- **Remember that lack of responsiveness doesn't necessarily indicate a lack of understanding.** Reasons for not responding can include insecurities, tiredness, passive-aggressive behavior, or many other things. It could be that the question simply has to be rephrased. Of course, it could also be that they haven't learned, and you need to go over it again.

How can I effectively use sub-groups and peer training?

Using sub-groups in a training program has many advantages for both the learners and the trainer. Many adults are quite willing to learn from each other and may be less threatened by their peers than by the instructor who is both an authority figure and typically an outsider to their work group. Peers might be better able to put new ideas and skills into terms and context of the workplace, thus making it easier for trainees to integrate new knowledge and transfer training. It also helps the trainees better understand and refine their own abilities and knowledge if they need to explain things to their peers, and it can provide an intrinsic reward, as well. The trainer who uses groups will have fewer people vying for his or her attention. Using groups can provide some time to catch your breath, deal with administrative items such as setting up equipment or reviewing lesson plans, or just enjoying a few minutes of quiet time.

That having been said, using groups in a training situation also poses some risks. Groups can make it easier for individual trainees to hide, as their peers cover for them or let them be "free riders" on the backs of others in the group who did the work or know the answers. Also, negative group dynamics may get in the way of effective learning if personalities or other issues keep the group from functioning properly.

Some of the many reasons you might want to use groups include:

- *Teambuilding.* If you have trainees who will be working together on the job, it can be very practical to have them also working together in training. Even if they won't be working with each other, most jobs do require some sort of people skills, and the training environment is a good place to develop them.

- *People can help teach each other.* Not everyone needs to get feedback from the trainer. Trainees who excel can help others to understand the lessons. It is good for everyone: the good students actually can learn more by having to structure their thoughts and explain to their peers; the weaker students get help from more sources; and the trainer can better use the class time.

- *More involvement.* Skills training, in particular, can benefit from several smaller groups in which participants can have more hands-on time, as long as safety or damage issues are not a concern. Even when dealing with knowledge, rather than skills, responses are coming from more participants. Reaching consensus happens more quickly in small groups than in large ones. Participants have a higher level of commitment in small groups.

- *Synergy.* Small groups can bond and better thinking (brainstorming, etc.) can occur in a small group than in a trainer-led larger group.

- *Varying the pace.* The use of groups can provide an option from the otherwise possibly tedious classroom format. It can also give the trainer a break to catch up on administrative matters, as mentioned before.

For short questions, groups of two ("turn to your neighbor") are quick and practical. Groups of three might be better for more richness or in situations in which you need an observer (such as role plays). Larger groups of four to six may be good for case studies, but the instructor may need to provide more structure and guidance, such as having the group elect a spokesperson, giving specific roles to different people, and so on. It's often a good idea to mix up the groups at least daily so varying strengths and weakness of individual trainees can be controlled, and so disparities in group levels don't become exacerbated.

Some other specific ideas for using groups effectively are:

- *Define the tasks very specifically.* If possible, provide a model or example of what you expect the group to accomplish.

- *Give different tasks to different groups* when appropriate.

- *Walk around during group exercises.* It's not a matter of spying, but of checking what kind of discussions are occurring. You might be able to head off trouble if you find a group wandering off on a tangent.

- *Tell the group how long they will have to work* and perhaps suggest an appropriate budget of their time: "Spend five minutes on each question, then leave ten minutes at the end to collect all the ideas and prepare a report." Make ending times specific: "Work on this exercise until 2:45," rather than, "I'll give you about twenty minutes for this exercise."

- *Let the group know if you're expecting reports.* This notice helps them get organized if they will be making reports and keeps them from getting prepared and excited, only to find out they don't get their chance to talk. Depending on the topic, it's not always necessary to have group reports.

- *Manage group reports effectively.* It's disappointing to trainees if they've discussed a topic for fifteen minutes, gotten some great ideas, and the first group to be called on uses all their ideas. A couple suggestions: Limit a group report to no more than two minutes, unless that's truly unreasonable. Also, consider having each group give just one or two things they discussed so other groups can add more ideas. At the end you can ask if any group has additional points that haven't been mentioned.

How do I deal with disruptive participants?

An infinite number of possible causes and remedies exist for common classroom disruptions. Usually the first step is to try to determine the cause of disruptive behavior. Causes can range from boredom to frustration, from use of drugs to just having an annoying personality, and so on. Some of these things, such as drug use, will be beyond your ability as a trainer to control, and you need to hand over the problem to the supervisor or appropriate office.

Here are some general categories of problem participants you may encounter:

- Someone who dominates the program, seeking attention and challenging the trainer or other participants (sometimes nicely and sometimes belligerently). This category can include the "class clown."
- People who arrive late, leave early, and are interrupted by multiple pages or other messages or work on personal activities during the training program.
- The unprepared person who did not come with prerequisite skills or did not do pre-work assigned for the training.
- Groups that sit together and talk or form cliques that have negative group dynamics. (Sub-groups can also be positive, but even positive groups can incur the ire of others in the training.)
- The non-participant participant who is present but silent.
- The over-eager participant who answers every question before others have a chance to think it through.
- The chronologically challenged participant who insists on discussing topics you covered ten minutes ago or will cover in another ten minutes.

As with any personality based issues, there are no sure fire answers. Some general ideas for dealing with people like these include:

- *Speak privately one on one with the problem trainee(s).* Public confrontations are no-win situations and usually escalate the problem. Try to deal with the problem on a break or when most of the group is otherwise engaged in some activity. Ask if they feel they don't need the training or otherwise try to determine the cause of their attitude. Empathize, if you can, and try to move on. Ask how you can make it better for them, putting the burden on them.

- *Try not to take sides.* Avoid making enemies or dividing the group. Also, avoid getting into a battle of wits, even if you're pretty sure you could win.

- *Deal with behavior, not with individuals.* Focus on what they are doing that disrupts the learning for others, rather than "dissing" them.

- *Let the group handle it, if you can.* They may know the problem individual well and have already developed ways of dealing with him or her, or they might be willing to just ignore the situation and get on with the learning, unless you make a big deal of it.

- *To get the group back on track, take a short breather.* Interrupt, if you need to, then summarize what has happened so far and focus again on the objectives and next steps in the training. Sometimes an unscheduled break is called for to get control back.

- *Finally, follow the suggestions elsewhere in this chapter and book.* For example, if you insist on starting on time, the late person is more likely to conform than if you wait for them.

How do I wrap up the program?

Although first impressions are important, so are the last ones. As the training comes to an end, a variety of tasks must be accomplished.

- *Have something meaningful to do near the end of the training.* Of course all of your training should be meaningful, but it's good to have some significant task that people can really get involved in and feel good about bringing to a closure.

- *Remind people what they've learned.* Recap the training using the schedule or the training objectives. Make sure to tie all the parts together and emphasize how the newly acquired knowledge and skills can be used on the jobs to which the trainees are returning.

- *Create action plans.* If the training subject matter lends itself to such a process, have the trainees put into writing in their own words how they plan to use the new knowledge or skills they have acquired. Some trainers keep these plans and mail them to the trainees at a predetermined future time as a reminder or reinforcement technique.

- *Complete any administrative requirements.* These requirements could include administering a post-test or final knowledge or skills test, handing out and collecting the program evaluations, getting any documentation signed or distributed (such as certificates of completion), and so on.

- *Prepare the trainees for any follow-up that will occur.* Will the trainees be asked to fill out any other documents once they return to their jobs? Will they be subject to any follow-up evaluation by their supervisors or by others? Will they be asked to participate in any further training? The following section, Improving Transfer of Training, covers these possibilities in more depth.

What can I do to improve on-the-job training?

Prepare the workplace and co-workers to make the experience as smooth as practicable. Like all other training, it's important to do a needs analysis of both the job and the trainee and to develop objectives and measures of learning out of that analysis. OJT must be planned; it won't just happen by accident. (See Chapter 7). Have a specific list of skills and/or knowledge that the trainee needs to learn and have a mechanism by which this learning will happen. Asking the famous "journalistic" questions "What, Who, When, Where, Why, How, and How much?" is a good starting point.

What should be taught first, and what can be delayed? As discussed in Chapter 10, some training has to be sequenced to cover basic skills before more complex ones. Most tasks can also be categorized into their levels of frequency and levels of importance. Teaching the most frequently encountered tasks first will get the trainee productive more quickly, but there may be some seldom-used knowledge or skills that also must be covered early, such as where the emergency shut-off button is located.

Who can best train the new trainee? It might be the supervisor or the best worker, but maybe not. Someone else may have the personality or common background to develop a better rapport with an individual. Someone else may be less busy or more patient.

When is the best time for training? It might be better to schedule new trainees for OJT at less busy times, such as second shifts or off-peak days or hours, or less busy locations if any are available. If OJT is coupled with off-the-job training, make sure that the trainee is still exposed to all of the different working environments of the job. Should off- and on-the-job training run concurrently or consecutively? Part of that decision will be influenced by how much conceptual knowledge must go with the procedural knowledge. For many jobs, procedural knowledge is all that's really necessary or has to be taught on the job or in a simulated job environment. Conceptual knowledge can often help a trainee learn the procedures better and faster, but it is usually best handled off the job.

Where should the training be done? Certainly, working with the exact equipment and in the true workplace has the benefit of eliminating transfer of training issues (covered later in this chapter), but if doing so unnecessarily exposes the trainee to distractions or dangerous situations, maybe a similar but more practical place can be found. As an example, a trainee feels conspicuous enough, so learning where the public or customers or even lots of co-workers will be watching can be unnecessarily stressful. Even training people in one location, perhaps a smaller or less busy one, then moving them to their final work site should be considered.

Why are we training this person? It's not a silly question. It just suggests that the needs analysis be reviewed again. Does the trainee (a) really need to know all the things in the training plan and (b) really not already know them? How skilled does the trainee need to be before he or she moves out of OJT and into just doing the job and asking for help when a new or confusing issue arises? Is the training for a primary job, or are people being cross-trained to help broaden the skill base in an organization so that people can be shifted to other positions to cover changes in workload and fill in for vacations or other absences?

How the training should occur is another question. (See Chapter 10, Developing the Training Plan.) In an overall perspective, on-the-job training can be handled through job rotation, delegating tasks from a higher level or different department, or as part of task forces in which people are put together to accomplish a special project. More likely, the training is the result of a new or newly transferred employee. The usual OJT approach is to first explain what must be done (tell), then demonstrate how it is to be done (show), and then have the trainee try it out (do). If the trainee doesn't pick up the skill after two or three tries, break it into smaller segments. The whole lesson plan must be developed with some flexibility to meet workplace demands.

How much training has to be done? The answer to this question should flow out of the needs analysis and be influenced by the ongoing evaluation of the trainee as he or she progresses in the job. Be certain to adequately document the trainee's progress toward meeting the objectives. Besides being important to knowing when the trainee is ready to work alone, such documentation can be useful in planning on-the-job training for subsequent trainees in the same work environment.

Improving transfer of training

As explained earlier in the book, ***transfer of training*** means that the trainees want to—and are actually able to—use what they learned during training when they get (or get back) to their jobs. Training that doesn't transfer represents wasted time and money. Therefore, a major concern in training is to make it relevant to the trainees and useful to the organization. This last part of the chapter discusses several specific ideas and suggestions to improve transfer of training.

What sort of things influence transfer of training?

Transfer of training is influenced by a number of factors, which can be grouped into those related to the *training*, the *trainee*, and the *organizational environment* in which they will be performing. Among these factors, the trainer probably has the most control over the training and the least control over the trainees. The degree of control the trainer has over the organizational environment will vary from place to place, but is probably also rather limited.

The ***training design factors*** include all of those things covered in the first ten chapters of this book: choice of training techniques, use of media, selection of facilities, skill of the trainers, sequence of the training, and so on.

The ***organizational environment*** includes how much management and general support exists for training, how quickly things change in the industry, the overall climate and culture of the organization, and so on. See comments in Chapter 1 regarding this last point.

Finally, *the **individual trainee*** is influenced by his or her personal skills and motivation, learning style preferences, any distractions that are occurring in their jobs and life that can affect learning, and many more issues.

How can transfer of training be improved through proper training design?

Training designers must do the work necessary to make sure that what they develop is really relevant to the trainees, as covered in Chapter 3. Very early in the program, the learners need to clearly understand when and how the new skills and knowledge will be used. *Just-in-time training*, meaning training that occurs immediately before it is needed, is best. If the application of knowledge or skills is hampered or delayed in the workplace, transfer of training will be less effective. Individual trainers also need to visit the workplace both before and after the training, and even during the training, if it doesn't all happen at one time. Such visits can be important to help discover any inconsistencies in the work and the training that is designed to support it.

Where it's feasible to do so, schedule training in extended rather than intensive blocks. A one-day session invites *"training tourists"* (people who look at training as a vacation from work) and crams a lot into a short time, without giving trainees a chance to practice it on the job. Assimilating the same content over a 4-week, two hours per week schedule will give them that chance, especially if they are encouraged to think of it as "homework." True, the extended schedule will increase the risk of people dropping out and incurring more scheduling conflicts, especially if the training is not conducted on site. But *distributed learning* (learning in smaller segments over a period of time) is the preferred technique to help people learn, and, therefore, to apply knowledge and skills more effectively.

Build in take-aways for the trainees that they can use as job aids. Take-aways can include such items as handouts, flash cards, lists of ideas, steps to follow, people to contact (including each other and the trainer), and even small tools—anything that can remind them to apply what has been taught. Similarly, have the trainees develop their own forms, lists, and perhaps even an action plan of what they intend to do with their new-found knowledge or skill once they return to the job. Besides just handing them lists of key ideas or cards to stick in their wallets, be sure to also review and summarize what has been covered in a bullet point fashion.

And, naturally, do the best job possible in designing the training to accommodate various learning styles, apply adult learning theory, use clear objectives, use appropriate multi-media, and so on.

How can transfer of training be improved by influencing the organizational environment?

As discussed in Chapter 1, organizational development ("OD") is a separate career path from training, but because of their very duties, trainers are frequently catalysts for organizational changes.

To the extent that trainers can influence the organizational culture, they may be able to positively affect transfer of training. This influence can be developed by working to establish and maintain a good reputation for the training department. If managers and employees see training programs as worthwhile, there will be more support for the trainers and encouragement for the trainees to apply what they've learned.

Trainers should work to keep management appraised of what is being done through regular formal and informal contacts, briefings, or newsletters. Many organizations set up a *steering committee* or *training advisory committee* to work with the training department to develop and prioritize training needs. A steering committee is an ad hoc group of interested persons, which can include—but is not limited to—potential or past trainees, supervisors, customers, employees from related departments, and trainers. The purpose of such a group is to help design and evaluate training programs.

The training department needs to be seen as an important part of the organization's operations. To reinforce the importance of training, many organizations use *training contracts* to formalize expectations and put the whole process of training on a business-like basis. These documents, often signed by the trainee, supervisor, and trainer, specify the objectives of the training, expectations for application, and measures of success. It's also a good up front place to specify expectations about such concerns as attendance, interruptions during the program, and so on.

Trainers frequently offer managers the opportunity to observe the training or even participate in either an abbreviated program or as part of a regular class. Participation helps managers understand what their workers should know or be able to do as a result of the training. Management involvement helps make training more relevant and assures the line managers that the training department is in touch with reality and not off in some ivory tower. It also minimizes the question of whether the supervisors will allow the trainees to use their new skills and knowledge when they return to the job, because the supervisors will be able to provide input during the training and will arrive at the same understanding of the content that their employees have gained.

Sometimes the trainer or training designer also has the skills to help the managers do assessments or engage in internal consulting. Although this work is typically handled by OD specialists, it can be a way of developing or improving the image of the training department within the organization.

How can transfer of training be improved by working with the trainees?

The trainer should focus on not only the content, but also on motivating the trainees to apply their learning back on the job. There are a number of ways to accomplish this goal. For some types of training, a "secret shopper" program could be set up in which the trainees are unknowingly put in a position to use the skills or knowledge taught them, then recognized and rewarded for doing it right. Other post-training assessments or different types of contests might also be developed.

If there is any choice about who comes to training and at what times, transfer of training will be improved if more than one person from a work area has the training. In this manner, the trainee has a coach or support person when they get back to the job. It's even better if the entire natural work group is trained at once. Such an arrangement may not be practical, but it should be considered when it can be done using substitutes to continue the regular work or by doing the training off-shift. Some training can be done in supervisor—employee teams, though the merits of such an arrangement should be considered before the decision is made. Will the presence of the supervisor inhibit the subordinate? What if the subordinate learns better than the supervisor? Will that create difficulties back on the job? Some companies arrange training to include various levels of employees, but do not put supervisors and their subordinates into the same group.

Bringing graduates of the training back for a review session or creating "alumni" groups can also be of some use to keep people connected after the training is over. It may increase the likelihood of them using what they've learned. Likewise, some organizations use newsletters that are created by the training department to both keep trainees in touch with each other and the trainers and to share any new ideas or approaches that have been developed since the training was completed. These newsletters can include success stories, interviews with graduates, and so on and can be either in hard copy or in electronic form.

Several books can suggest additional approaches to transfer of training, notably *Transfer of Training: Action Packed Strategies to Ensure High Payoff from Training Investments*, by Broad and Newstrom.

12 Assessing Training Programs

"What gets measured gets done . . . even imperfect measures provide a strategic indication of progress, or the lack thereof."

—Tom Peters

The professional trainer wants an honest answer to the question, "How did we do?" It's not only for his or her own satisfaction, but because the overall purpose of training is to foster a better organizational environment. Being professional means taking responsibility for follow through and correcting any problems.

■ ■ ■

In Chapter 6, you read that it is often difficult to differentiate between *learning* and *program* evaluations—*i.e.*, whether the trainees have learned what was taught, versus whether the training occurred in an efficient and appropriate manner. The discussion in this chapter considers program evaluations: evaluating the entire training process, not just whether the specified objectives were met. This chapter is divided into two parts: theory and practice.

The theory of training assessment

Why and how do we assess training?

A useful summary of why and how to do training assessment was created by The American Association for Higher Education.[1] The remarks below are based on that model, but adjusted and expanded utilizing *training* terms, rather than *higher education* jargon.

A good assessment process will:

- Begin with valuing training and development.
- Recognize the complexity with which trainees learn and demonstrate that learning.
- Be based on clear and explicit training objectives and goals.
- Consider outcomes, but also the experiences that lead to those outcomes.
- Operate continuously from before until well after the training.
- Involve representatives from across the organization.
- Begin with why training happens and focus on issues the organization and its employees really value.
- Be part of a larger set of conditions that promote change.
- Provide an effective means for trainers to ensure they have met their obligations to the organization and to the trainees.

Continuing with the AAHE comments, each of the above main points requires some expansion, but provides a good starting point for understanding the concept and philosophy of program assessment.

Assessment of training begins with organizational values. Assessment is not an end in itself, but a vehicle for improvement. When questions about organizational values are skipped over, assessment threatens to be an exercise in measuring what's easy instead of being a process to improve what we really care about. What is important to an organization, and how can the training function support that? Are ethics important to the organization? How about reducing employee turnover? Or, perhaps, fostering creativity is an organizational goal. Training programs must support (or at least not undermine) what is important.

Assessment is most effective when it reflects an understanding of learning as multidimensional, integrated, and revealed in performance over time. Learning is a complex process. Assessment should reflect this complexity by employing a diverse array of methods and using them over time to reveal change, growth, and increasing degrees of integration to help improve the trainees' learning experiences. When new employees are involved, for example, the entire process from initial orientation through skill training and the on-the-job training that follows should all be assessed. Although most learning objectives can be measured during the training, evaluating the training program will have to wait until the employee is settled into the job.

Assessment works best when the programs it seeks to improve have clear, explicitly stated purposes. Assessment must compare results and goals of the program. Goals include the training objectives, as well as larger elements of a business plan. When program purposes are not specific, assessment is difficult or impossible.

Assessment requires attention to outcomes, but also and equally to the experiences that lead to those outcomes. Information about outcomes is important—trainers need to know where the trainees "end up." But to improve outcomes, it is also necessary to know about trainee experience along the way. Assessment can help to understand which trainees learn best under which conditions, and with such knowledge comes the capacity to improve the whole of their learning. Did trainees learn because of the training design and instruction, or in spite of it?

Assessment works best when it is ongoing, not episodic. Assessment is a process whose power is cumulative. Though isolated, "one shot" assessment can be better than none, improvement is be best achieved using a linked series of activities undertaken over time. The point is to monitor progress toward intended goals in a spirit of continuous improvement. Along the way, the assessment process itself should be evaluated and refined in light of emerging insights.

Assessment fosters wider improvement when representatives from across the organization are involved. Trainee learning is an organization-wide responsibility, and assessment is a way of enacting that responsibility. Trainers play a role, but assessment should also involve individuals from beyond the training program, whose experience can enrich the sense of appropriate aims and standards for learning. Training and developing the workers is, after all, a responsibility of managers. It says so in their job description. Assessment of training is not a task for small groups of experts, but a collaborative activity by all parties with a stake in its improvement. Certainly it should involve the trainers and trainees, but also their supervisors, customers, and anyone in the organization who is in a position to assess quality and quantity of work by the trainees.

Assessment makes a difference when it begins with issues of use and illuminates questions that people really care about. Assessment recognizes the value of information in the process of improvement. But to be useful, information must be connected to issues or questions that people really care about. Assessment must be done using approaches that relevant parties find credible and applicable to decisions that must be made. It is a process that starts with involving the decision makers. Collecting data just because it is available is impractical; not collecting data simply because it requires primary rather than secondary investigation also can be a bad decision. Usually the ultimate "bottom line" is money, and more will be said about the influence of money on assessment later in this chapter.

Assessment is most likely to lead to improvement when it is part of a larger set of conditions that promote change. Assessment alone changes little. Its greatest contribution comes in organizations in which the quality of training is visibly valued and pursued. As discussed earlier in the book, training is not the only vehicle for change. If things are not going according to plan, training may or may not be an appropriate remedy. It's not enough to just understand that training is working or not working; assessment must be able to refine the reasons why it is or isn't, and—ideally—suggest appropriate actions to improve the situation. Assessing and discovering problems with training is expensive, frustrating, and can be a wasted effort unless something is done to resolve those problems.

Through assessment, trainers meet their responsibilities to the trainees and the organization. Trainers have responsibilities to the trainees and the organizations for which the training is done. This obligation goes beyond just reporting such information; the deeper obligation is to improve the trainees, the organization, and society in general.

That's a big challenge, and so far the discussion has been exclusively conceptual. How can this challenge be met?

How can we set the stage for training assessment?

When trainers assess training, a strong tendency exists to use "training oriented" approaches and theorists such as those by Rob Brinkerhoff, Donald Kirkpatrick, and Jack Phillips. All of these people have done excellent work in the field of training evaluation. The truth is, however, outside of the training field, most line managers have never heard of any of these folks. To effectively communicate across the organization, trainers need to consider which approaches can be used without the benefit of a translator. Phillips has done this nicely by using the widely understood concept of ROI (return on investment) as a basis for evaluation, rather than using training-specific terms. ROI, however, is not the only answer.

Unquestionably, an opportunity exists to use more general assessment concepts and theories that are understood by mainstream management. Training is a service, and although service evaluation is not yet as well understood as product evaluation, a whole body of literature is emerging in that area. Besides, using some of these other approaches might help trainers to understand training in ways never before considered.

Though a service, training apparently differs in some as yet undefined ways from other services. As one example, a study attempted to use Herzberg's widely accepted motivator-hygiene theory that was originated to describe job satisfaction and has also been successfully applied to the customer satisfaction field. This theory failed miserably when applied to the training field.[2] The study showed that whether people learned (i.e., met Kirkpatrick's levels two or three evaluations), had no effect on their level one ratings of the program. Further, even trainees who believed the program was badly handled were still equally likely to give it a good level one evaluation.

As was discussed in Chapter 6, very little relationship exists among the four levels of traditional evaluation. Regardless of how the program assessment is framed and structured, its purpose is to answer the question, "Could the training have been done better, faster, or cheaper and achieved equal or better results?" As businesses are increasingly reluctant to support activities that can't prove that they are worth their cost, trainers and training departments need to develop better ways to justify their own existence. Still, it is perhaps surprising that ASTD reported in 2003 that only 11% of courses offered by companies in their "training investment leaders" category were evaluated at Kirkpatrick's level four (and much less for other organizations).[3]

The practice of training assessment

What specific steps should be followed in design of a training program assessment?

First, make sure everyone is clear on exactly what training program is to be assessed and why. Who wants to know, and what do they want to know? This information influences decisions about how to design the assessment, what sorts of questions might be included, and where the information to answer those questions is gathered.

Next, use that information to create a specific list of questions and search out what data are available to respond to those questions. Who has this data and how can it be collected? What biases might be inherent in the data, and how can they be compensated or minimized?

Finally, once the data has been gathered, compare it to the original expectations of the training program and note any discrepancies. Is there an identifiable reason for these differences? Although quantitative data is often most prized by managers and other decision makers, one should not discount some qualitative data, as well. Even the current leaders in the field of training measurement acknowledge that it is often necessary to accept evidence, rather than proof.

These steps are summarized in the figure below.

Box 12-1   The Assessment Process

Planning:
1. Which program is to be assessed?
2. Why is the program being assessed?
3. Who is interested in the assessment?
4. What specific questions should be asked, based on the original program goals, standards, and implementation?
5. What data can be collected to illuminate these questions?
6. What tools are necessary to collect that data?

Implementation:
1. Collect the data
2. Analyze it in comparison to the original standards
3. Document (and explain where possible) any discrepancies
4. Summarize both the objective and subjective results of the analysis
5. Present the summary to the interested parties

Which program is to be assessed? Not every training program needs to be assessed. To begin with, not all training programs are designed with level three or four objectives; some, such as safety training, teambuilding, orientation, sexual harassment, and so on, can even be created with only level one (attitude or awareness) objectives. This fact is, of course, part of the reason that a much smaller percentage of programs is evaluated at the higher levels. A program that contains no level four objectives can't be evaluated at level four.

But don't all training programs in some way hope to affect the bottom line of an organization? Most do, but sometimes this relationship is so tenuous that any measurement would be specious. If a program is not going to be repeated, there may be very little practical use for the data that would come from an assessment. If a training program serves only a few people a year, or is only a couple hours in duration, it might not be worth the time and effort that a good assessment would require. That leads to the next question:

Why is the program being assessed? Usually it's because it is an ongoing high volume, high visibility, or high cost training program. If there have been problems with the program, an assessment is appropriate to see about correcting them. A change in the way the organization uses the knowledge and skills taught in the program could be another reason. Sometimes the organization or outside agencies require annual or other time-based assessments. A good question for the analyst to ask is, "What will be done with the program based on the outcome of the assessment?" If the answer is nothing, don't do it.

Who is interested in the assessment? The answer to this question can suggest a number of things, including how formal the assessment should be. Typically, the trainers and their supervisors are first on the list. Managers of the trainees also will want the information, as may any number of other decision makers in the organization. Finally, if the organization is subject to any outside private or governmental oversight agencies, there can be additional considerations. Examples of the latter might be if the company has ISO certifications, accreditation requirements (such as in hospitals, nursing homes, educational agencies, etc.), or any number of state and federal agencies that require training as part of their mission (Nuclear Regulatory Commission, Occupational Safety and Health Administration, Federal Aviation Administration, etc.).

What specific questions should be asked, given the original program goals, standards, and implementation? Some of the answer to this question will be based on the responses to the previous questions. In general, most assessments want to know if the trainees are satisfactorily performing in the jobs for which they were trained. Further, such issues as completion rates of the training, turnover of employees following training, differences between trained and untrained employees, amount of OJT needed following formal classroom training, and many other questions may be appropriate. A more emotional and less quantitative issue is how trainees felt as a result of the training. Did people finish the training with a feeling of satisfaction or relief? Was the process too fast or too slow to be comfortable? (Remember that individuals learn at different rates.) Do they feel they were treated fairly? Now that they've been on the job, what was included in the training that seems to have been superfluous? Was anything not treated thoroughly enough? Can the former trainees or their supervisors suggest any improvements?

What data can be collected to illuminate these questions? Certain productivity data is perhaps easiest to collect, especially where it exists for both before and after training, or where trained and non-trained employees are performing the same job. Hundreds of types of data could apply depending on the job of the trainees, so a complete list is impossible. Appropriate types of data would include turnover, scrap, time per unit produced, commissions, customer complaints, and other quantifiable items. If no specific records exist, can a reliable estimate be made? Always look for the most credible sources of any estimates. Attitude surveys can also provide some useable data, albeit subjective rather than objective. How has morale been affected because of training? How confident do people feel about their jobs? What is the employees' opinion of the organization? What is the opinion of the training department?

What tools are necessary to collect that data? The list of tools is essentially the same as was listed in Chapter 3. Any of the nine categories suggested by Steadham may apply. As already indicated, though, some of these categories might require professional expertise that is beyond the skill of the typical trainer. If outside experts such as auditors, industrial engineers, researchers, and so on are needed, the trainer should work with them early on as the questions are being formulated.

What steps are necessary in the implementation stage of a training assessment?

How should we go about collecting the data? As with most data collection, there will be a tradeoff between level of detail and ease or speed of collection. Begin with data that is already available in existing reports (in research terms, this type of information is called *secondary data*). Besides being the easiest to collect, it usually has the advantage of already established credibility. If it's necessary to collect additional information in a new form (called *primary data*), always try to do it in the least intrusive manner. For example, observations and work samples are less intrusive than interviews and tests, if they will give adequate data. Finally, if various sources of data conflict in ways that can't be easily resolved, opt for the more conservative data.

What does the analysis tell us about the training when compared to the original standards and expectations? What skill or knowledge outcomes were expected as a result of the training? Did these outcomes occur? What departmental or organizational level changes were expected as a result of training? Have these changes occurred?

Are there any discrepancies that must be documented and explained? If the training did not meet the expected goals, why not? Did the trainees meet level one, two, and three objectives during the training? If so, the training might not be the problem, but transfer of training to the job. Other possible causes of discrepancies include ineffective hiring or selection of trainees. Perhaps they don't have the intellectual or emotional or physical ability to perform on the job. (See the opening quote for Chapter 3.) Perhaps the job was not effectively analyzed or has changed in regard to technology, worker approach, market or customer requirements, or in some other fashion since the analysis. If, however, workers with the appropriate aptitudes did not emerge from the training with the expected skills or knowledge, then the training design or implementation must be questioned.

What can be done to summarize both the objective and subjective results of the analysis? The case is most clear when something close to a scientific research model can be used, with pre-training and post-training data, control groups, limits on potential outside influences such as changes in market, equipment, and so on. Such circumstances are a rare occurrence in the real world. It is usually necessary settle for evidence rather than proof. From a management decision maker's perspective, a training assessment should answer the question of whether the value received from the training was worth the cost of the training. Although not everything related to training can be reduced to a dollar amount, much of it can. Tally up the wages of the trainees and the trainer during the program, add in the cost of materials used and facilities and any travel or related costs, estimate the cost per program of developing the training. If it's a one-time training, use the full cost, both fixed and variable; otherwise, divide it by the number of expected offerings.

There might be other opportunity costs and so forth that a financial specialist could reasonably estimate. Once the cost is known, calculate how much the training has saved (or will save) the organization. Savings include reductions in scrap, employee turnover, accidents, lost sales, and other such measures when performance of the trained employees is compared to that of untrained employees who have not gone through the program being assessed. The savings divided by the cost should be more than 1.00. If it's only 1.00, that means the company broke even. Jack Phillips documents numbers of well over 1,000 in his work, meaning the training was repaid by savings of over 1,000 times as much as the training cost.[4]

What is the best way to present the summary to the interested parties? The answer to this question is largely dependent on the first question asked in this process: who is interested? Outside agencies such as accrediting bodies, state and Federal regulatory offices, and so on, will probably impose their own required formats. If a large number of program evaluations are being done, an organization should consider developing a standardized report form. The content and level of formality will ultimately be determined by the relationship between the training staff (or outside analysts) and the individuals or departments that receive the report. In most cases, some form of written report is probably appropriate. If changes are recommended, the suggestions in Chapter 4 can provide a structure for making the proposal.

What other questions and issues should be considered?

Should the assessment be done internally by training staff or other in-house specialists, or should outside expertise be brought in? Two major issues will affect this decision: availability and credibility.

First, are there individuals available within the organization to adequately handle an assessment on the scale being proposed? Most trainers have skills in dealing with Kirkpatrick's levels two and three, but it takes more depth of understanding to effectively handle levels one and four. Level one (attitude or awareness) requires understanding the subtleties of questionnaire design and analysis. Level four (job behavior) may require a mix of skills including financial, market analysis, industrial engineering, statistical, and other higher order talents that are not part of the typical trainer's repertoire. Even designing the study and collecting the data is a specialized expertise.

The second question, that of credibility, is equally important. There has been much in the news in recent years regarding corporate auditors who choose to overlook questionable accounting practices. At some level, most organizations have concerns when the people responsible for an activity are the ones who evaluate that activity. Certainly management should encourage employees to analyze their own work and suggest improvements on a routine basis. However, when this analysis has implications beyond the immediate individual's job, concern appropriately arises about possible bias in the report. If not an intentional bias, at least management should be aware that sometimes people don't want to look too hard to expose their own faults. There is no universal answer to this issue. Hiring an outside analyst to do training assessments will be expensive, both in time and money. Decision makers in the organization must determine whether the increased objectivity is worth the cost.

Whether the organization uses internal or external analysts to undertake the assessment, an excellent list of questions to ask as part of the process is suggested by Rob Brinkerhoff. The answers to the questions posed by Brinkerhoff, and the structure and context proposed by the American Association for Higher Education, described earlier in this chapter, will take the trainer and others in the organization well along the way to understanding the efficiency and effectiveness of any training program. An example of an assessment process is illustrated in Figure 12-1. It follows the format of questions posed earlier in this chapter.

Box 12-2   Brinkerhoff's Guiding Evaluation Questions[5]

Phase 1—Formulating Training Goals that are Linked to Business Needs
- Are training goals linked to business needs?
- Are learning objectives clear and specific?
- Are clear and specific job performance behaviors linked to each learning objective?
- Are business goals clearly and specifically linked to desired job performance behaviors?
- How important are the business needs to which the training is linked?
- Do the business needs justify the training investment that is likely to be made?
- Can training make a substantial impact on the desired job behavior, or are learning results likely to be overcome by negative systemic factors?
- Is training really necessary? Or could some other, cheaper, intervention be more effective (job aids, or incentives, for instance)?

Phase 2—Planning Training Strategies
- Does the training strategy adequately define necessary "before" and "after" management, supervisory and trainee preparation behaviors, and other critical factors?
- Does the training strategy aim to deliver training as close to the workplace as possible?
- Does the training strategy provide for just-in-time, just-enough learning to optimally impact performance?
- Does the training strategy provide for the least possible disruption of production and other critical activities?
- Are trainee selection procedures likely to get the right, and only the right, people into training?
- Does the training strategy provide for sufficient job aids and other post learning support activities?
- Is the learning design likely to produce the intended level of competence?
- Does the learning design provide for sufficient feedback and practice to assure mastery of the learning objectives?

Box 12-2 Brinkerhoff's Guiding Evaluation Questions[5]
(Continued)

- Is there sufficient high and mid-level commitment to the training and for providing the necessary after learning support?

Phase 3—Producing and Assessing Learning Results
- Are all critical elements of the training strategy (selection, delivery of the pre learning materials, etc.) taking place effectively and on time?
- Are learners clearly informed of and committed to the training they are receiving?
- Do learners understand and agree with the need to change their post-learning job performance as desired?
- Do learners understand and agree with the job objectives and business goals that are linked to the training they are receiving?
- Are learners receiving timely and accurate feedback about how well they are learning?
- How completely have learners mastered intended skills and knowledge?
- Are training leaders receiving timely and accurate feedback from learners about their issues, concerns, need for help, and perceived strengths and weaknesses of the training?
- Are trainee supervisors and other key stakeholders being kept appropriately informed about the progress of learning activities?

Phase 4—Supporting Learning Results so They are Sustained and Effectively Used
- To what extent are trainees correctly using new learning in their jobs?
- What factors are facilitating and supporting usage?
- What factors are blocking usage?
- To what extent are the supervisors providing the support and coaching needed to improve usage?
- Which trainees are making the best usage of their new learning? How? Why?
- Which trainees are making the least effective usage? What about their usage is least effective? Why?
- To what extent are the business needs that drove training being positively impacted?

Source: Brinkerhoff, R. 1995 "Using Evaluation to Improve the Quality of Technical Training" in The ASTD Technical and Skills Training Handbook, L. Kelly, ed., McGraw-Hill: New York pp. 399–400. Used by permission of the McGraw-Hill Companies.

Figure 12-1   Example Assessment Plan (using the format recommended in this chapter)

Planning:
- *Which program is to be assessed?*
  - Staff Sales Basics. This is a three day program required of all new retail associates before they can sell on their own.
  - The program was started about six months ago. Seventy-five trainees have gone through it since then, of whom 49 still work for us.
  - The original goals were that turnover would be reduced by 10%, and that sales per associate would be increased by 10% based on the training program.
  - Why is the program being assessed?
  - Sales records suggest that performance differs very little between new hires who have taken the program and long-term employees who have not because they were hired before the program was instituted.
- *Who is interested in the assessment?*
  - Operations director Alice Franks and Senior Trainer Tom Petry.
- *What specific questions should be asked, based on the original program objectives (standards) and implementation?*
  - Is the turnover among sales associates who have gone through the training different than for persons hired before six months ago? How?
  - Is the performance (unit sales) among trained associates different from performance in the untrained group? If so, is it influenced by other factors such as shift or department assignments, repeat customers who may request prior sales persons, changes in the market, and so on?
  - What is the attitude of the associates toward training, now that they're on the job? Is it different between the early groups and the later groups? Do the floor managers see any differences, and how do they validate that?
- *What data can be collected to illuminate these questions?*
  - Human Resources can check on turnover data.
  - Order entry and accounting can provide by-sales-associate reports for comparison. Alice has necessary data to compare shift and departmental issues.
  - Follow-up level one surveys on the training have been designed and will be distributed and collected for analysis by a professor of marketing from the local college. The same individual will conduct a focus group with several floor managers.

Figure 12-1 Example Assessment Plan (using the format recommended in this chapter) (*Continued*)

- A secret shopper will be trained to understand the process taught in the program, then will randomly approach ten of the newer salespeople to see if they are following the procedures as trained.
- *What tools are necessary to collect that data?*
  - (From Steadham's list): Records and reports, interviews, observations, questionnaires, and group discussion.

Implementation:
- *Collect the data*
  - The secret shopper is being trained this week and the level one surveys will be distributed by mail to associates' homes next week. The floor manager focus group will be held while we await the return of the surveys.
  - HR and Accounting will have their reports by the end of the month.
- *Analyze it in comparison to the original standards*
  - The above questions will be analyzed using the data collected to determine whether a difference exists between pre- and post-training hires in turnover or unit sales per associate.
- *Document (and explain where possible) any discrepancies*
  - Specific turnover and sales data will be compared.
  - The attitude surveys and focus group data will be analyzed by the consultant (professor) for any suggestions that might be helpful in decision making about the Staff Sales Basics training.
- *Summarize both the objective and subjective results of the analysis*
  - A report will be prepared by the end of this quarter. In the meantime, no additional offerings of the Staff Sales Basics class will be scheduled. (One is being held this week and another in three weeks. Further classes will await the results of this analysis.)
- *Present the summary to the interested parties*
  - Alice and Tom will review the data and present it to the trainers involved in this program to obtain their reaction and comments. A subsequent report will be forwarded to the executive staff for a decision on any changes or action regarding the class.

13 The Future of Training

"Map out your future, but do it in pencil."
—*Jon Bon Jovi quoted in* Reader's Digest

"I had hoped, vainly it turned out, that by talking to enough people I could discern some coherent picture of where the profession, if it is a profession, is headed."
—*Pat Galagan in* T+D magazine

The professional trainer stays aware of trends and considers appropriate responses to developments that may affect the organization, the industry, the training profession, and the culture as a whole. The business of training is changing, right along with the rest of the jobs in today's world, and constant adaptations can be required. "Be prepared" is more than just a scout motto; it's essential to long term survival.

■　■　■

The December 2003 issue of *T + D* magazine ran a cover story titled "The Future of the Profession Formerly Known as Training."[1] In it, the author asks if the field is about to kill off its brand equity [i.e., being known as "Training" for over 60 years] just as it begins to acquire some? A potential change in name for the business of training is just one of many things that may—or may not—happen in the next few years.

Where is the business of training headed?

In many ways, the business of training is headed the same direction as businesses of other kinds. It will be more international and employ increasing amounts of technology. There will be increased fragmentation within the ranks of the training business resulting in the need for more partnerships and outsourcing, as well as for decentralization of the training function. Productivity and quality issues will become more important, resulting in—among other things—an increased emphasis on level two, three, and four measures. The importance of training to most organizations will grow, as we already have seen with the implementation of the title of Chief Learning Officer as a major corporate business function in a number of well-known companies. As business strives to do more with less, the human factor must become more flexible, and people are the only "economic factor of production" that cannot be easily copied and mechanized. The premiere way to actively develop the people who work for an organization is through training.

The multitude of changes listed above will require much more and better training of trainers in the future. Not all trainers in the future will be standing in front of live classes—many already aren't—but the need for employees, customers, clients, and other trainees to learn facts, concepts, and procedures will continue to expand as long as society exists.

What are some of the causes and effects of internationalizing training?

The American Society for Training and Development changed its name several years ago to simply "ASTD," building on a market recognition study and the fact that the *A* for American was no longer representative of the organization's inclusiveness. At the 1999 ASTD international conference leading up to that name change decision, for example, over 30% of the registrants were from outside the United States. Training is a universal concept, and—as mentioned in Chapter 1—many countries spend proportionately more on it than the United States does.

News media almost daily seem to carry stories of jobs being "offshored," and not just the low level drudge jobs of manufacturing. Quite sophisticated jobs are now being done in regions and countries where most observers would not have expected them to be only a couple of years ago. Such jobs as computer programming, customer service, and product design and engineering are being done successfully by U.S. and other nations' corporations in what most Americans would consider third-world countries. In a recent keynote address to ASTD at its international conference and exposition,[2] Dr. Lester Thurow, author, economist, and former Dean of Business at MIT, pointed out that as we move from a national economy to a global economy, untrained people no longer get the economic benefit of living in a rich nation. If they don't have higher level skills, they may live in a first-world country but can only earn a third-world wage. Likewise, skilled persons in third-world countries—at least those countries stable enough to attract major business operations—can earn the equivalent of a first-world wage.

Most of the jobs sent from the U.S. to other countries go because of lower wages for persons who can perform them, fewer environmental restrictions, and in some cases, different work ethics. Other important reasons for globalizing include the need to operate where the customers are, to meet or take advantage of local content laws and resources, to be open for business across multiple time zones, and to accommodate cultural dynamics. Trainers, perhaps more so than other business professionals, will need to understand and reconcile the cultural differences. Chapter 8 explained that it's not good practice to take an existing training program and simply automate it; likewise, taking a training program designed for U.S. employees and simply changing the language in which it is presented is not good practice. Cultural differences of all kinds need to be considered, including such mundane things as the choice of colors used in presentations, religious and cultural references, and even delivery methods.

Among the effects of internationalizing training are a need for more translation services (both written and oral), perhaps more travel requirements for trainers, though that will be balanced with increases in distance learning, and an increased need to focus on cultural differences for both soft skills content and all kinds of training delivery. For technical training topics (e.g., how to install and maintain an electronic control component), there can be more need to use technology-based training. This kind of training reduces travel costs and standardizes the delivery, but still requires effective translation and consideration of any culture differences that would affect the training.

How can trainers cope with constant change in an organization?

The opening quote from Alvin Toffler used in Chapter 8 summarizes this whole area of change quite succinctly: *"The illiterate of the twenty-first century will be those who can not learn, unlearn, and relearn."* Raymond Noe[3] recommends viewing the entire field of training from a change model perspective. He suggests a process that uses the trainer as a change agent. Chapter 1 of this book noted that one of the competencies for a trainer is to facilitate change, and later that a collaboration with organizational development (OD) professionals who specialize in helping implement change is often a good idea for trainers.

Another important skill that trainers will need to develop and hone in the future is how to take the overwhelming and ever increasing amount of data to which we are subjected, sort it out, and turn it into information. Data is facts that have no particular context, like the television sports reporter who (a bit under the influence) announced, "And now for today's scores, ladies and gentlemen. Twenty-six to ten, fourteen to nine, and in a real surprise, sixty to forty-one." That's data. To make it information, you need to also know the teams that were playing and which sport. The basic process of keeping track of things in an organized way is becoming more important and increasingly poorly done. Trainers have always needed to organize facts, procedures, and concepts into appropriate training plans, but the proliferation and sometimes random nature of data with which we need to interact puts a new face on this challenge.

What kind of changes present the biggest challenge to the trainer? Some of the key ones include when, where, and how people will work, constant upgrades in the technology of the job, more diversity in the tasks and skills expected of a trainer, and the already discussed internationalization issue.

A well-established trend, even among domestic and local-only companies, is a significant increase in *virtual work arrangements* for employees. Virtual work arrangements refers to the option to work electronically from other locations than an office or plant (such as from home or the beach) through the use of technologies such as e-mail, voicemail, fax machines, Internet connections, courier services, and so on. Sometimes the term is also used to incorporate other alternative work arrangements such as flex-time, job sharing, and so on. These options become a challenge to training in its traditional form, and are likely to increase the incidence of both technology-based training and the general fragmentation of the way in which training departments accomplish their responsibilities. Trainers will have to deal with more virtual work arrangements in the future, including providing training on both (a) how to do the jobs and (b) how to work independently from home or as one-person office locations.

Professional trainers who teach technology skills (such as how to install and use new software) face a double challenge. Their subject matter content is always changing, as well as their presentation methods. Others, who deal strictly with soft (interpersonal) skills in traditional classroom environments, might not be challenged quite as much. They are more likely to just deal with changes in presentation technology, though CBT is making inroads into the soft skills area, as well.

Most people who have been around computers long enough to move from a DOS environment to early Windows® versions such as 3.1, through Windows 95, 98, XP, and so on, would not be willing to go back. Though the process of learning the new technology may have been slow and occasionally painful, the end result is being able to do more, faster, and more conveniently. It's human nature to not like any change that doesn't jingle in our pockets. But, change is inevitable and constant, so people and organizations must go through a continuous training and learning process.

A recent survey asked practitioners which names should be used for the training profession.[4] The most popular among the over 1,300 respondents was "Workplace Learning and Performance." This title suggests a broader level of influence for the field than simply "training." The International Society for Performance Improvement—as the name would suggest—has long espoused a multi-faceted approach to workforce improvement. How can trainers cope with the expanded responsibilities and organizational chaos that comes from these changes? Part of the answer is in understanding the nature of change itself.

Organizations resist changes for many of the same reasons as individuals:

- *Change requires effort.* One has to unlearn and relearn ways of doing things (which is why training is a key element in implementing change).
- *Satisfaction with the status quo.* If people see no problems with the present situation, there's no need to change.
- *Fear of the unknown.* Even when one doesn't like things as they are, there's the feeling that a change might make them worse. Change upsets established patterns and relationships.

Additionally, organizations (as opposed to individuals) tend to have an even greater inherent inertia. Inertia is the concept in physics that says that any object at rest will stay at rest and any object in motion will stay in motion in a straight line, unless acted upon by an outside force. The larger the organization, the more force is required to change it from its present path. It has also been said that change triggers an organization's immune system: many organizational elements just naturally conspire to prevent change from happening.

In general, changes will be more easily accepted if they are as small as possible, presented and explained simply and clearly, based on a need, supported by key individuals, and open to discussion. Managers in an organization can encourage acceptance of changes by clearly explaining the reason for the change. They also need to encourage and reward involvement, deal with the "me" issues for their employees, and over-communicate and overtrain. Their employees are most concerned with how a change affects them, so that effect should be explained in detail. Most managers believe they have told the employees more than the employees think they have been told. Finally, managers should expect and plan for resistance to change (it will happen), but try to do so without creating a bureaucracy.

Why is more fragmentation expected in the training field?

Trainers in the future will have to function in a more diverse and disconnected manner for many reasons. Two have already been mentioned: the job of training will require more diverse skills, and fewer people will be on-site for training programs. Another issue is that training departments will be required to form more partnerships with external sources.

Training departments will find an increasing need to collaborate with vendors and external subject matter specialists as the level of sophistication of workers increases. Few, if any, training departments will be able to handle the training content needs of a broad-based organization. Also, as the international nature of the employee base increases, companies will be forced to rely on technology-based training, or decentralized operations to meet the needs of a dispersed workforce.

As part of the 2004 campaign for re-election, President George W. Bush, as well as his opponent, Senator John Kerry, both were pushing an agenda of better training for workers, and both spoke highly of the community college structure as a means to do that. In truth, the quality and capacity of community colleges varies dramatically among states, and even within states. Nevertheless, they have been fairly quietly serving in this role for nearly four decades. The baccalaureate schools, and particularly the graduate schools such as Harvard, Wharton, Wisconsin, Penn State, and many others, have also been training the top managers of the business world in their executive programs. Businesses have been paying for their up and coming managers to go to these institutes for years. Likewise, thousands and thousands of businesses have developed tuition refund programs as a part of their employee benefits programs, and these have paid for not only four year degrees, but for associate degrees, certificates, and even individual courses at all kinds of institutions of higher learning. Many of these programs actually do focus more on training, rather than education, and many are quite willing to develop customized training for companies and industries.

The *Training* magazine 2004 Industry Report found that the percentage of training conducted internally but either designed or delivered by external agencies is increasing, and accounted for well over a quarter of all the non-OJT training.[5] Besides the universities and community colleges, who else is partnering with business and industry to meet their training needs? Various industry organizations have long contributed to the training requirements of their member organizations. The American Banking Association, for example, used to do a large part of all the formal non-OJT training done in the banking industry. Today, as banks have merged and grown and generally become much larger, many individual banks have developed their own internal training. But many, if not most, industries have gone the opposite direction, with individual companies becoming smaller, and thus needing the help of independent trainers, consultants, professional and trade associations, and a multitude of other sources. Increasingly, the membership in such organizations as ASTD has become a higher proportion of independent contractors and less of internal trainers.

With smaller organizations, fewer people are required to do any one job within the company. Trainers, therefore, have fewer potential trainees in any topic yet still have a wide range of topics that must be covered. This situation leads to a natural reliance on people who are good trainers in a specialized area who can serve several companies. It also leads to more supervisors and peer leaders being asked to take on the role of trainer in the organization. The natural result of this evolution is an increase in training partnerships. Concurrently, with the increase in technology-based training, companies such as ToolingU (mentioned in Chapter 8) and hundreds of others are preparing training that meets the needs of hundreds of organizations and thousands of employees, customers, and clients through on-line training classes in various forms. The colleges and community colleges are seeing a big movement in the direction of on-line courses, as well.

How can productivity and quality be improved in training?

Sam Adkins says, "In treating training like the business process its practitioners have wanted it to be, these [outsourcing] companies— Accenture, IBM, Deloitte Consulting, and others—are exposing what's productive and what isn't. Instructional design, for example, shows up under this scrutiny as a bottleneck, and trainers' salaries are viewed as expenses with little connection to results."[6] Wow!

Certainly one of the long term issues in the field has been that training has not treated itself like a business.[7] Training departments in the past have often not been required to justify their existence. Results in training are far less measured than results in academia. Kirkpatrick's level four measures (i.e., has the training made a difference to the organization's bottom line?) occur in single digit percentages of training situations.[8] Among the most popular topics at recent national training conferences, such as those put on by ASTD or *Training* magazine, is **ROI** (return on investment). As discussed in Chapter 12, recent work by Jack Phillips, Rob Brinkerhoff, and others is suggesting new and improved ways to document the value of training.

Accountability will be a new watchword, according to Goldstein and Ford. "The amount of emphasis concerning evaluation methodology, including information about criterion development, evaluation designs, values, and ethics, and problems with performance evaluations in organizations has exploded."[9] They discuss an increasing emphasis on benchmarking best practices, something well-established in ASTD's recent annual reports. The professional trainer will need to develop more skills in this area.

Will the role of trainer have more status in the future?

Wexley and Latham[10] say, "If training is to become respected as a science of behavior, we cannot retreat from the crucial task of specifying what it is that employees are supposed to learn." They continue, recommending four areas in which we need better research and understanding: (1) differences among trainees that require the use of different training techniques; (2) how different organizational variables affect training efforts; (3) the usefulness of different training techniques; and (4) how to create the culture of a learning organization. Although this book has touched on these topics, the reader is encouraged to investigate further by reading some of the books referenced in the bibliography, as well as using the Internet. (See the website listing at the end of Chapter 1.)

Trainers will not gain status by continuing the status quo. The era of "Those who can, do, while those who can't, teach," is long past. The increasing importance of the training field in helping organizations deal with changes has led to more research and professionalism in the field. Wexley and Latham go on to say that we don't know enough. Training is a complex field. In the sixty plus years since ASTD was founded, we have developed some structure and processes as shown by the detail in this book, yet there is still far to go.

Epilogue

Where do you go from here?

That's up to you. This book has covered the basics of the training process. It started with information about the field of training and the typical organizational environment in which training happens. Next, it covered the topics of adult learning, determining individual and organizational training needs, gaining management support for training, writing objectives, and planning for the evaluation of learning. Then it presented a number of questions to ask when deciding on techniques to use for the training and considering facilities and media support that might be needed. Finally, it dealt with writing effective lesson plans, and how to ensure that the training is working as effectively as possible. That's a lot of topics!

Even so, the key word in the above paragraph is *basics*. Any of these chapters could have been expanded to a complete book in itself, and—in fact—the references often suggest complete books on topics that were covered in only a page or two in this book. Training is obviously a complex field with many competencies required to do it well. And, in addition to knowing all this detail about how to train, it's generally expected that the trainer also needs to be a subject matter expert, as well!

The opening quote for Chapter 7 says, "We have a propensity to learn. We also have a propensity to teach." People who train others find themselves learning all the time. This is one of the most exciting and challenging aspects of being a professional trainer.

I wish you the best in this exciting, ever-changing, and complex career, and good luck in fulfillment of your personal and career goals.

Notes

Chapter 1

1. Based on the ASTD 2004 Competency Study. www.mymodel.astd.org.

2. Bernthal, P.R., *et al. The ASTD 2004 Competency Study: Mapping the Future.* Washington DC: ASTD Press.

3. The 1997 ASTD Leadership Conference report stressed that *trainers should spend their time on the activities that create the most value for businesses.* It was based on data from a book by The Forum Corporation entitled "The Customer-Driven Training Organization."

4. *Ibid.*

5. Industry Report 2004, *Training Magazine,* October 2004, p. 24.

6. Marquardt, M.J., *et al.* 2002. International Comparisons: ASTD's Annual Accounting of Worldwide Patterns in Employer Provided Training. Washington, DC: ASTD.

7. Carnevale, A. Statement made in 1999 ASTD produced video titled "Train America's Workforce."

8. Sugrue, B. *2003 State of the Industry.* Washington, DC: ASTD p. 12.

9. Industry Report 2004, *Training Magazine,* October 2004, 22–36.

10. *Ibid.*

11. Bassi, L.J., and McMurrer, D.P. 1998. Training Investment Can Mean Financial Performance. *Training & Development,* 52, no. 5: 40–42.

12. Schein, E. *Organizational Culture and Leadership.* 1985. San Francisco: Jossey-Bass Inc. and other references.

13. Such organizations as The OD Connection and the Organizational Development Institute can provide further information.

Chapter 2

1. Goldstein, I.L. 1993. *Training in Organizations* 3rd ed: Pacific Grove, CA: Brooks/Cole Publishing.

2. Kolb, D.A., and Boyatzis, R.E. 1991. Assessing Individuality in Learning: The Learning Skills Profile. *Educational Psychology: An International Journal of Experimental Educational Psychology* 11, no. 3–4: 279–295.

3. Gagné, R.M., *et al.* 1988. *Principles of Instructional Design,* 3rd ed. New York: Holt, Rinehart and Winston, Inc.

4. See www.Langevin.com.

5. Blanchard, P.N., and Thacker, J.W. 1999. *Effective Training: Systems, Strategies, and Practices*. Upper Saddle River, New Jersey: Prentice-Hall.

6. Stolovitch, H.D., and Keeps, E.J. 2002. *Telling Ain't Training*. Alexandria, Virginia: American Society for Training & Development.

7. Knowles, M., and Hartl, D.E. 1995. The Adult Learner in the Technical Environment. In *The ASTD Technical and Skills Training Handbook*, ed. L. Kelly. New York: McGraw-Hill, Inc.

8. Snelbecker, G.E. 1993. Practical Ways for Using Theories and Innovations to Improve Training. In *The ASTD Handbook of Instructional Technology*, ed. G.M Piskurich. New York: McGraw-Hill, Inc.

9. Chang, R. 1990. *Creating High-IMPACT Training*. Irvine, CA: Richard D. Chang Associates, Inc., Publications.

10. Laird, D. 1985. *Approaches to Training and Development*, 2nd ed. Reading, Massachusetts: Addison-Wesley.

11. Thiagarajan, S. 1993. Just-In-Time Instructional Design. In *The ASTD Handbook of Instructional Technology*, ed. G.M Piskurich. New York: McGraw-Hill, Inc.

Chapter 3

1. *Source:* Paraphrased from Steadham, S.V. 1980. Learning to Select a Needs Assessment Strategy. *Training and Development Journal* 30 (January 1980).

2. For further information, see www.siop.org or follow links from other references cited at the end of Chapter 1.

Chapter 5

1. Kroehnert, G. 1995. *Basic Training for Trainers,* 2nd ed. Sydney: McGraw-Hill, Inc.

2. Mager, R. 1997. *Preparing Instructional Objectives*. Atlanta, GA: Center for Effective Performance.

3. Bloom, B., ed. 1984. *Taxonomy of Educational Objectives, Handbook I: Cognitive Domain*. Reading, MA: Addison-Wesley. Also, Bloom, B., ed. 1984. *Taxonomy of Educational Objectives, Handbook II:Affective Domain*. Reading, MA: Addison-Wesley.

4. Laird, D. 1985. *Approaches to Training and Development*, 2nd ed. Reading, Massachusetts: Addison-Wesley.

5. Dave, R. 1967. *Psychomotor domain*. Berlin: International Conference of Educational Testing.

6. Simpson, E. 1972. *The Classification of Educational Objectives in the Psychomotor Domain: The Psychomotor Domain*. Vol. 3, Washington, D.C.: Gryphon House.

7. Harrow, A. 1972. *A Taxonomy of the Psychomotor Domain. A guide for developing behavioral objectives*. New York: D. McKay Co.

8. Shapiro, L.T. 1995. *Training Effectiveness Handbook*. New York: McGraw-Hill, Inc.

Chapter 6

1. Based on a comparison of the ASTD 2001 & 2002 State of the Industry Reports.

2. Kirkpatrick, D. 1996. "Great Ideas Revisited: Revisiting Kirkpatrick's Four-level Model." *Training and Development Journal* 50:1 pp. 54–57.

3. Phillips, Jack J. 1998. *Handbook of Training Evaluation and Measurement Methods* 3rd ed. Houston, TX: Gulf Publishing.

4. Sugrue, B. *2003 State of the Industry Report.* ASTD, p. 18.

5. A *Likert scale* is a rating system such as 1 to 5, with 5 defined as "excellent," 1 as "terrible," etc. It's named for Rensis Likert, who popularized its use.

6. Mager, RF. 1997. *Making Instruction Work,* 2nd Edition. Atlanta, Georgia: Center for Effective Performance.

7. Sugrue, B. *2003 State of the Industry Report.* ASTD, p. 18.

8. Brinkerhoff, R. 1995. Using Evaluation to Improve the Quality of Technical Training. In *The ASTD Technical and Skills Training Handbook,* ed. L. Kelly. New York: McGraw-Hill, Inc.

9. Donaldson, L., and Scannell, E. 1986. *Human Resource Development: The New Trainer's Guide,* 2nd ed. Reading, MA: Addison-Wesley Publishing.

10. Glaser, E.M. 1976. *Productivity Gains Through Worklife Improvements.* New York: Harcourt, Brace, Jovanovich.

11. Phillips, J.J. 1997. *Return on Investment in Training and Performance Improvement Programs.* Houston, TX: Gulf Publishing.

12. Vaughn, R.H. 2001. Sad, but true: "The Big Bird Syndrome" in Training. *Excellence in Teaching Newsletter* 2, no.1. pp. 2–3. Lakeland Community College, Ohio. (Based on doctoral dissertation.)

Chapter 7

1. A good selection can be found at www.trainerswarehouse.com.

2. For more information, check out this award-winning book: Rylatt, A., and Lohan, K. 1997. *Creating Training Miracles.* San Francisco: Pfeiffer. 68–78.

3. Noe, R.A. 2002. *Employee Training & Development–Second Edition.* New York: McGraw-Hill Higher Education.

Chapter 8

1. Galvin, T. 2002 Industry Report. *Training Magazine,* no. 39: 10–25.

2. Thompson, C., *et al.* 2002. *Training for the Next Economy: An ASTD State of the Industry Report on Trends in Employer-Provided Training in the United States.*

3. Moore, M., and Keasley, G. 1996. *Distance Education: A Systems View.* Belmont, CA: Wadsworth Publishing Co.

4. Koenig, A.E., and Hill, R.B. 1967. *The Farther Vision—Educational Television Today.* Madison, Wisconsin: University of Wisconsin Press.

5. Gagné, R.M., *et al.* 1992. *Principles of Instructional Design.* New York: Harcourt, Brace, Jovanovich College Publishing.

6. Clark, R.E. 1983. Reconsidering Research on Learning from Media. *Review of Educational Research* 53, no. 4: 445–459.

7. Bergeron, C. 1999. A model for estimating the development cost of e-learning models. Unpublished paper.

8. Galvin. *ibid.*

Chapter 9

1. Laird, D. 1985. *Approaches to Training and Development,* 2nd ed. Reading, Massachusetts: Addison-Wesley. 204.

Chapter 12

1. Liberally edited, based on *Principles of Good Practice for Assessing Student Learning,* (undated) sponsored by The American Association for Higher Education, and supported by the Fund for the Improvement of Postsecondary Education. Permission for use granted in the original text.

2. Vaughn, R.H. 2001. Sad, but true: "The Big Bird Syndrome" in Training. *Excellence in Teaching Newsletter* 2, no.1: 2–3. Lakeland Community College, Ohio. (Based on doctoral dissertation.)

3. Thompson, C., *et al.* 2002. *Training for the Next Economy: An ASTD State of the Industry Report on Trends in Employer-Provided Training in the United States.* p. 33.

4. Phillips, J.J. 1998. *Handbook of Training Evaluation and Measurement Methods,* 3rd ed. Houston, TX: Gulf Publishing.

5. Brinkerhoff, R. 1995. In *The ASTD Technical and Skills Training Handbook,* L. Kelly, ed., McGraw-Hill, Inc. New York.

Chapter 13

1. Galagan, P. 2003. The Future of the Profession Formerly Known as Training. *T + D* 57, no. 12: 26–38.

2. Thurow, L. Part of keynote presentation at May, 1999, ASTD International Conference and Exposition, Atlanta, GA.

3. Noe, R.A. 2002. *Employee Training & Development—Second Edition.* New York: McGraw-Hill Higher Education.

4. Galagan, P. 2003. The Future of the Profession Formerly Known as Training. *T + D* 57, no. 12: 29.

5. Industry Report. 2004. *Training Magazine,* October 2004.

6. Galagan, P. 2003. *Ibid.*

7. There's even a book on it: VanAdelsberg, D., and Trolley, E.A. 1999. *Running Training Like a Business: Delivering Unmistakable Value.* San Francisco: Berrett-Koehler.

8. Thompson, C., *et al.* 2002. *Training for the Next Economy: An ASTD State of the Industry Report on Trends in Employer-Provided Training in the United States.*

9. Goldstein, I.L., and Ford, J.K. 2002. *Training in Organizations,* 4th ed. Belmont, CA: Wadsworth Publishing Co.

10. Wexley, K., and Latham, G. 2002. Developing and Training Human Resources in Organizations, 3rd ed. Upper Saddle River, NJ: Prentice Hall.

References

Industry Report 2004, *Training Magazine,* October 2004, 22–36. http://www.trainingmag.com/training/reports_analysis/index.jsp

Bassi, L.J., and McMurrer, D.P. 1998. Training investment can mean financial performance. *Training & Development* 52, no. 5: 40–42.

Bergeron, C. 1999. A model for estimating the development cost of e-learning models. Unpublished paper.

Bernthal, P.R., *et al.* 2004. *The ASTD 2004 Competency Study: Mapping the Future.* Washington, DC: ASTD Press.

Biebel, M.G. 1995. Instructional Design Basics. In *The ASTD Technical and Skills Training Handbook,* ed. L. Kelly. New York: McGraw-Hill, Inc.

Blanchard, P.N., and Thacker, J.W. 1999. *Effective Training: Systems, Strategies, and Practices.* Upper Saddle River, New Jersey: Prentice-Hall, Inc.

Bloom, B., ed. 1984a. *Taxonomy of Educational Objectives, Handbook I: Cognitive Domain.* Reading, MA: Addison-Wesley.

Bloom, B., ed. 1984b. *Taxonomy of Educational Objectives, Handbook 2: Affective Domain.* Reading, MA: Addison-Wesley.

Brinkerhoff, R. 1995. Using Evaluation to Improve the Quality of Technical Training. *The ASTD Technical and Skills Training Handbook,* ed. L. Kelly. New York: McGraw-Hill, Inc.

Broad, M., and Newstrom, J.W. 1992. *Transfer of Training: Action Packed Strategies to Insure High Payoff from Training Investments.* Reading, MA: Addison-Wesley.

Carnevale, A.P., et al. 1990. *Workplace Basics Training Manual.* San Francisco, California: Jossey-Bass Inc.

Chance, P. 1995. The Technical Training Function: Growth of Technical Training Professionalism. In *The ASTD Technical and Skills Training Handbook,* ed. L. Kelly. New York: McGraw-Hill, Inc.

Chang, R. 1990. *Creating High-IMPACT Training.* Irvine, CA: Richard D. Chang Associates, Inc., Publications.

Charles, C.L., and Clarke-Epstein, C. 1998. *The Instant Trainer.* New York: McGraw-Hill, Inc.

Charney, C., and Conway, K. 1998. *The Trainer's Tool Kit.* New York: AMACOM.

Clark, R.E. 1983. Reconsidering Research on Learning from Media. *Review of Educational Research* 53, no. 4: 445–459.

Dave, R. 1967. *Psychomotor domain.* Berlin: International Conference of Educational Testing.

Davis, J.R., and Davis, A.B. 1998. *Effective Training Strategies.* San Francisco: Berrett-Koehler.

Donaldson, L., and Scannell, E. 1986. *Human Resource Development: The New Trainer's Guide,* 2nd ed. Reading, MA: Addison-Wesley Publishing.

Friedman, P.G., and Yarbrough, E.A. 1985. *Training Strategies from Start to Finish.* Englewood Cliffs, NJ: Prentice Hall, Inc.

Gagné, R., *et al.* 1992. *Principles of Instructional Design,* 4th ed. Fort Worth, TX: Harcourt, Brace, Jovanovich.

Glaser, E.M. 1976. *Productivity Gains Through Worklife Improvements.* New York: Harcourt, Brace, Jovanovich.

Goldstein, I.L. 1993. *Training in Organizations,* 3rd ed. Pacific Grove, CA: Brooks/Cole Publishing.

Goldstein, I.L., and Ford, J.K. 2002. *Training in Organizations,* 4th ed. Belmont, CA: Wadsworth Publishing Co.

Harrow, A. 1972. *A Taxonomy of the Psychomotor Domain. A Guide for Developing Behavioral Objectives.* New York: D. McKay Co.

Jacobs, R.L. 2003. *Structured On-the-Job Training: Unleashing Employee Expertise in the Workplace, 2nd Edition.* San Francisco: Berrett-Koehler.

Kelly, L., ed. 1995. *The ASTD Technical and Skills Training Handbook.* New York: McGraw-Hill, Inc.

Kirkpatrick, D. 1996. Great Ideas Revisited: Revisiting Kirkpatrick's Four-level Model. *Training and Development Journal* 50, no. 1: 54–57.

Kirkpatrick, D.L. 2004. *Evaluating Training Programs, 2nd Edition.* San Francisco: Berrett-Koehler.

Knowles, M., and Hartl, D.E. 1995. The Adult Learner in the Technical Environment. In *The ASTD Technical and Skills Training Handbook,* ed. L. Kelly. New York: McGraw-Hill, Inc.

Kolb, D.A., and Boyatzis, R.E. 1991. Assessing Individuality in Learning: The Learning Skills Profile. *Educational Psychology: An International Journal of Experimental Educational Psychology* 11, no. 3–4: 279–295.

Koenig, A.E., and Hill, R.B., eds. 1967. *The Farther Vision—Educational Television Today.* Madison, Wisconsin: University of Wisconsin Press.

Krempl, S.F., and Pace, R.W. 2001. *Training Across Multiple Locations: Developing a System that Works.* San Francisco: Berrett-Koehler.

Kroehnert, G. 1995. *Basic Training for Trainers,* 2nd ed. Sydney: McGraw-Hill, Inc.

Laird, D. 1985. *Approaches to Training and Development,* 2nd ed. Reading, Massachusetts: Addison-Wesley.

Leed, J., and Leed, K. 1993. Designing Training Rooms. In *The ASTD Handbook of Instructional Technology,* ed. G.M Piskurich. New York: McGraw-Hill, Inc.

Mager, R.F. 1997a. *Making Instruction Work,* 2nd ed. Atlanta, Georgia: Center for Effective Performance.

Mager, R. 1997b. *Preparing Instructional Objectives.* Atlanta, GA: Center for Effective Performance.

Mager, R. 1997c. *Measuring Instructional Results.* Atlanta, GA: Center for Effective Performance.

Marquardt, M.J., *et al.* 2002. *International Comparisons: ASTD's Annual Accounting of Worldwide Patterns in Employer Provided Training.* Washington, DC: ASTD.

Mellander, K. 1993. *The Power of Learning: Fostering Employee Growth.* Burr Ridge, IL: Irwin Professional Publishing.

Moore, M., and Keasley, G. 1996. *Distance Education: A Systems View.* Belmont, CA: Wadsworth Publishing Co.

Noe, R.A. 2002. *Employee Training & Development,* 2nd ed. New York: McGraw-Hill Higher Education.

O'Connor, B., et al. 1996. *Training for Organizations.* Cincinnati, OH: South-Western Educational Publishing.

Phillips, J.J. 1998. *Handbook of Training Evaluation and Measurement Methods,* 3rd ed. Houston, TX: Gulf Publishing.

Piskurich, G.M., ed. 1993. *The ASTD Handbook of Instructional Technology.* New York: McGraw-Hill, Inc.

Race, P., and Smith, B. 1996. *500 Tips for Trainers.* Houston, TX: Gulf Publishing Co.

Robinson, D.G., and Robinson, J.C. 1996. *Performance Consulting.* San Francisco: Berrett-Koehler.

Robinson, D.G., and Robinson J.C., eds. 1998. *Moving from Training to Performance: A Practical Guidebook.* ASTD / San Francisco: Berrett-Koehler.

Russel, J.D., *et al.* 1993. Systematic Planning for Materials and Media Utilization. In *The ASTD Handbook of Instructional Technology,* ed. G.M Piskurich. New York: McGraw-Hill, Inc.

Rylatt, A., and Lohan, K. 1997. *Creating Training Miracles.* San Francisco: Pfeiffer.

Sadler, P., and Barham, K. 1988. From Franks to the Future. *Personnel Management* 20, no. 5: 48–51.

Schein, E. 1985. *Organizational Culture and Leadership.* San Francisco: Jossey-Bass Inc.

Shea-Schultz, H., and Fogarty, J. 2002. *Online Learning Today.* San Francisco: Berrett-Koehler.

Shapiro, L.T. 1995. *Training Effectiveness Handbook.* New York: McGraw-Hill, Inc.

Silberman, M. 1990. *Active Training: A Handbook of Techniques, Designs, Case Examples, and Tips.* New York: Lexington Books.

Simpson, E. 1972. *The Classification of Educational Objectives in the Psychomotor Domain: The Psychomotor Domain.* Vol. 3, Washington, D.C.: Gryphon House.

Sisson, G.R. 2001. *Hands-On Training: A Simple and Effective Method for On-the-Job Training.* San Francisco: Berrett-Koehler.

Snelbecker, G.E. 1993. Practical Ways for Using Theories and Innovations to Improve Training. In *The ASTD Handbook of Instructional Technology,* ed. G.M Piskurich. New York: McGraw-Hill, Inc.

Swanson, R.A., and Torraco, R.J. 1995. The History of Technical Training, in *The ASTD Technical and Skills Training Handbook*, ed. L. Kelly. New York: McGraw-Hill, Inc.

Steadham, S.V. 1980. Learning to Select a Needs Assessment Strategy. *Training and Development Journal,* 30: 56–61.

Stewart, T.A. 1997. Brain power: Who owns it ... How they profit from it. *Fortune* 135, no. 5: 104–110.

Stolovitch, H.D., and Keeps, E.J. 2002. *Telling Ain't Training.* Washington, DC: ASTD.

Sugrue, B. *2003 State of the Industry Report.* Washington DC: ASTD.

Tannenbaum, S.I., and Yukl, G. 1992. Training and Development in Work Organizations. *Annual Review of Psychology,* 43: 399–431.

Thiagarajan, S. 1993. Just-In-Time Instructional Design. In *The ASTD Handbook of Instructional Technology,* ed. G.M Piskurich. New York: McGraw-Hill, Inc.

Thompson, C., et al., 2002. *Training for the Next Economy: An ASTD State of the Industry Report on Trends in Employer-Provided Training in the United States.*

VanAdelsberg, D., and Trolley, E.A. 1999. *Running Training Like a Business: Delivering Unmistakable Value.* San Francisco: Berrett-Koehler.

Vaughn, R.H. 2001. Sad, but true: "The Big Bird Syndrome" in Training. *Excellence in Teaching Newsletter,* 2, no.1. Lakeland Community College, Ohio. 1–2.

Watson, C.E., and Grzybowski, A. 1975. What your company should know about tuition aid plans. *Business Horizons,* 19 no. 5: 75–80.

West, E. 1995. Technical Training Facilities and Equipment. in *The ASTD Technical and Skills Training Handbook,* ed. L. Kelly. New York: McGraw-Hill, Inc.

Wexley, Kenneth N., and Latham, G.P. 2002. *Developing and Training Human Resources in Organizations,* 3rd ed. Upper Saddle River, NJ: Prentice Hall.

Index

About the Author

Dr. Robert H. Vaughn, author of ***The Professional Trainer,*** has personally worked with more than 2,500 people over nearly three decades to help develop their training skills. He's created training programs and materials used by such diverse organizations as The U.S. Air Force's Air Training Command and The American Management Associations, among others. As a speaker at local, regional, and national conferences, and a faculty member at several different colleges, Dr. Vaughn knows the world of business and the business of training. Both his masters' thesis and his doctoral dissertation related to the subject of organizational training. As the founder and president of Arvon Management Services, he has consulted or conducted training programs for nearly 100 different corporations and professional associations, mostly focusing on writing, supervision, and training skills. His client list includes divisions of such companies as General Electric, TRW, Babcock & Wilcox, Lincoln Electric, Eaton, Allen-Bradley, and others.

Dr. Vaughn is a three-time president and twelve-year board member of the 400-member Greater Cleveland Chapter of ASTD (formerly the American Society for Training and Development) and received the 2002 Distinguished Faculty Service Award from Lakeland Community College in Ohio, where he is a Professor of Management and former Dean of Business. He holds undergraduate degrees in industrial management and education (journalism), a Master of Business Administration, and a Ph.D. in Business Administration; he has also done doctoral-level work in adult education. He earned Beta Gamma Sigma (business honorary) recognition for his doctoral work, and he is listed in Who's Who in Business and Industry. Dr. Vaughn is also the author of ***Decision Making and Problem Solving in Management: Tools and Techniques for Managers and Teams*** (2000) published by Lakeshore Communications, Inc.

Berrett-Koehler Publishers

B errett-Koehler is an independent publisher of books
and other publications at the leading edge of new
thinking and innovative practice on work, business,
management, leadership, stewardship, career development, human resources, entrepreneurship, and global
sustainability.

Since the company's founding in 1992, we have been
committed to creating a world that works for all by
publishing books that help us to integrate our values with
our work and work lives, and to create more humane and
effective organizations.

We have chosen to focus on the areas of work, business,
and organizations, because these are central elements in
many people's lives today. Furthermore, the work world is
going through tumultuous changes, from the decline of job
security to the rise of new structures for organizing people
and work. We believe that change is needed at all levels—
individual, organizational, community, and global—and our
publications address each of these levels.

To find out about our new books,
special offers,
free excerpts,
and much more,
subscribe to our free monthly eNewsletter at

www.bkconnection.com

Please see next pages for other books
from Berrett-Koehler Publishers

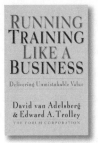

Running Training Like a Business
Delivering Unmistakable Value

David van Adelsberg and Edward A. Trolley

Hardcover
ISBN 1-57675-059-0
Item #50590-415
$27.95

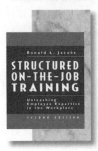

Structured On-the-Job Training
Unleashing Employee Expertise in the Workplace

Ronald L. Jacobs

Paperback
ISBN 1-57675-242-9
Item #52429-415
$34.95

Effective Training Strategies
A Comprehensive Guide to
Maximizing Learning in Organizations

James R. Davis and Adelaide B. Davis

Hardcover
ISBN 1-57675-037-7
Item #5037X-415
$49.95

Online Learning Today
Strategies That Work

Heather Shea-Schultz and John Fogarty

Paperback
ISBN 1-57675-143-0
Item #51430-415
$18.95

Berrett-Koehler Publishers
PO Box 565, Williston, VT 05495-9900
Call toll-free! **800-929-2929** 7 am-9 pm EST

Or fax your order to 1-802-864-7626
For fastest service order online: **www.bkconnection.com**